WITHDRAWN

THE IRANIAN REVOLUTION:
THANATOS ON A NATIONAL SCALE

The Iranian Revolution: Thanatos on a National Scale

Gholam R. Afkhami

WASHINGTON, DC 1985
THE MIDDLE EAST INSTITUTE

DS
318
A65
1985

Copyright 1985 by the Middle East Institute.
All rights reserved.
Library of Congress Catalog Card No. 85-61787
ISBN 0-916808-28-9

Designed by Maria Josephy Schoolman
Manufactured in the United States of America

*To The Memory
of My Father*

Contents

	PREFACE	ix
	INTRODUCTION	1
1	POWER AND DEVELOPMENT IN POST-WAR IRAN: AN OVERVIEW	17
2	POLITICAL STRUCTURE AND POLITICAL POWER UNDER THE SHAH	47
3	THE SHATTERING OF THE IMAGE	83
4	THE DILEMMA OF THE MILITARY	113
5	FOREIGN POLICY: PSYCHOLOGICAL COSTS OF OVERDEPENDENCE	145
6	LIBERAL MISPERCEPTIONS: THE ROOTS OF THANATOS	173
7	THE KHOMEINI PHENOMENON: A STUDY IN ALIENATION	197
8	THE FUTURE: IS THERE A REASONABLE WAY OUT?	223
	POSTSCRIPT	255
	BIBLIOGRAPHY	259
	INDEX	269

I Preface

This book represents an effort by a member of the Iranian political hierarchy under the Shah to make sense of the events which led to the Iranian revolution. It is the result mostly of personal observation placed in a theoretical framework. Its judgments are based on many years of association with the Iranian Imperial Court, government bureaucracy, party system, and the academe, as well as the common people in villages and small towns with whom the author came into close contact between 1975 and 1979 as secretary general of Iran's literacy movement. It is not intended as history, even though it emphasizes the role played by historical phenomena in the evolution of Iranian political culture. Its frame of reference is the general characteristics of the politics of the Third World. It tries to bring together themes from both development and dependency theories. It assumes that the reader has some familiarity with recent Iranian events.

Much of the impetus for writing this book has been generated by a sense of moral obligation to friends and colleagues who lost their lives to the revolution but were never allowed to present their case. More so because the emotional weight of the revolutionary process and the acerbity which the world brought to the condemnation of the Pahlavi era devastated the survivors of the regime so thoroughly that even today, six years after the revolution, many of them hesitate to look the past squarely in the face, or defend their otherwise remarkable record of collective achievement. This book is also a response to the need for balance, for putting the record straight when warranted by facts.

The most compelling phenomenon of the Pahlavi regime, however, remains its ultimate failure. This failure includes not only those who struggled to achieve the transformation of Iranian society, but, as demonstrated by subsequent events, also those who remained in the periphery as critical observers or self-righteous detractors. To understand the causes of this failure is the central purpose of this book.

Finally, this study is more concerned with the kinds of interpretations of the Iranian revolution which can either derive from or lead to propositions of a general nature. In this sense, values assigned to personalities, processes, structures and functions are largely determined by their susceptibility to more general, if not universal, application. The Shah's political attitudes, for example, remain of great interest; but more important are factors which help produce such attitudes. The same may be said with regard to the character of political power, patterns of economic growth, or manner of confronting dissidents.

I am indebted to a number of friends, colleagues, and institutions whose assistance made this book possible. The Hoover Institution on War, Revolution and Peace made an original grant that launched me on this endeavor. My special thanks are due to Professor George Lenczowski who not only introduced me to Hoover, but also read the whole manuscript and made many valuable suggestions. My friends and colleagues of the National University days, Professors Amin Alimard and Ahmad Ghoreishi, read all and part of the manuscript respectively; their comments helped me clarify both my facts and ideas. Readers and editors in the Middle East Institute were instrumental in helping me bring to the book better organization and greater lucidity. The shortcomings, of course, are solely mine.

And last but not least, to my wife goes my deepest gratitude for her intellectual and moral support, and her unceasing willingness to share with me remembrances of tragic moments, past and present.

I Introduction

The 1970s began in Iran with the celebration of the 2500th anniversary of the establishment of Iranian monarchy by Cyrus the Great. Almost all of the Iranians living in this period had been born during the Pahlavi era, a great majority of them during the reign of Muhammad Reza Shah, the second of the dynasty's monarchs. Most of them had been brought up under a political-educational system which had formally extolled the pre-Islamic history of Iran as the proper basis for the manifestation of Iranian nationalism and the reconstruction of the new Iran. The Achaemenid King Cyrus, therefore, provided a proper symbol. Not only had he founded the first great Persian Empire, history had also proclaimed him a noble king. He had brought prosperity and security to his people. He had introduced new principles of equity and fairness in the government. He had respected local customs, laws and religions. He had liberated helpless people from the bondage of captivity. Most important, as a source of greatness for his people, he had been blessed with "divine glory", the *khvarnah*,[1] and had shown the world that great leaders can produce great things.

The new Iran, too, would recapture its past glory under the leadership of a great king. The ground had already been prepared. The White Revolution of 1963 had established a framework for the realization of new principles of political equality and socioeconomic justice. The cumulative thrust of such revolutionary ideas as land reform, political and social equality for women, ownership and profit-sharing schemes for industrial labor, nationalization of basic natural resources, and the reorganization of educational and administrative systems, formulated under an integrated plan and supported by the stability of the political system, had encouraged many people throughout the world to conclude that Iran's future was indeed pregnant with happy possibilities. The government's claim that there were reasons for thanksgiving and celebration did not seem unfounded.[2]

Less than a decade later, on January 16, 1979, the symbol of Iran's stability and progress, the Shah, was forced to leave his country under the pressure of one of the most extraordinary revolutionary upheavals in the history of the Third World. The Shah departed ostensibly for rest and recuperation from illness and extreme fatigue—a formula considered by practically everyone as a face-saving device not to be taken seriously, though later events proved that he was indeed grievously ill and had been so for many years.

The news of his departure was greeted with widespread jubilation in Tehran. Tens of thousands of men, women and children, in cars and on foot, invaded the streets. They honked their horns, turned on their headlights, laughed, cried, embraced, and raised their hands and fists in celebration of the imminent victory. Later in the evening, the Shah's statues, those which still remained upright, were brought down, one by one, amid shouts of "God is great" and "Death to the Shah." In the revelry of the moment, those who were conscious of the extent of the calamity which had befallen their country were indeed few. The nation's divorce from reality was almost total. Like Ahab, Iranians had embarked upon a beast whose nature they did not know and could not comprehend. In an ironic moment of history, responding innocently and faithfully to well-rehearsed cues, the revelers sang in earnest a parody of the beautiful *ghazal* of the poet Hafiz signifying that the "devil" had left and the gate had opened to embrace the "angel."[3]

This change in the mood of the country was in many ways remarkable. It occurred abruptly over a short period of only a few months. It affected an exceptionally large number of people drawn from an unusually diverse and variegated spectrum of the society. Still, for many Iranians, neither its origins were clearly understood, nor its trajectory cogently mapped. The combination of fundamentally terroristic acts exhibited in the riots, pillage, and arson, and the profoundly serene and soberingly orderly marches of hundreds of thousands of people from a large variety of classes, strata and professions, dazzled and confounded most people, not least of all those who constituted the core of the street demonstrations. Indeed, except for some of the activists who had worked at establishing its infrastructure, the revolution caught a majority of people among both the Shah's supporters and opponents by surprise. The result was certain immediate and at times impulsive reactions which often tended to form the intellectual foundation of theories purporting to explain the Khomeini phenomenon.

Among the Shah's friends, the revolution created confusion, self-doubt, and aggression toward the man they had considered omnipotent. The edifice they had believed unshakable was crumbling before their eyes. The man they had spoken of as the Supreme Leader appeared helpless, unsure, incapable of showing them the way. They sought the explanation in stereotyped answers: American treachery, Communist conspiracy, British tricks—a variety of devil theories. They condemned the Shah for his weakness, lack of resolve, softhearted liberalism, and aversion to strong action in the face of adversity.

The Shah's clerical enemies attributed the whole phenomenon to divine will, translated into the will of a people who had accepted martyrdom as the proper way to eternal salvation. His liberal opponents stressed repression, SAVAK atrocities, corruption, blind modernization, cumulatively resulting in the curtailment of human rights by a one-man tyrannical regime. The leftists denigrated him as an imperialist stooge who had destroyed the nation's economic infrastructure, had turned Iran into an outpost of American imperialism, and now, bowing to the dictates of history, was going down in abject defeat before the ire of proletarian masses, in spite of aid and comfort he received from his imperialist friends.

The effect of this array of conflicting judgments on Iran's political climate in the fall of 1978 was to produce a sense of bewilderment leading to manifestations of intellectual and political behavior that we have characterized in this study as *thanatos*[4] on a national scale. The mood was epitomized by the behavior of the Iranian middle class. One by one, the intellectual, the entrepreneur, the technocrat, the public servant, jumped on the bandwagon of a revolutionary movement which could not possibly hold values that remotely resembled their own. Almost willfully, they suppressed their better judgment, refused to involve themselves in meaningful analysis, insisted on total denigration of the prevailing system, fabricated evidence of the nation's socioeconomic destruction, exaggerated the reality of political tyranny, and clung to a utopian panacea that simply was not contained in the premises of the revolution.

This study questions the validity of many of the opinions and theoretical postulates advanced during and after the revolution as explanations of the fall of the Shah's regime, not because some of them do not comprehend at least some aspects of the truth, but mainly because individually and collectively they fail as explanatory tools when applied to comparable situations in other Third World countries. In many cases, they tend to be essentially generalizations of some observable set of contradictions in Iran, as in other parts of the Third World, which had been traditionally used by certain ideologically antagonistic groups as a way of opposing the Shah's regime. Curiously, the most pessimistic accounts of the system have been often given by those who do not represent a radical ideology and therefore appear to be meticulously objective. These types of arguments tend to add together all of the factors stipulated in the antagonistic ideologies and find the reason for the Shah's fall in some combination of all of them. The result is a picture of misery, corruption, repression and political savagery which can in no way be sustained when objectively compared to the reality of the Iranian society in the 1970s.

One of the confounding dimensions of that reality is that the Shah's system fell when both the Shah and his system appeared quite strong and were judged so by seemingly knowledgeable observers. Strong systems, of course, do not normally go down in defeat unless they are attacked by stronger forces. Hence, the tendency of the Shah and his friends to place the blame on the West as the only power presumably capable of overthrowing the Iranian political system, and a corresponding tendency in the West to attribute to religion in Iran a far greater power, prestige, and influence than it in fact enjoys.

The debate over the role played by the West in the fall of the Iranian monarchy is still zealously pursued by a respectable number of knowledgeable Iranians. The Shah himself passed away apparently convinced of the West's culpability in the overthrow of his regime. The available evidence, however, does not corroborate the role attributed to the West, even though there is no doubt that some Western politicians and functionaries were anxious to see the Shah fall.[5] But even if one assumes that the convergence of positive and negative forces in the West resulted in an inclination to see the Shah go, it is difficult to see how it would have been sufficient to cause the regime's fall if the Shah's system were really strong and stable. Both logic and the evidence of the West's experience with unfriendly Third World countries tend to negate the proposition.

The observable instrument of the revolution was, of course, religion. To many analysts, the fact that the revolutionary momentum appeared to be sustained by Khomeini's popularity and the revolution finally consummated under his religious banner, suggested a hitherto undetected strength in the Shia religious establishment capable of overthrowing a powerful secular authority once a number of extremist clerics had resolved to do so. The proposition, however, is difficult to sustain once we take into account the Iranian political scene in the periods before and after the heat of revolutionary fever. A year before the revolution, there was really very little indication of the phenomenal expressions of religious devotion observed in the fall of 1978; a year after, Khomeini's popularity had plunged beyond recognition. Furthermore, religion succeeded at a time when a majority of the people whose cooperation was crucial to the success of the revolution, namely the various sectors of the modern middle class, had very little affinity with the brand of religion that spearheaded the revolution and took over the country after the collapse of the system. In fact, available evidence suggests that the clerical leaders were just as surprised as others at the turn of events. They simply were not prepared to take over the reins of government; hence Bazargan's so-called interim government, and Khomeini's rather hasty fall from popular grace shortly after the revolution.

The conclusion, therefore, must be that in spite of all appearances, the Shah's system had become truly debilitated. But how and why? Was the cause corruption? Was it repression? Too rapid modernization? The destruction of the economic infrastructure and a wholesale abandonment of the country to imperialist scavengers, as some Marxists would have us believe? God's will as explained by the clerics? Or, perhaps, all of the above?

Six years after the revolution, now that passions and frustrations have somewhat subsided, most observers have come to agree, more or less, that if these were the real causes of the revolution, many other countries should have succumbed before Iran did. This study will in part demonstrate that many of the above arguments were utilized as revolutionary propaganda and many of them were grossly exaggerated. Besides, historically speaking, Iranians were quite accustomed to both corruption and repression, even though the social transformation they experienced was for them a novel phenomenon.

Was it then that the Shah was personally too weak, too despotic, too evil, and therefore, hated beyond relief by his people?

We shall argue that the Shah, while not very strong, was not too weak; that while operating within an authoritarian system, he was far from being despotic; that in fact he was of a benevolent character and a nationalist wanting the best for Iran and the Iranian people; that he was in many ways weary of denying not only to his friends, but even to his enemies, their supplications, even when their demands were patently against his interests; and that he was certainly not hated by a majority of the people because, for archetypal reasons, a majority of his people could not have conceived of hating him.

On the other hand, during the last 15 years of the Shah's regime, the country had moved forward, often with exceptional vigor, in the economic, social, and cultural realms. In addition, the Shah had at his disposal a formidable army, a seemingly capable security organization, and a great reservoir of material and human resources which, at least in theory, should have rendered him invincible to the kinds of attacks he was likely to face.

Where then in the Shah's regime lay the Achilles' heel? Why did a seemingly powerful system collapse with such relative ease? Evidently, the answer must be looked for in the structural characteristics of the system. The fragility of the Iranian political system resulted from the contradiction between the pattern of accumulation of political power and the institutional properties of the Crown. Paradoxically, the weakness of the Shah's regime was a function of the strength of the institution he personally represented. The Crown had certain institutional properties that determined the form and range of responses available to its incumbent. We shall argue that once the society had moved beyond certain levels of socioeconomic change, the institution of the monarchy could no longer accommodate centralized and concentrated patterns of political relationships, and therefore could be maintained only if power could be successfully moved toward decentralization and deconcentration.

In fact, however, during the period that is of interest to us, political power in Iran, as in all other Third World societies, demonstrated a palpable propensity toward centralization and concentration. The reason was that with time lags of no more than a few decades, in all countries now known as the Third and Fourth Worlds, political systems have undertaken to introduce basic changes in their social, economic, and cultural environments.[6] This fundamental reversal of relationship between the political and other subsystems of the society was historically necessitated by an evolving world situation that has been generally subsumed under some variant of the concept of colonialism.

The colonial experience, which is conceived in this study as resulting from a historically-mandated relationship between social systems of fundamentally unequal economic and technological capabilities, thrust the Iranian political system into the forefront of the developmental process, and thus transformed the traditional mode of relationship between the polity and the society. It affected the generation and evolution of Iranian nationalism by subjecting the form and substance of internal change to the hegemonic characteristics of external forces. Hence nationalism became a phenomenon in which the outside world constituted the essential dimension. Since the essence of the colonial experience came to be perceived as economic and technological, the drive for political emancipation and the drive for economic and technological development became inextricably intertwined. Thus, the Iranian political system was forced to shoulder the mantle of development, a condition that would separate the future mode of development of the nation from the patterns experienced in the past. For the first time in history, it became a conscious mission of the state to transform its socioeconomic base in order to attain the goals of socioeconomic development.[7]

By introducing a logic of development alien to the ethos of

the Iranian traditional culture, the colonial experience forced an uneven pattern of development that exacerbated the emerging contradictions and cleavages within and among the components of the society, including those of the political system.[8] It created tensions of a dialectical nature. The following may be taken as examples:

A. The colonial experience led to a cultural fragmentation of the society. Quite obviously, the structural insulation of vast sectors of the society caused by class barriers, widespread illiteracy, lack of geographic and social mobility, poor communications, poverty and the like did not allow for a uniform distribution of alien values or norms through the society. As a result, the intellectual reorientation which is associated with the awareness of development occurred unevenly in different social sectors, depending on the character of the prevailing subculture and the nature and intensity of the encounter with the new norms. The implications of the resulting cultural fragmentation for the notions of legitimacy and authority in government are self-evident. In Iran, it meant that at least since the Constitutional Revolution of 1905–6, no governmental system could have hoped to be accepted as legitimate by all of the people. The use of force, therefore, became an inherent property of governance.

B. Under the conditions of cultural fragmentation discussed above, the quest for systemic power, that is, the capacity of the political system to mobilize its resources for the specification and implementation of its goals, led to the salience of personal styles of leadership. Due to the limitations of the consensual base and the weakness of the evolving institutions, power, wielded by the leader, became the arbiter of social choice. The country's socio-economic and cultural characteristics also strengthened this tendency, so that in the preliminary stages personal power appeared as an indispensable catalyst for the unification of the elite and marshalling of the nation's human and material resources.

C. The structure of the Iranian political system comprised a number of rationally conceived organizational frameworks[9] (bureaucracies, political parties, councils, parliaments) designed to act as institutional media for the transaction of the society's political business. Institutions, however, are ordinarily the result of recurrent patterns of behavior based on values and emotions to which participants are more or less ethically and aesthetically bound. When these patterns of behavior are followed in a rational organizational framework, they tend to become more efficient. Conversely, when rationally conceived organizations are not allowed to perform their proper functions, and are thereby alienated from the purposes for which they have been established, their value content loses its potency, and they in turn diminish in their possibilities of becoming viable and effective institutions.

In Iran, as in other developing countries, the prevailing political culture favored the institutionalization of the structures that dealt with the political system's implementation functions, and hindered the institutionalization of the structures that were meant to deal with the specification of goals. Thus, channels of political action best geared to the requirements of central authority and least resistant to political command tended to flourish. In the Third World, these channels are ordinarily the military, the public bureaucracy, and the mobilizing political party. In Iran, due to the characteristics of the Crown, political parties never really took root. As a result, the channels in question were confined, for the most part, to civil and military bureaucracies.

The major reason for these structural proclivities was that in the early stages of socioeconomic development centralized power operating through the intermediary of command-oriented structures was better geared to the accomplishment of the goals of the state, as these goals were defined and determined by the elite. In due course, however, the process of socioeconomic development transformed important parts of the social base. New economic, social, and cultural power groups emerged, which needed to be inducted into the political process and their power translated into political capability, if systemic power was to grow at a rate commensurate with the new demands and expectations generated in the society. In order to respond to the new circumstances, the political system needed to undergo a set of appropriate structural changes to provide channels of political participation necessary for the negotiation of new realities in the societal power structure. The Iranian political system failed in this effort, and as a result became progressively underdeveloped relative to the changes it had helped generate in its environment.

As the above paragraph suggests, in this study economic, social, and cultural developments are conceived of as properties of the human resource base; whereas political development is seen as a function of the structural arrangements whereby the evolving demands within the society may be processed through reasonably appropriate channels to arrive at authoritative decisions in the name of the community.[10] As a result of the impact of the colonial experience on the evolution of national impulse and the ideology of development in Iran, the economic, social and cultural developments occurred unevenly within a contradictory frame of interrelationships. The transformation of the society led initially to quantitative increases in the demands made on the political system (e.g., a rise in demands for more and better education, hygiene, fertilizers, etc.). Continuous transformation of the society's organizational, technological, and sociopsychological dimensions led to conditions in which it became progressively more difficult for the government to respond effectively to the newly emerging and constantly increasing demands without the introduction of significant structural change in the goal-specification and goal-implementation domains of the political system. The tensions arising from the discrepancy between the increasing vitality of the resource base and the relative inertia of the political system helped to transform the nature of the demands from higher shares of values to demands for participation in the decisions concerning the allocation process. This dialectical transformation—a qualitative jump—was historically determined because (a) subjectively, its promise was contained in the Constitution as well as in the ideologies of nationalism and development, and (b) objectively, in the absence of effective political participation the capabilities of the political system remained more or less confined to bureaucratic potential and therefore were inadequate to the development requirements.

Two questions need to be asked at this point. First, why was the Iranian political system not able to respond appropriately to the new circumstances, and second, assuming that the system's inability to react led to its fragility, was this phenomenon by itself sufficient to create the explosion? In other words, was the Iranian Revolution self-generating?

The answer to the second query is probably no, at least not in immediate terms. Political fragility leads to vulnerability, but not to the necessity of revolution. There is therefore a dimension to the Iranian Revolution which has been only partially studied, if at all:[11] the organization, strategy, and background of the revolutionary forces. Where did they come from? How and by whom was their strategy and theory of organization conceived? What were their lines of command? How did they get their intelligence? At a different level, but within the same genre, another set of questions may be asked: Would the Shah's regime have fallen, for example, if instead of a Carter administration a Nixon or a Reagan administration had been in office in the United States? Indeed, most Iranians are convinced that under either of the above alternatives the revolution would not have succeeded, which leads them, understandably, to question the West's political savvy, if not political motives.

The first question, of why the Iranian political system was not able to respond appropriately to the new circumstances, is more involved, and in fact constitutes the theme question of this study. Our argument, as mentioned above, is that the Shah, in fact, found himself in a dilemma which ended in tragedy. While the form of accumulation and concentration of political power in Iran followed the pattern dictated by historical forces present in all Third World countries, the institution of the monarchy could not accommodate that pattern of power relations, due to its special kind of historical relationship with the nation. As a result, power converged on the Shah in the period when centralized power was essential to the requirements of goal-specification and goal-implementation; but once the society had moved beyond certain levels of change and complexity, he could no longer convert it to systemic capability because the institution he represented required that the conversion process take place within a decentralized and deconcentrated framework. In other words, while monarchy as an institution would have succeeded only as the *guarantor* of the system's movement toward an open and participative polity, men who occupied the major positions of the political system were not able to negotiate a reversal of the universal trend of power accumulation in the Third World. They succumbed to the temptation of power and, dazzled by the system's success, tended to attribute much of it to a happy combination of leadership capability and historical legitimacy uniquely assembled in the person of the Shah: a characteristic which in their minds separated Iran from the rest of the Third World. The result was an exaggerated emphasis on Iran's national character, its institution of kingship, its unique history and its political-religious faith in the Shia branch of Islam, which tended to obscure the contradictions that were developing between the form and structure of the political system on one hand, and the changing character of the sociocultural and economic environments on the other, as the society experienced a formidable transformation under the proddings of its increasingly divergent elites.

In the end, a system that had much potential for success imploded in a vacuum of power, because the structure it had assumed was diametrically opposed to the objective requirements of its only effective political *institution*, namely, the Crown. The process of disintegration was precipitated by a misperception of the roles both of monarchy and the Shah by the latter's liberal opponents. As a result, even when the vacuous character of the regime's power had become apparent, the liberal elements still reacted to power as if it belonged to the Shah and not to the Crown. The image had become so solidly ingrained, that for most people it had assumed phantom-like properties. Like Don Quixote, they charged windmills that were no longer there.

The ensuing chapters in this study address the above questions in the hope of shedding some light on the issues that bore on the demise of the Shah's regime and the rise of the Islamic Republic. The first six chapters deal with the Shah's regime: its accomplishments, strengths and weaknesses, as well as the reasons for its final defeat. Chapters 1 and 2 discuss the structure of the Iranian political system before the revolution in terms of its history and culture. Chapter 3 explores the regime's responses to environmental pressures, the reasons behind the options taken by the regime, and the roles these options played in the encouragement of the revolutionary movement. Chapter 4 analyzes the military command's dilemma in the last months and suggests a number of reasons as to why the confluence of internal and external forces finally checkmated the military by forcing it into positions from which it could not retrench. Chapter 5 discusses the effect of Iran's special relationship with the United States on the patterns of responses made by the Shah and his adversaries to the revolutionary upheaval. Chapter 6 addresses the problems and shortcomings of the Iranian liberal community and particularly its presumed political arm, the National Front, in the light of the role they played in the fall of the regime. Their particular mode of response to the events of 1978 is taken as a basis for the suggestion in this study that *thanatos* may be an appropriate concept for the characterization of the behavior of the Iranian middle class during the Khomeini assault.

Following this examination of the recent past, Chapter 7 looks at the Khomeini regime and finds it ideologically alien to the historical ethos of the Iranian nation in the last quarter of the 20th century. In so far as colonialism is a function of fundamental unevenness in the economic and technological capabilities of different societies, this section sees the historical meaning of the Islamic Republic as the prolongation of the colonial era in Iran. Contrary to the prevailing opinion, this study finds the Khomeini regime relatively weak and, given the fact that its legitimacy is inextricably geared to its fundamentalist world view, doomed to failure. If so, future possibilities should be of interest not only to Iranians, but also to other countries with interest in the regional and global implications of Persian Gulf politics. Chapter 8 addresses future options and concludes that, given the characteristics of Iranian politics, specifically the properties of Iranian political culture, constitutional monarchy remains the most appropriate form of government for Iran.

Notes

Introduction

1. The idea of the *farr-i izadi*, the divine glory, and the Avestan "khvarnah", the light that shone upon the brow of consecrated ancient Iranian sovereigns signifying their legitimacy, was archetypally ingrained in the Iranian mind. The purest form of khvarnah in the *Shahnamih*, Firdawsi's heroic epic of the kings, is perhaps expressed in the tragedy of Siyavash. See Shahrukh Miskub, *Sug-i Siyavash* (Mourning for Siyavash) (Tehran, 1355).
2. The following are excerpts from the preface to the 1971 edition of *Area Handbook for Iran:*

    "Reform programs initiated in 1963 under the rule of Muhammad Reza Shah have profoundly affected the people's social, political, and economic life, as well as their attitudes toward internal and external situations. . .

    "The new reforms initially created strong opposition from some of the landed aristocracy, Islamic traditionalists, and dissident opportunistic political factions. The resulting social turmoil and public order disturbances prevalent in mid-1963 were soon surmounted and general parliamentary elections were held in September. Candidates supporting the reforms were elected, presenting the opportunity to lay the groundwork for a modern and stable society. . .

    "Economic progress also was continued, with important changes highlighted by the increasing importance of industry in the economy and by a rising economic growth rate. . . The country's stability and independence have enhanced its status and prestige in the Middle East and throughout the world. Its importance in the Persian Gulf region, in particular, will assume increased significance after the withdrawal of British forces from the area. . ."
    Harvey H. Smith, et al., eds., *Area Handbook for Iran* (Washington, DC: American University Foreign Area Studies, 1971), v–vi.
3. The author was a witness to the demonstrations. The relevant verse in Hafiz is:

"Khalvat-i dil nist ja-yi suhbat-i aghyar,
Div chu Birun ravad, Firishtih dar-ayad".
4. *Thanatos* is a Greek word meaning instinctual destructiveness or death instinct, used in this study in contrast to the Freudian concept of eros, or life instinct. See also note 1, chapter 6.
5. Zbigniew Brzezinski, *Power and Principle* (New York: Farrar, 1983), 354 ff.; Jimmy Carter, *Keeping Faith: Memoirs of a President* (New York: Bantam Books, 1982), 431 ff.
6. For a general discussion of power in relation to the developing countries see John H. Kautsky, *Political Change in Underdeveloped Countries: Nationalism and Communism* (New York: John Wiley and Sons, 1962), 38–9. This is probably the most logical explanation for the elevation of the need for economic development to the level of a moral imperative. See also Wilbert E. Moore, "The Social Framework of Economic Development", in Ralph Braibanti and Joseph Spengler, eds., *Traditions, Values, and Socio-Economic Development* (Durham, NC: Duke University Press, 1961), 57–82.
7. Chapters 1 and 2, below. The essence of much Western liberal analysis remains Marxist, related to a Lockean frame of reference in which society precedes the polity both logically and chronologically. The reality of the Third World appears to be much closer to a Hobbesian and/or Leninist scheme in which the political precedes the economic and the social. The difference is crucial not only for political analysis, but also for construction of developmental scenarios.
8. Chapters 1, 2, and 3, below. For examples of general exposition and review, see *inter alia*, Samir Amin, *Unequal Development: An Essay on the Social Transformation of Peripheral Capitalism* (New York: Monthly Review Press, 1976); André Gunder Frank, "The Development of Underdevelopment," *Monthly Review* 18 (September 1966), 17–31; André Gunder Frank, "Development and Underdevelopment in the New World: Smith and Marx vs. the Weberians," *Theory and Society* 2 (Spring 1975), 431–66; Celso Furtado, *Development and Underdevelopment*, trans. Ricardo W. de Aguilar and Eric C. Drysdale (Berkeley: University of California Press, 1975).
9. Samuel P. Huntington, "The Change to Change: Modernization, Development, and Politics," in Norman W. Provizer, ed., *Analyzing the Third World* (Cambridge, MA: Schenkman Publishing Company, 1978), 63.
10. See the concept of politics as forms of "authoritative allocation of values," in David Easton, *A Systems Analysis of Political Life* (New York: John Wiley and Sons, 1965).
11. See Marvin Zonis, "Iran: A Theory of Revolution from Accounts of the Revolution," *World Politics* 35, no. 4 (July 1983).

1 | Power and Development in Post-War Iran: An Overview

The legal framework of the Iranian monarchy under the Pahlavi dynasty was provided by the Iranian Constitution of 1906. The original document referred only to the establishment of a National Consultative Assembly, or *majlis*, composed of the representatives of six classes of people whose major functions were to approve and to oversee the revenues and expenditures of the government. A year later a supplement was added to the original document, containing a bill of rights and defining the powers and responsibilities of the Shah, as well as those of the various branches of the government. While specifically designated as the head of the executive branch, as the embodiment and symbol of the majesty of the state, the person of the Shah was pronounced inviolable; responsibility, therefore, devolved on his ministers who were presumed answerable before the assembly but who, nevertheless, were appointed and dismissed by the Shah.[1]

The 1906–7 Constitution established the ideal of a representative government tempered by the tradition of monarchy as the symbol of unity of the state. The tensions between the executive and the parliament, however, resulted in mutual hostility and a lack of trust that marred the system to the last days of the Constitution.

Parliament, as an institution, never took deep roots in Iran. Historically, parliamentary ascendancy corresponded to periods of political chaos in which forces of dispersion threatened the integrity of the state. The 1905–6 Constitutional Revolution introduced the emerging middle class, mostly consisting of merchants and small traders, into the Iranian political system, but it did not materially change the Iranian social system. With the exception of the first two assemblies, up to the period of the White Revolution the Iranian parliament reflected the semifeudal and tribal composition of the society.[2] Great men and leaders had sometimes bestowed on these assemblies an aura of national consciousness and moral transcendence, but, in practice, they had generally failed to overcome the feudal and tribal parochialism of their associates. That parochialism lent itself to manipulation by interested foreign powers far more easily than it did to the call of patriotism raised by national heroes. Thus, the weakness of national consciousness and the tribal composition of the society exacerbated the geopolitical vulnerability of the state to the extent that, in the absence of a strong, unifying executive, the country was faced with constant threats of actual dismemberment.

On the other hand, strong executives never allowed the parliament to develop as an institution. Before he became Shah, while still prime minister and commander in chief of the armed forces, Reza Khan, the first of the Pahlavis, had already reduced the parliament to a formalistic rubber stamp to legitimize his decrees. During the 20 years of his rule, only those who had accepted their role as the functionaries of the executive were allowed to be elected to the Majlis. The country was never without a parliament and the parliament, in turn, rarely showed an inclination to oppose the Crown's wishes.

Reza Shah's historical mission, as he saw it, was to quell the centrifugal forces that threatened the unity and the integrity of the country. No doubt his personal qualities were of cardinal importance in performing this task. The historical requirements of Iranian national independence under the prevailing conditions of the period demanded strong, straightforward action by a powerful, dedicated and relatively simple leader.[3] These requirements favored Reza Shah, but, regardless of who took the helm of power, it would have been impossible not to move toward centralization of authority and, therefore, contraction of the potential democratic space. Conversely, no leader with democratic aspirations would have survived, much less succeeded, in the accomplishment of the historical requirements of forceful, straightforward, and essentially military action.

With the outbreak of the Second World War, Reza Shah was forced to resign in favor of his son, Muhammad Reza, and go into exile, ostensibly for his pro-German sentiments. More plausibly, he was forced out because the Allied powers' requirements of freedom of movement in Iran clashed with the existence of a centralized, powerful, sovereign state. The Iranian national consciousness, for example, could not have accepted the presence of Soviet troops in its territory. The system, therefore, had to be broken down and the authority of the state shattered. The Allied occupation of Iran broke down the central authority and, in effect, encouraged the development of political conflict among different and ideologically diverse social types in order to ensure the simultaneous achievement of two major aims: free and unhampered use of Iranian facilities needed for the satisfaction of the Allies' military requirements, and mutual political accommodation relative to their respective postwar ideological and economic interests, tactfully executed so as not to jeopardize their basic imperatives of cooperation.

The Allies' twin objectives of military and political accommodation brought to the surface and exacerbated the fragmentation of the Iranian political culture; they did not, however, create it. That reality was the result of a continuous process of social mobilization that had started before Reza Shah had assumed power, although it had obviously speeded up under his programs of economic and social mobilization. It was a product of the expansion of education, of urbanization, of rationalization and Westernization of the legal and governmental systems, of communication, and of industrialization. And yet, compared to what was obtaining in Iran in 1978, these processes were only in their initial stages: In the decade of the 1940s no more than 25 per cent of the population lived in the urban areas; per capita income did not exceed $85; and student enrollment hardly reached 700,000.[4]

Reza Shah's deportation in 1941, therefore, released the relatively meager political energy of the forces he had kept under control into an institutional void dominated by the presence of the Allied occupation forces. This pent-up energy exploded in a formless political arena in violent and conflicting expressions for which parliament, as a convenient channel of political expression, provided an important outlet. The experience of these years, wistfully referred to as the "democratic era" in Iranian politics, is most revealing for the understanding of Iranian political culture. This was also the most formative period in the development of the young Shah's perception of the political requirements of Iran and his role as its king and leader.

The politics of Iran in the decade after the Second World War, culminating in the fall of Prime Minister Muhammad Mossadiq in 1953, might be construed as a classical example of the clash of factional powers in a political arena wanting in institutional capability. Reza Shah's rule in Iran had ushered in significant changes in the areas of bureaucratic rationalization, urbanization, education, and military reorganization and preparedness. It had commenced the first steps in the construction of a relatively modern economic infrastructure. Most important of all, it had unified the country by forcing existing parochial powers to yield to the requirement of central authority. But it had left the structure of the Iranian social system substantially intact.[5]

At the end of his reign, Iran was still basically semi-feudal and agricultural; its sociopolitical manifestations ascriptive-filial; its world view subnational, geared to the preservation of parochial interests. The countryside, containing more than three-fourths of the population, had remained under the effective political control of the feudal and tribal landlords who defended their interests in the capital through their representatives in the Majlis and the bureaucracy. Their power issued from their legal position as landowners and the resulting political and economic control of the peasants who worked and lived on their lands. Given the relative insulation of rural society from urban centers, national issues had little bearing on the landowners' power base in local communities. They could thus move freely in and out of different power cliques with a facility rarely enjoyed by the urban-based politicians.

As the power of the feudal and tribal leaders was based on the effects of the insularity of rural society, so their politics tended to perpetuate the causes of that insularity. If the effects were superstition, poverty and bondage, the causes were lack of communication, immobility, paucity of educational facilities, illiteracy, prejudice, and illogical and unjust patterns of land ownership. Their political power represented a vicious circle feeding on ills it helped to perpetuate. The politics of Iran between 1943 and 1963 clearly showed that their control of the

Majlis had effectively precluded the possibility of any meaningful social legislation within the country's constitutional frame of reference.

The tribal landlord aristocracy had found its natural ally in the country's religious establishment. Jealous of its newly achieved prerogatives, and conscious of its sway over the traditional mind, the clergy had a vested interest in the perpetuation of the traditional society. The experience of the Reza Shah era had made them acutely conscious of the danger of a strong and centralized secular authority and inclined them instinctively to side with the forces of dispersion and distraction. The lower clergy, the *mullahs* and the *akhunds*, fed on the society's superstition and ignorance, while the learned and the exalted drew their influence from the control of vast tracts of agricultural *waqf* land and the payments of religious dues, *khums* and *zakat*, by the faithful. Their urban base was centered in the bazaar, which controlled not only the flow of money, but also many of the business transactions in food and primary consumer goods, through extended chains of retail stores.

The political influence resulting from this combination of moral and material power in the hands of the higher clergy had made them one of the most important factors in any political equation concerning the policy options of the society. Nevertheless, it is wrong to assume that they were all united in their approach to political power. Temperamentally, their approaches ranged from the sublime and religiously transcendent posture of Ayatollah Burujirdi, the most exalted prelate in the Shiite realm, to the terroristic activities of groups belonging to the *fada'iyan-i Islam*, the precursor of the main religious elements constituting the backbone of the revolutionary movement that some 30 years later transformed Iran into a theocracy. The political ideology of Shiism, however, tended to make religious opposition to antisecular militancy extremely difficult, if not impossible.

We shall have occasion to speak about the political ideology of Shiism at greater depth in our discussion of the Khomeini phenomenon and the Iranian Revolution. But it is necessary to mention at this point the essential characteristics of this ideology within the general framework of Islamic political theology. The *ethos* of Shiism lies in its glorification of the concept of the *Imam* as the manifestation of the primordial light, blameless and infallible. Unlike Sunni Islam, in which the supreme authority resides theoretically in the *ijma'* (consensus) of the community of believers, in Shiism, the Imam is the repository of all knowledge and the sublime shepherd of his flock. The Imams were the Prophet Muhammad's descendants through his daughter, Fatima, and, in the line of 'Ali, his son-in-law and cousin. According to the Shiite faith, the twelfth and last Imam, the promised *Mahdi,* the rightly guided one, went into a short occultation at the age of four in 872 AD, when he appeared only to a select few of his deputies known as his *na'ibs;* in the year 939 he commenced the long occultation that would last until God wills him to reappear.[6]

Esoteric Shiism recognizes no deputies during the Mahdi's long absence. Nevertheless, it prescribed *taqlid,* or the imitation or adoption as authoritative of the utterances of a *mujtahid,* a man of proven high morals, learned in Islamic jurisprudence and allowed to interpret religious sources, as a religious duty. To the layman, however, the source of *taqlid,* commonly known by the title of *ayatollah,* assumes some of the characteristics of the Imam, especially, holiness and infallibility. The combination of emotional and intellectual attachment to the ayatollah in turn, gives him almost absolute power over his followers, including, at times, over life and death, as when he orders his followers into *jihad,* the faithfuls' war in support of religion against the manifestation of infidelity.

Since Islam does not allow for clear separation of the temporal and spiritual realms, the tension between the secular and the religious authority has always remained a cardinal aspect of Iran's political life. This tension poses a latent challenge to the legitimacy of the secular authority. The most palpable and immediately perceived example of such a challenge is the propagated notion of the immorality and unlawfulness of paying taxes to the secular government. Instead, the faithful are encouraged to pay their religious dues and the Imam's share. The question of money, therefore, has always been of prime importance in the relationship between the government and the clergy.

The higher clergy use their income for various causes, including the support of theology students in religious schools and the lower mullahs. Since these elements, in effect, constitute the core of the higher clergy's field forces, ability to support them is the sine qua non of the preservation of each ayatollah's relative political influence. Traditionally, the secular authority has taken advantage of clerical vulnerability and tended to channel the required money to the more amenable among them. Obviously, the stronger the government, the less the perceived need to court the clergy; conversely, the more unstable the political system, the greater the clergy's leeway in drawing income from the government's coffers. This contentious relationship has tended to strengthen the ideological inclination of the religious elements toward the weakening of the secular authority. It is therefore not surprising that religious animosity to secular authority in Iran traditionally reached its peak when the clergy's sources of income were seriously threatened. Relevant examples are the religious opposition to the land reform of 1963, which envisaged the distribution of part of the clergy-administered waqf lands to the peasants, and the almost unanimous attack on the monarchical system after 1977, when government subsidies to the higher clergy were reduced in the name of frugality and moral rectitude.

Formidable as the alliance between the landed aristocracy and the clergy was, its negative effects were exacerbated by the formlessness of the urban political forces that had emerged after the fall of Reza Shah. These forces ran the gamut of political ideologies from Stalinist communism, represented by the Tudeh party, to fascist bands like the *sumka* and the *shahin*. The interested foreign powers, especially the British and the Soviets, aggravated the situation by playing these factions against one another according to the exigencies of their political and economic interests, and depending on the characteristic of the existing groups.

The most flagrant manifestations of interference in the internal affairs of Iran were exhibited by the Soviet Union not only through its direct support of the Tudeh, but also by the establishment of the puppet regimes in the Iranian provinces of Azarbaijan and Kurdistan. Unlike the other Allied powers, the Soviets refused to honor their pledge to leave Iran after the war until the threat of force by the United States government and, even then, only after they had exacted a concession of northern Iranian oil from Iran's prime minister, Ahmad Qavam (Qavam al-Saltanih), a concession later repudiated by the Majlis.[7]

The British, having lost much of their prewar influence in the area, were nevertheless strong in the country as a result of their control of the Anglo-Iranian Oil Company and their close contact with the clergy, as well as their relationship with both urban and rural traditional political notables. While both the British and the Soviets were a curse on Iranian politics, their concurrent presence had the salutary effect of mutual neutralization and, therefore, the provision of a breathing spell during which the country's more conscientious statesmen could strive for the preservation of the nation's integrity and independence. Consequently, they welcomed the added presence of the Americans as a third force, initially as military advisers and later, toward the end of the 1940s, as members of the Point Four (technical assistance) program.

A great number of "parties" emerged and faded away in relatively short intervals.[8] Except for the Tudeh party, whose organization and ideology were informed and aided by the experience and resources of the Communist International, the rest were often no more than ephemeral gatherings of people around political notables of personal charisma or power. Such semi-Marxist, anti-Soviet ideological groupings as Khalil Maliki's Third Force, whose socialist concepts in domestic politics and nonaligned posture in world affairs gave it a semblance of a party based on ideas rather than charisma, were either dwarfed by the towering personalities of political figures like Qavam, Mossadiq, and General Haji 'Ali Razmara, or drowned in the encompassing effect of such emotionally charged, single-issue politics as oil nationalization.

Given the paucity of institutional channels for political communication, power tended to gravitate to individuals whose political base was either traditionally sanctioned, organizationally effective, or politically popular. Thus, religion and the Crown, as the only deep-seated institutions of the country, sustained political power bases never equalled in tenacity by other groups. Organizationally, the army and the Communist party were probably the major forces affecting the political process, whereas, at different times, a host of ideologically divergent personalities commanded public opinion, whose volatile manifestation in the streets was largely responsible for the political ascendancy of its beneficiaries. These spheres, of course, were not mutually exclusive, as evidenced by the constant political interaction among personalities whose influence often transgressed the boundaries of their own base and pervaded the others. The political alliances between Mossadiq and Ayatollah Sayyid Abul Qasim Kashani, Mossadiq and the Tudeh, and, finally, Kashani and the Shah, demonstrate the intricate nature of political give and take in these turbulent years.

What is called the democratic era in Iran was in reality a period of personal power politics in an institutional vacuum exacerbated by the pressure of economic despondency. The sanctity of the Majlis and the Constitution was the battle-cry of those out of power. Once in power, the situation was transformed, priorities changed, and sanctimonious statements about democracy and the rule of law assumed novel meanings. The most telling evidence of this fact is afforded by Mossadiq's premiership between 1951 and 1953.

The consensus among liberal Iranians is that Mossadiq was not only the most patriotic and honest leader of his time, but also demonstrably devoted to democratic ideals. That is, at best, a dubious statement. His record as prime minister shows that he used power as he saw fit, irrespective of democratic precepts and constitutional injunctions.

Mossadiq belonged to one of the most exalted families of the nation and was related, through the Iranian aristocratic web system, to most of the traditional power bases in the society. He had opposed Reza Shah in the name of freedom and democracy, had been exiled, saved from posssible execution through the crown prince's intercession, forgiven, and, for the most part, forcefully kept out of politics. After Reza Shah's fall, he emerged anew in the Iranian political scene as an outstanding nationalist politician, the champion of the people, a force on the side of respect for democratic institutions, and, finally, as the most popular secular leader of the country. He was, therefore, the natural candidate for the leadership of a national front to fight against foreign domination.

In opposition, Mossadiq had used the Majlis, as the most sacred and inviolable bastion of national sovereignty and popular will, to wage war against leaders whose stand on domestic and foreign issues he opposed. By 1949, when the question of the Anglo-Iranian Oil Company became the nation's overriding political issue, his reputation as a nationalist leader and his command of militant public opinion had placed him at the apex of the political forces in the country, so that, upon the assassination of Prime Minister Razmara in 1951, the Shah eventually had no choice but to call on him to form the new cabinet.

Once in power, Mossadiq never hesitated to overrule the

Majlis or use nonparliamentary means, including martial law, the referendum, mob action, and extraordinary executive powers, to have his way. The same Majlis that he had defended before as the bastion of civil and political rights, he now denounced as a nest of foreign and reactionary agents. In fact, his relationship with the parliament left a legacy of abuse which was later utilized to contain the parliament's impulse to affect the decision-making process. His popularity, however, was hardly touched by such deviations from the democratic path.[9]

The point to be noted here is that Iranian culture was far better geared to the appreciation of personalities than to that of legal and constitutional structures and procedures. The check on Mossadiq's power never was the law of the land but, rather, other powers whose bases were different and strong enough to withstand him. The Shah, the clergy, the army, the Tudeh, the khans, each had a far greater effect on defining the boundaries of his power than the constitutional limitations of his office.

The trauma of the Mossadiq era convinced the Shah of the necessity of asserting and consolidating his political supremacy in the country. The conviction was, in part, a cultural phenomenon resulting from the recollection of the historical role of his office and, in part, a consequence of dialectical forces affecting the nature and operation of political power under the transitional socioeconomic conditions of the country.

Historically, kingship in Iran had often been conceived of as the repository of supreme political power.[10] While it is true that, in reality, the Crown was more a matter of contention among the more powerful tribal elites, it was nevertheless natural to expect great kings to strive to give substance to the ideological conception. Thus, in spite of his relatively gentle and tolerant nature, the Shah had to lend himself to policies and machinations that were not always congenial to his psychological makeup.[11]

From Cyrus to Reza Shah, glory had belonged not to the meek and the civil, but to the strong and the warlike. The tribal origin of most of the dynasties that had ruled Iran favored a ruthlessness of character more at home in the dispensation of primitive justice than with the more refined ideas of equity and fairness. To be a great king was to expand the boundaries of the kingdom, to bring one's adversaries to their knees, to look unchallengeable to friend and foe. The Iranian tradition of heroics is replete with accounts of victories of great kings on the battlefields, to the exclusion of any meaningful account of the prevailing socioeconomic and moral conditions. Even a man like Nadir Shah, of the Afshar tribe, whose genius centered on plunder and bloodshed, was held in higher esteem than others in whose time the country had lost in territory or in prestige. Closer to our own time, Reza Shah was held in awe, not because of what he had built on the ruins of the latter Qajar period, but rather for the strength of character he had shown in beating others into submission and, finally, forging a nation out of the chaos he had inherited. It is not surprising, therefore, that a significant part of the available wisdom in Iran should consistently stress the need for a strong leader. Nor is it surprising that many people should have felt that the role had to be shouldered by the Shah lest some emerging hero usurp it.

The decade between 1953 and 1963 still represented a continuation of Iran's postwar politics, even though, relatively speaking, the Shah's power had become palpably more pronounced. Both the first and last prime ministers in this period, General Fazlollah Zahidi and Dr. 'Ali Amini, belonged to a political world that could not tamely accept the political supremacy of the king as unchallengeable. Even such men as Asadollah 'Alam, Dr. Manuchihr Iqbal, and Engineer Ja'far Sharif-Imami, who held the office of prime minister for the most part in between, and whom the Shah held in highest trust in his years of near-absolute power, conceived of the role and office quite differently than Amir 'Abbas Hoveida, who presided over the Iranian cabinet for 13 of the 15 years of the Shah's supreme leadership. These men viewed the Constitution as still a viable and meaningful document to be considered in the discharge of their duties. It is, however, wrong to assume that their perception was the result of some innate and ingrained respect for the document; rather, it was more the result of the prevailing checks and balances within the framework of the operating power structure, and not the other way around, as evidenced by their behavior in the 1960s and 1970s, when, as the Shah's closest friends and advisers, they stifled any debate concerning the constitutional implications of the regime's actions.

Nevertheless, these were the years in which the bases of the Shah's political supremacy were laid down. That supremacy was based, in part, on the powers conferred upon him by the Constitution as the commander in chief of the armed forces, the head of the executive branch of the government, a partner in the legislative functions, and, finally, as the head of state, with all the pomp and ceremonial privileges ordinarily reserved for that position in a traditional society. In greater part, his political supremacy resulted from years of hard work on the consolidation of political support, both in and out of the country, and the elimination of enemies, sometimes by means of suppression, more often through cooptation. The fact that he was heir to millenia of Persian monarchy, and thus the archetypal father of his nation, placed him in a fundamentally strong political position in a country where other political institutions were either nonexistent, or had not yet matured much beyond the stages of infancy.

The year 1963 may be considered a political divide in Iran's postwar constitutional history. 'Ali Amini's assumption of office in 1961 was construed as a response to the gathering political turmoil centered around a new resurgence of the National Front, whose activities had remained minimal since the fall of Mossadiq in 1953. That resurgence, in turn, was in part a reflection of the perceived changes in the international political atmosphere stemming from new expectations generated by the John F. Kennedy presidency in the United States. By the end of 1962, Kennedy's practical experience in world politics, his encounter with Soviet premier Nikita Khrushchev in Vienna, the Bay of Pigs, the Cuban missile crisis, and his ever-increasing involvement in Vietnam, had sufficiently changed the climate to suggest a dampening of enthusiasm for continued democratic change around the world.

With the dismissal of Amini in 1962, the Shah took the reigns of power into his own hands. The 1963 referendum, in which the Iranian people expressed support for his policies, was, to his mind, an affirmation of his vision of Iran's future and, thus, a legitimization of what he considered to be his mission to move Iran out of the quagmire of political turbulence and economic stagnation. Henceforth, governments would be organs of administrative action to put his policies into effect. As we shall see, his success in generating the empirical conditions favorable to his intentions was largely due to a confluence of political and economic forces that were not entirely of his own making and which proved to be his downfall in the end.

On January 26, 1963, the Shah's six-point program constituting the ideological basis for his White Revolution was submitted to the people in a nationwide referendum and received an overwhelming popular approval. Since the parliament had been dissolved on May 9, 1961, and was not reconvened until October 1963, the legality of the referendum was based on Article 26 of the Supplementary Fundamental Law of the Constitution which stated in part that "powers of the realm are all derived from the people." Although the Constitution had not envisaged referendum as a form of legal action, the precedent for it had been set during Mossadiq's popular premiership and his insistence on the legitimizing effect of the popular will as the supreme determinant of political action. In the event, however, the relevant points of the White Revolution were later ratified by the Majlis and a constituent assembly and thus received the sanction of legality within the framework of the Iranian Constitution.

The following six principles were contained in the original six-point program: (1) land reform; (2) nationalization of forests and pastures; (3) sale of state-owned factories to the private sector as security for land reform; (4) profit-sharing schemes for employees in industry; (5) reform of the electoral law to allow for the political participation of women; and (6) the creation of a literacy corps to wage war against illiteracy, particularly in the countryside.

Between 1963 and 1977, some 13 new principles were gradually added to the original six within the framework of what came also to be called the Shah-People Revolution. Individually and cumulatively, the new principles were meant to expand and strengthen the basic philosophy governing the ideological underpinnings of the first six. They ranged from the ideologically trivial, such as struggle against inflation (presumably a policy that any government would pursue), to such fundamentally significant steps as the nationalization of natural resources and administrative and educational revolutions.[12]

The White Revolution aimed at a fundamental transformation of Iranian society. On the rural side, its basic objectives were to liberate the peasant from the shackles of historical bondage by transforming the legal and traditional rules that governed his relationship with the land and the landlord, to allow for the development of a new pattern of cooperative action to provide financial and technical support as substitutes for the landlord's traditional responsibilities, and to educate the peasant in order to enable him to take advantage of his new possibilities. The land reform legislation, the cooperative movement, the establishment of the Literacy Corps and the National Committee for World Literacy Program were directed at the accomplishment of these objectives.[13]

On the labor front, the profit-sharing scheme was later buttressed by the mandatory sale of up to 49 per cent of legally specified private industrial shares and 99 per cent of government plants to industrial laborers, rural cultivators, and the general public, in order to expand the ownership base in the society.[14] The underlying idea was to allow labor to share in the profits resulting from the increased productivity of capital based on modern technology, as well as to provide it with new incentives for the development of labor productivity.

The Ministry of Labor was charged with the responsibility of administering the law and arbitrating labor-management disputes through committees drawn from the ranks of labor, management, and third party neutral elements. In practice, the ministry, as a rule, threw its weight in support of labor, judging by the constant complaints of the managerial elements who had contacts in high political circles.

Socially, the issue of women's liberation, subsumed under the fifth principle of the White Revolution, proved one of the most promising, though volatile, aspects of the transformation of Iranian society. The principle aimed at changing the electoral law to allow for women's participation in the political process. In reality, it became the basis for a rather widespread and concerted effort on economic, social, political and cultural levels to transform the archetypal image of the woman as man's mother, wife, and sexual companion to that of a citizen with equal rights and privileges. In the 1970s, the Women's Organization of Iran became the focal point of these efforts, as it developed into a substantial ideological and organizational force significantly affecting the government's political and socioeconomic decisions concerning women on both domestic and international levels.[15]

Statistically, the most spectacular successes of the Shah-People Revolution[16] were registered in the economic realm. Indeed, the progress achieved in Iran's economy between 1963 and 1977 was routinely hailed by a majority of observers, inside and outside of the country, as nearly unique among Third World nations.[17] Compared with Iran's economic picture at the beginning of the Pahlavi dynasty's ascent to the Peacock Throne in 1925, by 1976 the GNP had grown 700 times, per capita income

200 times, domestic capital formation 3400 times, and imports almost 1000 times.[18] Much of this growth, of course, had taken place during the later years of the regime.

Between 1963 and 1976, the average annual industrial growth exceeded 20 percent while the number of industrial plants and the size of the industrial work force doubled. The GNP increased 13 times from $4 billion in 1961/62 to $53.5 billion in 1975/76. Per capita income went up eight times from $195 to $1600 in the same period.[19] By 1978, it had passed the $2000 mark. Most economic and social indicators showed appreciable progress, from education to labor, from production to consumption, from infrastructure to social welfare.

The changes in the domestic scene also had their counterpart in foreign policy. By the end of 1960s, Iran had begun to move away from an essentially one-sided association with the United States and was gradually assuming a more even-handed policy with respect to the East and the West. As a result, its relations with the Soviet Union and the East European Communist bloc decidedly improved, as exemplified by the continued growth in the volume of trade. On the Western side, the Iranian economic policy took painstaking care to diversify Iran's trade relations between Europe and the United States, so that practically every interested country had become a partner in some aspect of the nation's international economic and trade activities.[20]

Iran's relations with the Arab countries of the Middle East also showed marked improvement. The solution of the Bahrain question, the aid to Egypt's Anwar Sadat in the 1973 Egyptian-Israeli war, the rectification of the Kurdish problem and the diplomatic peace reached with Saddam Hussein of Iraq paved the way for the establishment of relatively friendly relations with all of the regional powers.[21]

China emerged as a new but promising partner in trade and diplomacy. The hostility between China and the Soviet Union naturally complicated Sino-Iranian relations. The Iranian government, however, seemed to succeed in presenting a neutral posture and thus, to some extent, in mollifying Soviet suspicions. Nevertheless, the visit to Iran by Chinese leader Hua Kuo-Feng in 1978 proved anew the underlying friction which remained in Russo-Iranian relations. By this time, however, Iran was in the throes of revolutionary turmoil, and the Soviet attitude toward the

Shah's government had begun to adjust itself overtly to this new situation.[22]

In the United Nations, Iran's aid and counsel were sought on a par with the most effective members of the Third World community. Even though her relations with Israel and South Africa remained a stumbling block in her dealings with some of the non-aligned countries of Asia and Africa, new and significant strides were made toward the establishment of closer ties and more friendly relations, as exemplified by Iran's voting record in the various chambers of the world organization in the latter part of the decade.

The most spectacular transformation, however, occurred in the Shah's power and his image as a national and regional leader. From a fragile young man, caught in the web of international and domestic political rivalries of the 1940s, he had grown into one of the world's most experienced and powerful leaders. The contrast between the humiliating reception he had been accorded in his own capital in 1943 by the leaders of the three Allied powers and the deference showed to him on the occasion of the 2500th anniversary of the Iranian monarchy in 1971 was symbolic of the fundamental transformation not only in the international stature of his country, but also of his personal standing among the leaders of the world. Then, as the official photograph shows, he had stood meekly behind a sofa on which Stalin, Roosevelt and Churchill had posed for pictures to commemorate their alliance; now, less than 30 years later, he could be seen on the world's television screens leading more than 70 heads of state and political luminaries of major countries, including those of the Soviet Union, the United States, and the United Kingdom, through elaborate state ceremonies. The contrast was impressive, intended not to be lost on the national sentiments of the Iranians.

Throughout his reign, the Shah had insisted that there was no honor in ruling over a poverty-stricken and backward country. Now, he boasted that Iran was moving into the company of the rich and the powerful. Although his role in the quadrupling of the price of oil in 1973 had been received unfavorably in most Western political and financial circles (a fact that may not have been altogether irrelevant to his later downfall) it had established new bases of economic and political power from which he could exercise unprecedented domestic and international influence. In the 1970s, Tehran became a major center of international economic and political activity. The Shah's audience and favor were continuously sought by financial and political leaders who converged upon the city to partake of the emerging opportunities.

In spite of his provocative criticisms of the West, the Shah's conception of a proper future for Iran was very much patterned after the Western experience. His idea of the "Great Civilization"[23] as the desirable picture for the future of Iran was a remarkable facsimile of a Western-style welfare state. In the promises of social security for all Iranians from womb to tomb, free and adequate nutrition for children in schools, equity in income distribution, nationalization of the country's basic natural resources, emphasis on private initiative, promotion of technology and efficiency, decentralization in the political process, and the people's participation in political decisions concerning their affairs, as in many other visions of the future, he echoed the ideals of Western liberalism in a society which had only begun to emerge from the bounds of traditionalism.

For most of his countrymen, the Shah's seemingly unassailable power, his air of self-confidence, his insistence on Iran's right to economic success and political grandeur, and his demonstrable ability to demand and receive international respect, were sources both of hope and despair. Often his pronouncements appeared exaggerated, unreal, at times even fantastic. On the other hand, his continuous success created a sense of awe, a feeling that he might be right, that it might be possible to break the vicious circle of underdevelopment in a short span of time, and that perhaps Iran could, under pressure, reach beyond her own grasp and achieve the impossible.

This almost schizophrenic dimension of Iranian politics was exacerbated by the nebulousness of the system's ideology. The relationship between Iran's past, present, and future was never satisfactorily explained, and the policies adopted were rarely justified by reference to some identifiable and cogent theoretical framework. The Shah-People Revolution was perceived by many as a series of policy propositions intimating a bright future, but designed essentially to preempt the political space from the influence of leftist and other adverse propaganda. The Shah's books,[24] and, later, the Rastakhiz party's manifesto,[25] were the closest approximation of an ideological statement. Their focus, however, was the history of the 2500 years of monarchy in Iran as a sine qua non of the nation's present stability and prosperity, and the necessity of the continued leadership of the monarch, at least for a period of time, in order to achieve a projected future presumably patterned after an advanced Western democratic welfare state. The linkages between present realities and future projections, however, were largely ignored. As a result, much of the Shah's pronouncements took on the hue of the pretentious statements of an ostentatious ruler; to some, they appeared as signs of megalomania.

Nevertheless, behind the system's ideological ambivalence there existed a set of theoretical premises which defined and governed the moral imperative of the nation's politics. While nowhere explicitly stated, included among them was a common belief that the relationship between the developed and the developing countries was basically a colonial one; that the essence of this colonial relationship was economic and that the economic hegemony of the developed nations derived mainly from their technological superiority; that under the prevailing historical circumstances, there was no escape from this unbalanced relationship. It was felt that Western technology had reached a stage where it had become self-propelling, that it moved on its own momentum and, so moving, it underwent qualitative change, exuding new dimensions of power. To face this power, it was essential to grasp the meaning of the technological revolution. This could not be accomplished in a vacuum. It had to be achieved through a bold historical encounter, by accepting interdependence with the West no matter how unbalanced the relationship, in order to achieve the capability of balancing it out gradually through a mutual journey into the future.

It was an option taken with a reasonable awareness of the economic, social and cultural costs entailed. From an ideological standpoint, three basic assumptions governed this choice. First, historically, Iran as a nation had faced numerous foreign military and cultural shocks and had succeeded in absorbing and assimilating aspects of the best of what they entailed, while maintaining its unique identity as a nation. The Islamic, Turkic and Mongol invasions, among others, provided eloquent testimony to the cultural and political resilience of the nation. It was argued that those who denigrated the country's attempt at rapid modernization did not appreciate the potential of this nation, or else had succumbed to the condescending attitude of those

Westerners whose cultural parochialism and economic selfishness prevented them from accepting as serious the concerted efforts of non-Western countries to move out of the vicious circle of underdevelopment. Iran could, and therefore must, do its utmost to find and regain its place among the progressive nations of the world.

Second, it was argued that economic and technological gaps between the advanced and developing nations were widening. The tempo of change in the West had brought about a drastic alteration in the meaning and impact of time. It was no longer possible for a country that hoped to achieve a semblance of parity with the West to move at its own accustomed speed. The political system had to muster the necessary mobilization capability to bring as many sectors of the society as possible into the developmental process, which meant, to bring them into contact with Western ideas and methods of operation. This was an endeavor beyond the reach of many Third World countries, for it entailed not only economic, social, cultural, and political upheavals, but also financial costs which not many of them could afford. Iran was fortunate in this respect because of its rich resource base and the income derived from oil. But oil was being rapidly depleted. It was estimated that within a period of 20 to 30 years, the country's known reserves as a meaningful source of foreign exchange would dry up. It was therefore incumbent upon this generation of Iranians to effect the transition from an essentially traditional agricultural society to a self-evolving industrial nation within the short span of a quarter of a century.

The economic, social, and cultural dislocations resulting from relentless pressure on the country's socioeconomic infrastructure were conceived to be serious but manageable. To the extent that there was an economic model guiding the developmental process, it was meant to achieve, as much as possible, a balanced growth pattern in the productive sectors even though it was assumed that the ideology of development necessitated a greater emphasis on industry.[26] In the event, political forces often imposed themselves on the economic plan, reinforcing the natural tendency of the economic forces toward greater polarization of the society.

Concerning the perennial issue of agriculture versus industry, the economic planners argued that it was impossible to achieve a sustained high growth rate without the establishment of a reasonably efficient and productive industrial sector, that, given the physical characteristics of the country's farmland and the limits of its water supply, agricultural productivity could not be raised beyond meager limits without the infusion of qualitatively different and superior technology, that the character of modern technology was such that it required profound psychological and orientational transformation, not to be confused with simple introduction of machinery in the rural areas, and that given the cultural framework of the Iranian farmland, such transformation could be effected mainly through a spillover function from the urban industrial and service sectors.[27] It was assumed that the land reform effected in the early 1960s would be a major stepping stone toward the achievement of this reorientation, because it would liberate the farmer from the limiting effects of his traditional pattern of sociocultural interrelationships. The literacy campaign, as the first step in the continuum of lifelong, nonformal education, and the introduction of cooperatives and farm corporations as principles of the Shah-People Revolution were meant to support the general policy of achieving cultural change in the rural areas.

The instrument of building the new society or "Great Civilization" was to be the private sector, aided by the government. As matters stood, the government not only channeled the financial resources it secured through the sale of the oil, but also controlled the nationalized sector, operated basic industries like steel, petrochemicals, and heavy industry, and set the norms for the private sector operations.

Nevertheless, in spite of a few signs of stress, the system's performance between 1963 and 1973 was by and large satisfactory. The advent of the 1974 oil boom, however, introduced new and drastic changes in the configuration of economic and social forces in the country. In spite of a rather lively debate about the absorptive capacity of the nation, it soon became apparent that no economic plan could withstand the force of a euphoric nationalism excited by the expectation of new possibilities opened up by the availability of these almost unfathomable riches.[28] Accordingly, it was argued that this was the chance Iran had been waiting for; that what was required was a sense of adventure, a boldness equal to the opportunity, an acceptance of calculated risk to reach the dreamland of self-sustaining economic and social development.

Between 1974 and 1977 Iran experienced an unprecedented economic boom. The GNP rose by a factor of 42 per cent in 1975.[29] Per capita income, no more than $85 in the mid-1940s, was around $2000 in 1977 and was expected to surpass $2400 by 1978.[30] Tehran, like a magnet, attracted businessmen and high-level politicians from all parts of the world. The combination of the newly acquired riches and the sociocultural change achieved in recent years imbued many Iranians with the feeling that they had finally arrived. Iranian businessmen, politicians, bureaucrats, and technical and scientific cadres felt, with tantalizing effect, that for the first time in the country's recent history they could hold their own in any international forum. In short, the prevailing mood among *au courant* Iranians in the first two years of the boom was one of dizzy and almost childishly optimistic expectation.

The planners, of course, recognized that the economy was going to be faced with at least two sets of basic constraints: an insufficient infrastructure, including a shortage of skilled manpower to handle and accommodate the volume of goods and services moving toward and through the country, and a widening of the economic gap between the rich and poor, urban and rural, and skilled and unskilled people. The negative effects of the boom, however, exceeded their expectations. Corruption, always a part of the country's economic and political landscape, now reached levels unparalleled in the nation's history in absolute terms, even though relative to the GNP, the evidence suggests that it had subsided.[31] The inflationary spiral resulting partly from internal mismanagement and partly from the weight of the increasingly higher prices of imports[32] particularly affected the middle-income fixed-salary white-collar worker. Its most telling manifestation was in the housing sector, where the shortage of capital goods and the pressure of speculation had practically priced housing out of the reach of the middle-income wage and salary earners in the government and the private sector. Significantly, the collapse of the Shah's regime was fundamentally facilitated by the breakdown of the government bureaucracy representing a major sector of the salary-earning middle class.[33]

Other economic pressures were also taking their toll. The declining value of the dollar in the international market in the mid-1970s led to a fall in the purchasing power of the foreign exchange obtained as payment for exported oil.

As a result, by the end of 1976 government expenditure was exceeding government income. The exorbitant wastage of money and material in 1974 and 1975, mainly due to a serious miscalculation of the absorptive capacity of the country's economic infrastructure, now forced the government to make an about-face in its approach to economic policy. The brunt of this policy change was to be faced by the social sector, reflecting a sharp reduction in the amenities and services people had become accustomed to expect. Lavish subsidies of primary consumer goods, as well as significant portions of welfare programs, were to be trimmed; government ministries were to scrutinize their budgets to prune as much of their housekeeping expenditures as possible, the tax structure was to be reexamined to be brought up to levels approximating those existing in other welfare states, and certain capital-intensive projects in the civil and military sectors, such as the naval base at Chah Bahar on the Indian Ocean, were to be discontinued.[34] Having failed to contain inflation by fiat, the government now was to embark on a belt-tightening deflationary policy. It was recognized that such a reversal of policy would inevitably exacerbate the existing economic and sociocultural tensions pervading the society, but the third assumption underlying the politics of development in Iran maintained that the political system was capable of containing the anticipated contradictions: an assumption that proved grievously wrong in the light of subsequent events.

The moral imperative of politics in Iran, as in other developing societies, derived, as we have seen in the introduction, from the consciousness of colonialism. Within that framework the leaders of the country believed, with considerable justification, that its successes in the economic, social, and cultural realms were substantial. In all of these areas, the capabilities generated within the society were of a nature which under propitious political circumstances could conceivably have catapulted the society out of the bounds of structural underdevelopment. The pressures placed on the society had created the necessary critical mass in a variety of fields ranging from domestic investment to scientific and industrial research. No doubt, social transformation in Iran had entailed substantial contradictions. But they were neither unique, nor particularly abnormal. The gaps in the socioeconomic development of Iran were easily perceivable in many other rapidly developing countries, from Mexico and Brazil to Taiwan and South Korea. The tragedy of Iranian politics was largely a consequence of a different sort of gap resulting from the evolving contradictions between a rapidly changing society with its growing social, economic, and cultural power systems, and a structurally petrified political system which had become progressively less capable of translating societal powers into systemic capability. The result was that the Iranian political system under the Shah became progressively underdeveloped relative to the development of its socioeconomic and cultural environments and thus became progressively more vulnerable to attack from both inside and outside the country.

The steps which the gradual process of political underdevelopment traversed are not very difficult to trace. Socially, the Shah-People Revolution led to a substantial breakdown of the traditional socioeconomic relationships by weakening the intermediary power structures in the farmland, among the tribes, and in the cities; by speeding up urbanization and education; by accelerating social mobility; and by transforming the traditional values of patience and submission into a new morality impressed by notions of acquisitiveness and expectation, systematically encouraged by a manifold increase in per capita income and consumption. Culturally, it exacerbated the existing social cleavages and created new social types as a result of the differential assimilation of new norms by differentially situated social sectors. Economically, while substantially increasing the number of middle class workers in white-collar positions in the trade, entrepreneurial, managerial, and service sectors, it also led to a widening of the gap between the city and the countryside, the rich and the poor, and the different geographic sectors.[35] In short, by accelerating the tempo of social mobilization, it generated new capabilities as well as new frustrations.

Politically, the Shah-People Revolution led to two interrelated processes. By breaking down the traditional parochial loyalties while increasing the mobility of the population, it facilitated the political atomization of the society, rendering a far greater number of people accessible to the authority and command of the central government. By focusing political attention on the Shah, it gradually eroded the authority of other central sources of power, leading to a concentration of power in the hands of the monarch. The realities of the Iranian political culture and institutions as well as the moral imperatives of

Iranian politics rendered the tendency toward centralization and concentration of power inevitable in Iran as they did in other Third World countries. The fact of concentration of power, therefore, does not in itself explain the vulnerability of the Iranian political system. Its concentration in the hand of the monarch, however, does. The tragedy of Iranian politics was, to a large extent, a consequence of the lack of proper understanding of the *institutional* powers of monarchy which imposed inherent limitations on the Shah's political options, a condition which separated him from all other comparable leaders who were not encumbered by such institutional limitations. Once Iranian society had moved beyond certain levels of socioeconomic transformation, the only alternative for the Shah was to open up the political space, and to deconcentrate and decentralize political power. The institution of monarchy did not allow him the option of totalitarian forms of accumulation of power, while traditional autocratic rule, in spite of the many benefits which it had bestowed on the people, was simply not adequate to the requirements of systemic power. This, as we shall see, is possibly the most likely explanation as to why the Shah's system proved so weak while the country was palpably on the move and he personally appeared so strong.

The myths and realities of the Iranian political system in the last decade of the Shah's rule will be discussed in the next chapters. Suffice it to say at this point that the Shah's command of domestic and international forces was conceived to be the basic pillar on which rested the hopes and aspirations of those who managed the process of socioeconomic change in the country. More than that, it was an essential ingredient of all calculations pertaining to policy options and, as such, its preservation or destruction became more important than the realization of the economic and social purposes it was supposed to support.

In the course of time, the relationship between the Shah and the political system assumed an unreal and personal character obscuring the objective weakness of the Shah's position, as reflected in the discrepancy between the purported aims of the system and the system's structural ability to achieve these aims. This obscurantist approach to politics mystified the notion of power by confusing its form with its substance. It began to equate statements of intent with the reality of action. In the end, this mystification was a basic source of deception not only for the proponents of the Shah's regime, but also and more importantly for otherwise astute domestic and foreign opponents, whose judgments had become clouded by this illusion of personal power. Their preoccupation with the Shah's power prevented them from seeing the larger issues of politics, thus facilitating the downfall of the regime precisely at a time when a historical opportunity had emerged for the reorganization of political power based on concepts of freedom, equality, and human dignity.

Notes
Chapter 1

1. See *Qanun-i asasi va Mutammim-i An* (The Basic Law and its Supplement) (Tehran: Chapkhanih Majlis, 1355); Herbert H. Vreeland, *Iran* (New Haven: Human Relations Area Files, 1957), 56–9.
2. See, for example, E. Abrahamian, "Factionalism in Iran: Political Groups in the 14th Parliament (1944–46)," *Middle East Studies*, no. 14 (January 1978), 22–55.
3. For a sympathetic treatment see Donald N. Wilber, *Riza Shah Pahlavi: The Resurrection and Reconstruction of Iran, 1878–1944* (Hicksville, NY: Exposition Press, 1975).
4. Julian Bharier, *Economic Development in Iran 1900–1970* (London and New York: Oxford University Press, 1977), chaps. 2 and 3, p. 42.
5. Amin Banani, *The Modernization of Iran 1921–1941* (Stanford: Stanford University Press, 1961); L. P. Elwell-Sutton, *Modern Iran* (London: Routledge, 1941); Hussein Makki, *Tarikh-i Bist Salih-i Iran* (The Twenty Years' History of Iran), (Tehran, 1945).
6. For an unadulterated account of Shiism see Seyyed Muhammad Hossein Tabataba'i, *Shiite Islam*, tr. by Seyyed Hossein Nasr (Albany: State University of New York Press, 1975). See also Fazlur Rahman, *Islam* (New York: Holt, Rinehart and Winston, 1966); Michael M. J. Fischer, *Iran: From Religious Dispute to Revolution* (Cambridge, MA: Harvard University Press, 1980); Shahrough Akhavi, *Religion and Politics in Contemporary Iran: Clergy-State Relations in the Pahlavi Period* (Albany: State University of New York Press, 1980).
7. George Lenczowski, *Russia and the West in Iran, 1918–1948* (Ithaca, NY: Cornell University Press, 1949).
8. L. P. Elwell-Sutton, "Political Parties in Iran: 1941–1948." *Middle East Journal*, 3, no. 1 (1949), 45–62.
9. For a favorable account of the Mossadiq era see Richard Cottam, *Nationalism in Iran* (Pittsburgh: University of Pittsburgh Press,

1964).
10. Pio Philippani Ranocni, "The Tradition of Sacred Kingship in Iran," in George Lenczowski, ed., *Iran Under the Pahlavis* (Stanford: Hoover Institution Press, 1978), 51–84.
11. "As time went on and I got to know the Shah better, I realized that he was not by nature a domineering personality. Indeed he was rather shy and withdrawn. I could never escape the impression that he was a gentle, even sentimental, man who had schooled himself in the maxim that the ruler must be aloof and hard, but had never succeeded in making it come naturally. His majestic side was like a role rehearsed over the years. In this he was prisoner, I suspect, of the needs of his state, just as he was ultimately the victim of his own success." Henry Kissinger, *White House Years* (Boston and Toronto: Little, Brown and Company, 1979), 1259. See also E. Bayne, *Persian Kingship in Transition* (New York: American Universities Field Staff, 1965); see also chapter 4 below.
12. For a list of the principles of the White Revolution see Lenczowski, *Iran Under the Pahlavis*, 478.
13. For background information on the traditional system of land tenure in Iran see A. K. S. Lambton, *Landlord and Peasant in Persia: A Study of Land Tenure and Land Revenue Administration* (London: Oxford University Press, 1953).
14. Thirteenth principle of the Shah-People Revolution, September 9, 1975.
15. See *Karnamih-i Saziman-i Zanan-i Iran* (The Balance Sheet of the Women's Organization of Iran) (Tehran: Center for Research on Women, 1978).
16. The title "White Revolution" was changed to the "Shah-People Revolution" on the occasion of the anniversary of the first decade of the revolution.
17. For an appraisal of Iranian economy for American business, see U.S. Department of Commerce, *Iran: A Survey of US Business Opportunities*, (Washington, DC: Government Printing Office, October 1977).
18. Jahangir Amuzegar, *Iran: An Economic Profile* (Washington, DC: The Middle East Institute, 1977), ix.
19. Ibid., 248. For a comparison with Iran's economic and social conditions at the turn of the century, see Bharier, *Economic Development*, chap. 1.
20. See Ahmad Faruqhi, "L'URSS et la révolution Iranienne," *Le Monde Diplomatique*, (July 1980).
21. See chapter 5, below. President Anwar al-Sadat's speeches and comments during his official visit to Tehran in June 1976 are indicative of the Arab world's changing perception of the Shah's

image. Sadat is particularly concerned with Iran's relations with other Arab nations and the Shah's position on the Arab-Israeli issue. Says he, "Your Majesty, the Arab nation keeps record of the fact that you stood by it in its legitimate struggle. . . . You supported the right of your Palestinian brothers to practice their political rights as an ancient nation with an undeniable civilization and political entity. . . . I wish to mention that Iran has voted in favor of eight U.N. General Assembly resolutions, at its thirtieth session, all of which aim at safeguarding the Palestinian people's rights and consolidating their international position. Futhermore, your stance towards the Jerusalem problem, of such vital importance to all Islamic nations, is a principled one compatible with our expectations and the spiritual ties that hold us together." See *Speeches and Interviews by President Mohammed Anwar al-Sadat during his Visit to Iran, June 15–21, 1976* (Cairo: Egyptian Ministry of Information, State Information Service), 11.

22. In fact, the account of the meeting between Hua Kuo-Feng and the Shah in the September 1, 1978 issue of *Izvestia* is rather conciliatory toward the Shah: "In his speech the Shah recalled that Iran's independent national policy is based on the principles contained in the United Nations Charter and the idea of 'friendly relations with countries that have different political, social and ideological systems'." *Isvestia* goes on to quote the Tehran daily *Ittila'at:* "Official Iranian circles emphasize that Iran is fully resolved to maintain its warm relations with the Soviet Union and does not wish to be drawn deeply into the conflict between the Soviet Union and the CPR." *CDSP* 30, no. 35, 5. Even the September 9, 1978, *Pravda* account of "Black Friday" (see chap. 3 below) is cautiously based on the reports of the Iranian Pars News Agency. It is only with the September 17 issue of *Pravda* that the Iranian events begin to be addressed in the Soviet press in purely ideological terms charging that the oil boom had not brought relief to the poor and blasting Iran's arms purchases from the United States. *CDSP* 30, no. 37, 20. Apparently, Alexander Bovin's analysis of the Iranian situation in *Literaturnaya Gazeta* of October 25, 1978 was the first full-length article appearing in a major USSR paper to blame the Shah's troubles on a long history of oppression. *CDSP*, 30, no. 44, 7.

23. The Shah's books and interviews remain the most direct sources for the study of his ideas. See inter alia, Muhammad Reza Pahlavi, *Mission for My Country* (London: Hutchinson, 1961); *The White Revolution* (Tehran: Kayhan Press, 1967); *Bih-su-yi Tamaddun-i Buzurg* (Toward the Great Civilization) (Tehran: Pahlavi Library, 1978); *Answer to History*, tr. by Joseph Ltd. (New York: Stein and Day, 1980). For an illuminating inquiry into the Shah's sociopolitical

attitudes, see Bayne, *Persian Kingship*.
24. The same publications as above.
25. See *Maramnamih-i Hizb-i Rastakhiz-i Millat-i Iran* (Manifesto of the Iranian Nation's Resurrection Party) (Tehran: Kayhan Publishing House, 1355).
26. See Plan and Budget Organization, *Iran's Fifth Development Plan 1973–1978, A Summary* (Tehran: PBO, 1973); also the *Summary* of the revised plan (Tehran: PBO, 1975). The Fifth Plan made a point of emphasizing social programs, rural-urban balance and fair income distribution. See also F. Najmabadi, "Strategies of Industrial Development in Iran," in J. W. Jacqz, ed., *Iran: Past, Present, and Future* (New York: Aspen Institute of Humanistic Studies, 1976), 105–22.
27. To the extent that the intrabureaucratic tensions represented divergent ideological outlooks, they were based on different perceptions of rationality in the modes of socioeconomic development. The country's economic success, however, gave the proponents of rapid industrialization a political edge over the agriculturalists. Prime Minister Hoveida, for example, often bragged that the country's splendid economic progress had been achieved in spite of the advice of economists.
28. See Amuzegar, Jahangir, "Oil Wealth: A Very Mixed Blessing," *Foreign Affairs*, Vol. 60, no. 4 (Spring, 1982), 814–35.
29. Bank-i Markazi-yi Iran (Iran Central Bank), *Annual Report, 1976*.
30. The unrevised Fifth Development Plan in 1973 had projected a GNP per capita income of approximately $1000 for 1978.
31. The high officials of the Iranian Government during the last years of the Pahlavi regime could be considered corrupt only in ideological and possibly moral terms insofar as they agreed to serve under the questionable moral conditions prevailing in the Iranian economic scene. By far the majority of them were untainted in personal terms. Indeed, not a single member of the Amuzigar cabinet could be plausibly accused of any financial wrongdoing.
32. See M. H. Pesaran, *World Economic Prospects and the Iranian Economy* (Tehran: Institute for International Political and Economic Studies, 1976).
33. See chapter 3, below.
34. See Robert Graham, *Iran: The Illusion of Power* (New York: St. Martin's Press, 1979), chap. 6.
35. For background analysis see M. H. Pesaran, "Income Distribution and its Main Determinants in Iran," in Jacqz, *Iran: Past, Present and Future*, 267–87.

2 | Political Structure and Political Power Under The Shah

The political business of Iran under the monarchy was transacted mainly through the bureaucracy and, after 1964, to a lesser extent through the Iran Novin party. The latter was the presumed conglomeration of the new popular forces centering on peasants, workers, women, and other social elements newly emancipated by the implementation of the principles of the White Revolution. The linkages among these social groups were provided by such organizations as rural cooperatives, labor syndicates, and guilds which acted more or less as transmission belts for the support and propagation of party policy. Since 1965, both systems were geared to the command position of the monarch through the intermediary of the late prime minister, Amir 'Abbas Hoveida.

Characteristically, Iranian political culture favored the elimination of ideologically rival and opposing elites from participation in the political process and the setting of national goals. Under favorable circumstances, however, this should not have excluded the possibility of collegiate decision-making by those sharing the same ideology. Sharing the same ideology obviously does not mean agreement on every specific issue; it suggests a willingness to shoulder responsibility, to insist on the right to affect policy decisions, and to accept the outcome as legitimate even though one may not completely agree with it. The sphere of legitimacy and authority may initially be limited, but the aim of the process is to expand its horizons to include progressively wider spectra of existing political forces. The success of the process depends not only on the structure of the political system, but also on the political attitudes of those who occupy its major positions. An analysis of the existing clusters of relevant and significant attitudes regarding politics and development, therefore, should shed some light on the realities of the Iranian political system.

Accordingly, two major intellectual currents dominating Iranian politics and administration in the post-war period may be identified and studied before an analysis of the salient structural characteristics of the political system is attempted. Both currents were products of Western intellectualism, and even though mutually antagonistic in appearance and content, their combination had the effect of paving the way for the centralization and concentration of political power. The first, American-inspired and marked by an aversion to "politics," dominated economic planning and administration. The other, essentially Soviet-inspired and distinguished by its totalitarian proclivities, dominated the political process.

The American influence on the patterns of economic and administrative thought in Iran dates from the end of the Second World War. Two basic reasons may be cited for the American preponderance in these areas. The obvious reason is that the United States had emerged after the war as the supreme Western power, whose interest in containing communism coincided with Iran's effort to maintain its independence in the face of the communist threat exemplified by the establishment of Soviet puppet regimes in Azarbaijan and Kurdistan and the growing influence of the Tudeh party.[1] The other was the favorable attitude of the Iranians toward the United States.

Unlike the Soviet Union and Great Britain, the United States had not left a memory of colonial domination in Iran. In fact, all through the 19th century, efforts by Iranian governments to secure American involvement in Iran as a hedge against Anglo-Russian domination had been side-stepped by United States administrations. The first serious American adviser in Iran, Morgan Shuster, had been forced to leave his mission on January 11, 1912, eight months after he had arrived, as a result of joint Anglo-Russian pressure. Morgan's account of his mission, entitled *The Strangling of Persia*, has remained a source book among Iranians as evidence of the nation's plight under colonial pressure. American missionaries had also made important contributions to the development of the country. The most renowned among them, Dr. Samuel Jordan, had founded the famous Alburz College, whose graduates constituted a significant portion of the Iranian intelligentsia in the years immediately after World War II.[2]

It was, therefore, natural for the Iranians to wish to send their children to the United States for higher education. The return of the first wave of Iranians educated in the United States coincided with the establishment of the Point Four technical assistance program, instituted in Iran in 1950.[3] The program proved to be a focal point for the employment of the young returnees, many of whom were gradually transferred to various government organizations engaged in economic development. Having the first claim on the existing positions and dominating policy process, the new managers attracted others with similar educational backgrounds. In due course, their employment policies were challenged and others began to penetrate their ranks, but their intellectual preponderance in matters pertaining to organization, method, and professional style remained intact.

The fundamental intellectual characteristic of the American-educated individual was his knowledgeability in matters internal to his field and a corresponding naiveté in matters pertaining to the relationship between his field and its sociopolitical environment. This apparent anomaly resulted from the overwhelming impact on the foreign student of the strength of the American socioeconomic system, the wisdom of the American Constitution, and the preponderance of American techniques for dealing with problems of administration and technology while the essential conservatism of the 1940s and 1950s precluded critical examination of the deep-rooted differences existing between the American way of life and social circumstances in Iran.

To the extent that theoretical stipulations concerning the international scene were advanced in American universities, they were couched in bipolar concepts reflecting the world as dichotomized between freedom and communism. The Third World would either develop after the pattern of the modern Western industrial nations, or, under the combined pressures of poverty and Soviet bullying, it would fall into the chasm of Communist bondage. Economic development defined as industrialization, freedom defined as anticommunism, and democracy defined as the approximation of Western institutions, were identified as the relevant panaceas for the future salvation of the world.[4]

This teleological undercurrent suggested a mandatory choice between the West and the Communist world. The result was a false sense of the universal applicability of the theories and principles derived from the Western experience to basically different socioeconomic and political structures. If the West were the preferred reflection of the future for Iran, that model had to be given reality by the identification and implementation of Western organization patterns and methods. For the technocratic mind, this process was confined to his own field, since, beyond the general philosophical orientation implied in the identification of development with Westernization, his intellectual tools were essentially geared to matters pertaining to the limited sphere of his specialty. His politics were also manifested within that framework. Thus, there existed constant tension about economic and social policy and complaints about the imposition of political preferences on economic policy, but rarely about the nature and organization of political power as the basic source from which political preferences derived their consistency. The effect was to reinforce a political structure that tended to exclude certain sectors of the society from influencing political decision-making.

The same may be said of administrative policy. Bureaucratic inefficiency had long been declared a major shortcoming of the Iranian political system. To combat the problem, students had been sent to various American academic and professional institutions to study ways and means of improving administrative efficiency. After the late 1950s, the responsibility for proposals concerning administrative policy and organization had passed to the graduates of these institutions who were organized into a newly established Civil Service Organization, as well as several colleges of which the prototype was Tehran University's School of Public Administration.

Steeped in the *POSDCORB*[5] tradition, these men and women were able to achieve some success in such esoteric areas as job classification, budget procedures, promotion policy and the like, but they never succeeded in confronting the basic administrative question in Iran: how to make the bureaucracy responsible to public interest. To confront the issue would have meant raising the question of the relationship between the bureaucracy and its socioeconomic environment in political terms. Since there were no independent channels of political communication comparable to the bureaucracy, there was no popular authority to which the latter could be rendered answerable. Power, therefore, tended to concentrate in the bureaucracy, transforming an organizational paraphernalia whose raison d'être was to serve the people into their unintended master. Administrative thought in Iran, meanwhile, tended to concentrate on issues internal to the bureaucracy, and by trying to streamline administrative process under conditions of bureaucratic hegemony exacerbated the problem of centralization and concentration of power.[6]

American- and Western-educated Iranians, therefore, unwittingly aided the development of a political system they did not particularly favor. Their preferences lay with democracy, but their conception of democracy was largely irrelevant to the realities of Iranian institutions. Half-recognizing this fact, they tended to sublimate politics in bureaucratic bickering, leaving most of the definition and justification of organizational patterns and styles of the interrelationship between the political system and its environment to a different genre of political actors. Pervading and widespread cynicism, demonstrably present in all echelons of the political system under the Shah, was largely a consequence of this unhappy consciousness.

The style of Iranian politics bore the mark of a radically different type of political personality. Desiring to expand its base of support or, at any rate, to neutralize oppositional forces, the system had embarked upon a policy of coopting the more agreeable members of the opposition. The coopting process took many forms: Some leaders of the National Front, for example, were engaged in lucrative economic ventures; others pursued their professions; still others were allowed to participate in the political process after recanting their old political beliefs. Among the latter, the rehabilitated Communists played a particularly important role in the shaping of the Iranian political style during the last decades of imperial rule.

The reformed Communists were coopted at all levels of the political system. They were found in high positions in the imperial court, among the upper echelons of the government bureaucracy, in leadership positions first in the Iran Novin and later the Rastakhiz parties, and in the sinews of the mass media, at the central as well as provincial levels. After the eclipse of the Tudeh party in the mid-1950s and the apparent flourishing of the Shah's regime, they placed their considerable political skills at the disposal of the government. Their cast of mind, molded in the intellectual spheres of totalitarian dedication, was particularly suited to the requirements of personalized power moving inexorably toward the apex symbolized by the person of the Shah. As the system flourished, so did they, by posing as architects of the new politics, extolling the virtues of obedience, inviolability of command, and the ubiquity and inherence of salvation, all geared to the majesty of the leader.

The Iranian experience reinforces the findings of a number of studies on the characteristics of the authoritarian personality, the most revealing of which, to date, remains the monumental work of Adorno and his collaborators on fascism.[7] The old Iranian Communists were supremely adept in jumping the scale of political values from the extreme left to the extreme right, never feeling at ease in the center. Their formidable talent in sloganeering dwarfed every attempt at moderation. Their exaggerated symbolism glorifying the leader and the leadership process surpassed all previous criteria. They set the style and the tone in professions of allegiance to the monarch while the linguistic characteristics of Persian culture, developed and perfected in symbolic deference to authority through millenia of practice in class-oriented gentility, encouraged a process of one-upmanship, carrying the language of worship to such extremes that it proved impossible for many otherwise loyal individuals to sustain it seriously.

On a more mundane level, the reformed Communists were instrumental in promoting methods of political manipulation. They introduced the concept of using labor syndicates and rural cooperatives as transmission belts to advance the government's political purposes. They denigrated the sanctity of private property, making it expedient for many in business to make their money as quickly as possible and transfer it to safer surroundings abroad once it was made. They treated the law as an extraneous factor to be used not as a foundation of policy, but as a mechanism for formalizing political options. They depersonalized and alienated the political process by legitimizing policies in reference to mass concepts, rather than group interests. They bastardized the concept of political parties by transforming the idea of Rastakhiz as a movement into an all-encompassing and therefore useless party coextensive with Iranian society.[8]

All this proved anomalous within the Iranian political context, because the system was essentially open, Western-oriented, and capitalist. The slogans, therefore, tended to lack conviction and to fade in the face of the reality. They succeeded, however, in creating disbelief, cynicism, and alienation.[9] They made it difficult for others to defend the system on logical grounds, because the system's use of language in its own defense was essentially illogical. The exaggerated symbolism, mystifying power, placed it out of the intellectual grasp of most people; they therefore tended to withdraw from it.

The prevalent style of politics, of course, brought out people by the thousands, from all walks of life, to cheer Iranian progress under the Shah-People Revolution. They filled the papers with expressions of gratitude to the monarch and blessed streets, squares, schools, monuments, and businesses with the names of members of the royal family. On balance, this was far more an expression of deep-rooted Iranian cynicism than straightforward political support. The command structure, however, operating through the bureaucracy and judging its performance by the echoes of its own proddings, consistently misread cynical acquiescence for political support.

The above should be considered in light of the general propensities of the system. We have already suggested in Chapter 1 that the personalization of power succeeded because it corresponded to the requirements of systemic power in the first decade of the Shah-People Revolution. The professionals helped the process by withdrawing from consideration of the essential issues of politics; the politicians enhanced the process by providing its basic mottoes, slogans, and justifications. Nevertheless, it is obvious that the two groups had very little in common and would have come to direct confrontation were it not for the historical accident of the presence of Amir 'Abbas Hoveida, who served as Iran's prime minister for 12 and one-half years, between January 1965 and August 1977.

Hoveida's pivotal position as prime minister for over a decade was instrumental in shaping the structure of the relationship between the Shah and those aspects of the political process that immediately affected the lives of the people. Compared to his, the role played by such political luminaries as Asadollah 'Alam, Manuchihr Iqbal, Jamshid Amuzigar, Hushang Ansari,

Ni'matollah Nasiri, and others, was at best marginal. No doubt, some of them might have been closer to the monarch and, thus, have shone more brightly in the luminosity of the court's apparent favor. But if the essence of politics is regarded as the process by which collective values are authoritatively allocated, it is indicative of Hoveida's importance that as far as the people were concerned, matters pertaining to allocations in the areas of jobs, prices, land, water, credit, education, hygiene, housing and the like were all implemented through the bureaucracy, at the head of which stood the prime minister. Furthermore, as an accomplished politician, Hoveida managed and manipulated the channels of political communication in ways unmatched by any other person or group. Yet his unassuming character inclined many observers to dismiss him as a force in Iranian politics. Others have unjustly accused him of the vilest crimes, including that of purposely betraying his country. The fact is that Hoveida tried to serve Iran as best he could. His ultimate failure was due more to the timing of his entrance into Iranian politics, to his perception of the world and to his personal traits, rather than to any lack of nationalistic fervor.

It is important to note that Hoveida was the first prime minister in the postwar Iranian history who had no personal experience and recollection of the office during the period when the Crown had not yet achieved the political supremacy and involvement associated with the years of the White Revolution. Through the intermediary of his relative, Hasan 'Ali Mansur, he had joined the Progressive Circle, a group of younger technocrats posing as a potential alternative to the more traditional politicians. Under Mansur's leadership, the Progressive Circle was transformed into the nucleus of the Iran Novin (New Iran) party in December 1963, and when Mansur was called upon by the monarch to form the new cabinet in March 1964, Hoveida was appointed minister of finance. When Mansur was assassinated in January 1965, the Shah called on his close relative and collaborator Hoveida to head the cabinet.

Ironically, Hoveida's lack of traditional political experience rendered him ideally suited for the occupation of an office whose functions were now to become mostly coordination and administration, rather than policymaking. It is probably false to assume, however, that his choice was governed by this consideration. A more plausible explanation would be that the Shah had committed himself to party government as demonstrated by the Mansur cabinet, whose members, except for the war and foreign portfolios, had been chosen exclusively from the ranks of the Iran Novin party. Given the political circumstances of the assassination, Hoveida emerged as a natural candidate, not only because of his special relationship with the deceased Mansur, but also because, as finance minister, he held a traditionally senior portfolio in the cabinet. As an explanatory factor, therefore, his personal traits relate more to his longevity in office than to circumstances of his selection.

What were those traits, and how did they relate to the requirements of power within the Iranian political system?

Hoveida had a complex personality which did not yield itself to facile psychological labels. His conception of the world appeared to include philosophical dimensions which tended to separate him from many of his colleagues and other contemporaries. Perhaps the most interesting attribute of his intellectual outlook was the strong sense of the absurd exuding from his sophisticated and often ensnaring cosmopolitan view of the world. He looked on life as a drama which unfolded on an expansive stage on which human actors sought meaning for their parts by vainly striving for the center of the limelight. In this competition in futility, everyone could be bought for a price. For some, the price was money, status and position, or praise to soothe their vanity; for others, more idealistic in their spheres of dedication, it was perhaps an opportunity to serve, to create, or to construct. In either case, men could be expected to succumb to clever manipulation by fate, by God, or by their own peers. His cynicism appeared to be fundamentally of a philosophical nature and, in that sense, extended to all, including himself. He remained in office for so long a time, quite possibly because he thought that, given the absurdity of it all, he might as well retain the center of the stage.

Socially, he was one of the most charming individuals ever to hold the office of prime minister during the country's constitutional history. He was witty in conversation, affable in manner, and cordial in his relationship with others. He did not show much interest in wealth, liked to mingle with ordinary people, insisted on driving his own Iranian-built Paykan, and generally gave the impression of a benevolent, folksy leader.

Politically, his skill in manipulating factions had allowed him to emerge as the champion of the line of least resistance, one consequence of which was that each pretender to his job tended to consider him preferable to all others. Thus, in practice, it had become very difficult to oppose him without seeming selfishly to covet his office. Furthermore, all through his tenure, in press interviews, in parliamentary debates, and in speeches across the country, he had loudly proclaimed the Shah as the real boss and gladly disassociated himself from any intimation that he had played a significant role in the progress of the country. Thus, perhaps unwittingly, he had succeeded in checkmating practically everyone, including the monarch, for if all success emanated from the Shah's sagacious leadership, how could he be separated from failures and shortcomings? How could problems be addressed forcefully without offending the Shah and casting doubt on his foresight?

Indeed, this was the predicament of the "loyal opposition," the Mardum party, whose leaders were called upon to criticize the government but often had to resign because their criticism seemed to implicate the Shah. Years later, in 1975, as a justification for the dismantling of the multiparty system and the inception of the Rastakhiz, the monarch stated that, while as the representative of the nation he was the prime force behind the Iranian national progress, the credit had been taken mainly by the majority party, while the minority politicians, loyal as they were, had been consistently left out of the governing process. The establishment of the all-encompassing party would presumably afford them the opportunity to participate in the making of a new Iran. Still, Hoveida not only retained his office as prime minister, but was also assigned the task of organizing the new party as its first designated secretary general. Clearly, the monarch was genuinely fond of him.

Hoveida's adeptness in politics had the practical consequence of keeping the lid on the basic contradictions of the Iranian political system and, thus, postponing their detection until efforts at their resolution proved too late. No other possible candidate in 1965 had the political talents Hoveida proved to have in later years. None had his sense of the absurd, his malleability concerning power, his capacity to laugh at criticism, his penchant for the almost stoic acceptance of his role as a political bridge for the gradual evolution of the notion of *fuehrer prinzip* and the military fixation of the monarch as the commander of the nation.

All others would have probably succumbed to the temptations of power, to vanity, to the pangs of conscience, or to nervous tension.

Obviously, Hoveida could not have endured for so long in office had other conditions not been favorable. In fact, he played his part in an exciting era unmatched in its manifestation of socioeconomic progress by any other comparable period recorded in the history of Iran. It is therefore wrong to assume from the foregoing that the intent of this discussion has been to fix the blame on him. On the contrary, it has been a central point of this study that no person nor any group of people could be held solely responsible for the determination of the destiny of a nation, and that destiny is shaped by a conglomeration of factors resulting from the interaction between the leadership process and socioeconomic forces whose characteristics are largely determined not by individuals as such, but by the history of the developmental process. Individuals and political structures may help or hinder timely detection of the evolving contradictions, depending on their characteristics. It is in this sense that reference has been made to Hoveida.

The organizational framework of Iranian politics hinged upon the bureaucracy. The bureaucracy was the main instrument not only of policy development and implementation but also of political communication. The major urban and rural mass organizations were related to the political system through the intermediary of the relevant ministries. In the rural areas, farm cooperatives had been organized and were led under the direction, first, of the Ministry of Agriculture and later the Ministry of Cooperatives and Rural Affairs. Labor unions were directly related to the Ministry of Labor, which acted as their sponsor. Guilds had close relationships with the Ministry of Commerce, although, due to the characteristics of the guild system, the ministry's tutelage was not as stringent. Thus, the Iranian bureaucracy was much more than the administrative arm of the government; it was relied upon also to perform the functions ordinarily reserved for political parties.

In fact, one of the basic problems of the Iranian political system was the intensely political nature of the public bureaucracy. But the structure of power was such that, logically, no significant change could be introduced to alter bureaucratic hegemony without a reformation of political ideology and reorganization of political power.

The central reason related to the constitutional position of the monarch. The Crown, as an institution, represented the whole nation. The king, therefore, could not engage in party politics without jeopardizing the institution of the monarchy. On the other hand, political parties could not grow in membership and stature without gaining meaningful political power. If they were to gain real political power, the monarch would have had to agree to refrain from interfering in at least a substantial sector of political decision-making. If he were not ready to do that, parties could not develop. Thus, since he was constitutionally the head of the executive branch of the government, the bureaucracy remained intensely politicized as the major vehicle of political influence. Political parties, on the other hand, tended to survive only as adjuncts of the bureaucracy. Individuals and corporate groups joined them in order to receive political favors, with the knowledge that in practice such favors could be meted out only through the bureaucracy.

The Iranian bureaucracy was structurally centralized, elitist in character, behaviorally formalistic, and functionally political. These characteristics were interrelated and collectively tended to make it culturally and socioeconomically hegemonial. Extreme centralization and politicization, however, appeared as the dominant factors—traits which helped the White Revolution in its first decade and debilitated it in its second.

As already stated, the White Revolution was a series of profound reforms instituted from above. It aimed at the introduction by legal means of socioeconomic changes in patterns of human and material interrelations in both rural and urban areas. These steps had, in turn, widespread political implications and, therefore, could not have been as smoothly instituted had they not been carried out through channels insulated from the ordinary patterns of political interrelationships.

By having a revolution by decree, legitimizing it outside of the normal political channels by referendum, and promulgating it through administrative action, the system avoided confronting adverse forces which would otherwise have created a great deal of political strife. Accordingly, the bureaucracy became the main instrument of administering the structural changes proposed in landlord-peasant relations, in labor-management relations, in the domain of women's rights, as well as in the relevant spheres of property and natural resources. Thus, fundamentally political acts were carried out by essentially nonpolitical individuals. One effect of this process was that drastic measures were taken in the name of the people, while the people's participation in making the relevant decisions was, at best, vicarious.

From the standpoint of systemic power, that is, the capacity of the political system to mobilize its resources for the specification and implementation of its goals, this mode of action proved efficient in the first decade of the revolution, because it bypassed the sources of friction that had historically made goal specification in these areas impossible, while the implementation capabilities of the political system derived from bureaucracy were sufficient to promulgate the relevant policies. The system began to face difficulties early in the 1970s because, by the end of the first decade, the mobilizational changes it had initiated had introduced substantial quantitative and qualitative transformations in the characteristics of its human resource base, producing new expectations and demands in economic, social and political realms, which the system could not satisfy without introducing a set of relevant structural changes in its relationship with its sociopolitical environment. It required the transformation of the bureaucracy from a hegemonial to a responsive position which, in turn, necessitated the establishment and promotion of viable and meaningful channels of political participation sufficiently powerful to keep the bureaucracy responsible.

Judged by its political announcements, the political leadership appeared to recognize the need for such structural changes. By 1975, the ideas of political participation and bureaucratic decentralization had been pronounced as official aims of the government. These statements of intent, however, were never translated into positive policy due to certain factors, of which the most cogent were those that had facilitated the concentration of power in the first place. The monarch was reluctant to relinquish power because of uncertainty about its political implications. Others exacerbated the matter by their interpretation of the two concepts. The bureaucrats tended to treat decentralization in purely administrative terms as delegation of authority to field officers, while politicians regarded political participation mainly as political education and indoctrination. The result was that the two concepts developed gradually into empty shells and turned into another source of frustrated expectations.

The phenomenon, however, should not be understood solely in terms of personal decisions. It was more a result of the systemic effects of the dialectics of power relations on one hand, and the environmental socioeconomic pressures on the other. Historically, decentralization and deconcentration of power have been more easily achieved under conditions of socioeconomic quiet and tranquility. Conversely, environmental pressures have generally tended to push toward greater centralization and concentration of power. The evidence of ancient hydraulic societies,[10] the depression years in Europe and the United States, and the conditions prevailing in contemporary Third World countries clearly demonstrate this tendency. The same conclusion is derived from the comparative study of complex organizations. Such studies demonstrate that, under turbulent environmental conditions, such organizations tend to collect themselves, pay greater attention to the lines of command, and generally reemphasize authority.[11]

In Iran, recognition of the need for decentralization and deconcentration of power characteristically materialized at a time when social and economic conditions had deteriorated and environmental pressures had intensified as a result not only of the discrepancies between the emerging requirements of the resource base and the limitations of the political organizations, but also of the international climate that was perceived by Iranians as clearly showing anti-Shah proclivities. The system's response was instinctively defensive: It fell back on emphasizing its symbols, stressing its achievements, and streamlining its lines of authority. The effect was to exacerbate the contradictions which the system was trying to resolve.

The Iranian political system in the 1970s was faced with a series of painful contradictions, the meaning of which it only partially understood. The decentralization of bureaucratic authority, for example, could not have been achieved without the institution of a system of checks and balances at the provincial and local levels, the focal points of which were the existing, though substantially dormant, local councils. The activation of provincial, city and village councils required the institution not only of relevant and effective channels for political participation, but also a panoply of demonstrable power that would give them meaning in terms of their effect on the socioeconomic condition of the community. Since the share of income from oil exceeded by far all other sources of government revenue, the activation of local councils meant, in effect, a decentralization in the decision-making processes concerning revenue sharing and resource allocation. Under the Iranian unitary system of government, the whole process required parliamentary legislation, the bill for which had to be prepared by the cabinet.

In the event, the general framework for the bill was prepared through the cooperation of certain members of Plan and Budget Organization, the Interior Ministry, and the Rastakhiz party. It was actively supported by the secretary general of the party and the state minister for plan and budget and subsequently, in late 1976, received in principle the approval of the monarch. The relevant ministries, however, while extolling the virtues of decentralization, killed the idea by objecting to it on several constitutional, political, and moral grounds.

The moral objection pertained to possible squandering of the money by corrupt local politicians. The political argument related to loss of central power and, therefore, control. The thorniest of all, the constitutional objection, was based essentially on Article 61 of the Supplementary Basic Laws of the Constitution that identified the ministers as individually and collectively responsible before the parliament for the affairs of their ministries. None of these arguments could withstand the test of serious analytic, legal, or experiential evidence and obviously derived symptomatically from bureaucratic antipathy to loss of power and organizational empire. Their combined influence, however, deflected the measure in such a way that the question was never again seriously considered during the remaining years of the Shah's rule.

Recent analytical studies of the Iranian political system have rarely paid proper attention to the systemic effects of the bureaucracy on Iranian politics. Quite possibly the political hegemony of the bureaucracy had far graver systemic consequences for Iranian politics than the combined effects of all other factors, including corruption and repression.

As the major source of the allocation of values, the centralized bureaucracy was instrumental in widening the gap between the rich and the poor, the city and the countryside, the educated and the illiterate, the skilled and the unskilled. The effect was systemic and resulted not from policy intentions, but rather from the differential impacts of the forces affecting the loci of decision-making. As the system grew more complex, the differential impact grew stronger. Those who were closer to the decision-making centers succeeded in arrogating to themselves more of what there was to be allocated, through the sheer weight of their proximity. Those who were closer, of course, were already in a more advantageous economic, social, or cultural position: the rich industrialist versus the poor artisan, the international importer versus the local merchant, the university professor versus the distant school teacher, the upper-city man versus the slum dweller,[12] the skilled technician versus the ordinary laborer, the laborer in richer industries versus the construction worker, the townsman versus the villager.

Those who focus on policies without attending to structures are likely to miss the basic point that policies affect people in the process of implementation. Implementation is often a tedious process over time, easily prone to deflection by forces and influences that converge on its trajectory. Elsewhere in this study, we have stated that the focal point of politics is power, while the proper referent of administration ought to be accountability.[13] Hegemonial bureaucracies are, by definition, accountable to themselves and under the effect of systemic influence end up responding mainly to the elite, in whatever field they may be found.

As the main instrument of value allocation, the bureaucracy was the major political arm of the Iranian government. Its politics, however, were naturally centered on interdepartmental rivalry. While it was not able to provide for popular participation or elicit political zeal, its insulation from the public, its hegemonial character, and its promises spelled out in development plans and spread out through the mass media, created expectations that could not possibly have been satisfied for all the people at the same time. The point is important politically, because the claim that progress has been made is broadcast uniformly to all the population, while the reality of progress is necessarily both limited and unbalanced. Thus, tripling the rate of adult literacy, quadrupling rural medical services, and raising the span of rural electrification tenfold in 15 years may be a great feat of accomplishment by any standard, but it still may leave half the adult population illiterate, 40 per cent of the population without meaningful medical care, and 30 per cent of the land without electricity.[14] Unless explained to them politically, all such statements appear as falsehood to those who have not received the benefits of the progress; and, in the hands of skillful agitators, failures can be made to loom far more importantly in the minds of ordinary people than successes.

The hegemonial bureaucracy cannot explain politically for two basic reasons: First, because, as the master of its environment, it does not have to, since its allegiance and accountability are to a different constituency—the superior hierarchs at the center, and second, because political understanding requires praxis, that is, that action and reflection be brought together. Bureaucracy is antiparticipative by nature: it follows its own esoteric rules, dictates its own patterns of behavior, responds only to the more powerful, and, finally, tends to alienate even those to whom it is supposed to give service.

The remedy is political decentralization. Hegemonial bureaucrats cannot, in practice, decentralize even when the state's policy calls for decentralization. Delegation of authority means the distribution of capacity to make and implement decisions. Taking such decisions involves risks for both subordinates and superiors. As the Iranian case shows, the subordinate tends to refuse to take independent decisions without hedging against the risk by obtaining the prior approval of the superior. The buck passes upstairs, and the law of delegated authority under these conditions is that of the ball thrown against a solid wall: it always bounces back.

Bureaucratic centralization was a major structural barrier against political participation. Conversely, without political participation, it was scarcely possible to effect decentralization. The interdependence between the two constituted a vicious circle that could not be broken without a comprehensive change in the characteristics of political power in the country. As the forces whose combined determination was needed to achieve the breakthrough were the immediate beneficiaries of the existing pattern of power relationships, efforts from within the system proved largely futile. Predictably, the major force blocking decentralization was the bureaucracy itself. Neither the Shah nor other nongovernmental beneficiaries of the centralized authority seemed particularly conscious of the political implications of decentralization. Taking their cues from the bureaucratic leaders, however, they tended to interpret it in purely administrative terms.

Political participation, on the other hand, was seen primarily as an education program by which the virtues of the political system, the sanctity of its symbols, and the correctness of the socioeconomic philosophy underlying the Shah-People Revolution were to be imparted to the people. The monarch represented the basic symbol of the educational process and was, therefore, a referent in all popular expressions of gratitude for the newly achieved stability, security, and progress under his benevolent leadership. Parties, unions, cooperatives, associations, and other mass organizations were expected and encouraged to demonstrate their support on national occasions by sending telegrams, advertising in the media, taking part in parades, and engaging in other demonstrative behavior.

The process was not unlike other leader-dominated systems in that essentially rootless, anomic expressions were interpreted and presented as evidence of significant political participation and support. Comparable patterns of political behavior can be readily identified in communist systems as well as in noncommunist Third World countries in which the weaknesses of the institutional frame of reference invariably thrust the leader to the fore. The difference in Iran was that the Crown, as an institution, had strength enough to limit the ideological and organizational choices open to the Shah and other political leaders.

The point suggests—and herein lies its importance—that contrary to the prevailing liberal and socialist opinion that holds the republican form of government historically and logically more progressive than the monarchy, given the characteristics of the Iranian political culture, only a monarchical system can guarantee the required limitations on the political system commensurate with the needs of institution-building and constitutional government. In fact, had it not been for the limitations which the Crown imposed on the Shah, he could have opted for organizational and methodological uses of political control that would have enhanced and preserved his power indefinitely. Conversely, options now open to the Iranian nation without the monarchy are basically limited to either a rightist-military, a Communist-leftist-military, or a variant of the two regimes. Only the most politically naive may still hope for a republican secular democracy.[15]

What were the inherent power limitations of the Crown as an institution? How were they related to the question of political participation?

The Crown as an institution could not carve out a sociopolitical sphere as its preferred domain and separate itself from the rest of the population. Traditionally, the Crown conceived of itself, and it was conceived of by the people, as comprehending the whole of the nation. Politically, therefore, it could not present itself as partisan, a point of great significance for the dismal state of the parties in Iran, but also, as we shall see, for the promise of a democratic party system under more propitious political conditions.

The Crown as an institution could not be revolutionary in terms of the prevalent modern notion of revolution as a class-oriented phenomenon. The so-called White Revolution, as mentioned earlier, was an effective reform operation that materially changed the structure of power relationships in the society. But even though it emphasized the farmer and the worker, it was careful not to sever itself from the landed or industrial and commercial capital. Consequently, it never developed the ideological framework or the organizational capability to allow it to mobilize and control the power inherent in some socioeconomic classes and strata in order to exterminate or totally control other classes or strata.

The crucial point here is that, while it is true that under totalitarian and semi-totalitarian systems, organizations like labor unions and farm cooperatives cannot dispose of independent political power, nevertheless, they are powerful organizations whose potential is developed and realized through the intermediary of the vanguard party's political ascendance.[16] In other words, by dominating basically powerful organizations, the party rides on the crest of their power and, by giving it shape and direction, dominates all other elements as well. Under the Iranian monarchy, such organizations were essentially powerless and were not allowed to achieve power, because the system could neither associate itself with them ideologically, nor was it inclined to withdraw so that they might develop independent power. The government tended to play the role of the arbiter under conditions in which the rights and responsibilities of labor and capital, as those of other contending factors, were determined by arbitrary and often esoteric notions of social justice. The result was alienation, even though all parties, in fact, gained socially and economically.

The Crown, therefore, was never able to develop the infrastructural power necessary for the development or perpetuation of either totalitarian or autocratic systems of government once the social base had achieved the dynamic dimensions associated with modernism. In order to survive, the Iranian monarchy would have had to move in the direction of greater openness in the political space and increasing pluralism in political relationships, choices that were stifled by the existing conglomeration of forces, but which could have been made if national as well as self-interest had been perceived more logically.

The plight of the Iranian political parties as the potential means of political participation points to the same conclusions. A cursory analysis of the Rastakhiz may illuminate the point.

The Rastakhiz party came into existence because the previous two-party system had failed. The system had maneuvered itself into a political impasse in which it had become virtually impossible for the opposition party to attack the government without appearing to criticize the Shah's policies. As the Shahsavar by-election of 1974 had shown, the failure of the two-party system had little to do with the people's propensity, or lack thereof, to participate in the political process. In that election, the popular response was overwhelming, even though it was carried out mainly for the purpose of gaining experience for the new leadership of the Ministry of the Interior, all of which had been recruited from other organizations including universities, and were substantially unacquainted with the management of the electoral process.

There were no specifically important issues involved. The mood, however, had changed because it was the first year of the new prosperity occasioned by the quadrupling of oil prices, and also because the new minister of the interior, Jamshid Amuzigar, was reputed to be independent of then Prime Minister Hoveida. Furthermore, on the occasion of the introduction of the new vice-ministers in a palace audience, the monarch had solemnly instructed the team that he sought, and expected, free and unhindered general elections the next year and that, contrary to the prevailing political rumors, both parties were equal in his eyes, and therefore he could have no preferences whatsoever as to which party would achieve a majority in the coming elections.[17] These points, of course, were duly brought to the attention of the public, including the people of Shahsavar.

The experience was instructive. Since practically all of the public and most of the private organizations were affiliated with the majority Iran Novin party, it took some persistence to convey the message of the ministry's resolve to carry out an unbiased election and to prevent undue government interference. The prime minister, as the head of the majority party, sent word that the result of the election would depend solely on the capacity of the cadres in each party to get the votes out. Eventually, most of the leaders of the two parties converged on the small town to help with the campaign.

By Iranian standards, popular participation was impressive. Over 60 per cent of the eligible voters participated. In addition to the electoral supervisory groups stipulated by law, each candidate was also allowed to have his special observer at each of the poll stations. In the event, the majority party won by the smallest of margins, a difference of some 200 votes, representing 50.1 per cent of the ballots cast to 49.9 per cent for the Mardum party. In comparison, in the previous general election in 1971, the Iran Novin candidate, whose recent appointment to a cabinet post had made the Shahsavar by-election possible, had drawn close to 90 per cent of the votes. In the Rastakhiz general elections of a year later, in 1975, the former Mardum candidate won by a comfortable margin.

The relative success of the Mardum party in the Shahsavar election encouraged the loyal opposition to prepare seriously for the coming general elections. The party's major dilemma was finding issues on which it could differ with the government without alienating the Shah. This proved extremely difficult, since over the past ten years the Hoveida government had made a point of identifying itself with the monarch on every conceivable issue. Even when the issues were narrowed down to the relatively benign questions of efficiency in operations, people in Tehran began to ask questions: if the government was so inefficient, why should the Shah have allowed it to stay in office for so long? The result was a political impasse that was finally resolved by the surprise announcement of the formation of the Rastakhiz party in January 1975.

The idea of the Rastakhiz had been suggested to the monarch in 1971, through the intermediary of the queen, by a group of relatively young intellectuals drawn from the universities and middle-level government offices. The group acted as an unofficial think tank for the queen, dealing with specific and limited issues of public policy and administration.[18] In time, it had come to the conclusion that the basic problem was political and required a structural reorganization of political power for the mobilization and participation of the people in the political process. Given the seemingly unshakable identification of the government with the monarch, and the fact of fragmentation of the Iranian political culture, the conclusion was reached that the appropriate way out of the impasse was for the Shah to use his power to effect a new relationship between the bureaucracy and its environment, not by separating himself from the government completely, but by extending the umbrella of his power to embrace popularly elected organs as well.

The theoretical justification for the move was suggested in the following terms. The first decade of the White Revolution was devoted to the implementation of infrastructural changes, particularly as they pertained to peasants, workers, women and natural resources. The changes were of a nature that could have been best achieved through legal and administrative acts. They were profound and had been accomplished with the least amount of political tension. Beyond this point, however, the revolution could not be consummated without popular participation in the political process. Popular participation, on the other hand, could be mobilized only if the process could be translated meaningfully into political decisions. But as long as political decisions were made by a hegemonial bureaucracy attached uniquely to the person of the Shah, the nexus between decisions and participation was impossible to achieve. Hence, the objective necessity of breaking this vicious circle.

In effect, the group suggested the democratization of the political process. But it also recognized that under the Iranian political culture, characterized as it was by fragmentation and institutional weakness, the democratization process could not be achieved without a consensus on the fundamentals of political process and content. Obviously, it would have been futile and anachronistic to have suggested a system in which the Communists or Muslim fundamentalists were also invited to participate. It was, therefore, proposed that the sphere of participation would encompass all who believed in the Iranian Constitution and the basic principles of the Shah-People Revolution, both of which would then be open to interpretation through the constitutionally accepted legal and political procedures. To this end, a political movement, not a party, called the Resurrection movement of the Iranian nation, the Rastakhiz, would be announced within which people would be free to join associations, unions, cooperatives, and political parties of their choice. Simultaneously, steps would be taken to decentralize the bureaucracy and empower local councils through appropriate legislation.

The monarch's power was seen as a sine qua non of the success of the proposition. It was assumed that his prestige, leadership qualities, constitutional position, command of the armed forces, and generally unchallenged power at the time, had placed him in a uniquely favorable position to effect the change. His role from then on would gradually evolve into that of an umpire, as the Constitution in effect had foreseen.[19] He would not involve himself directly with every political issue, but rather take care that the political process was not abused. He would remain on top of the policy options concerning such relatively esoteric but vital matters as foreign policy, oil, military, and national security for the foreseeable future; but all other economic, social and cultural questions would be decided through the evolving political process within the general consensual framework. It was assumed that in the early phases, the sphere of popular participation, particularly among the intelligentsia and portions of the middle class, might be limited, but as they came to believe in the honesty and efficacy of the system, it would gradually expand to increasingly wider horizons.

The significant factor in the group's position was that it was conscious of the dialectical nature of the problem confronting the Iranian political system. It recognized the contemporary reality as well as the fundamentally meager potentials of the existing political power structure. It also recognized the intellectual paucity of purely normative propositions in favor of liberal democracy. The Iranian Constitution, except for its never-used article concerning the religious determination of the propriety of the laws,[20] was indeed a purely Western document, and perhaps for that very reason had never been honored except in the breach. The fundamental question, therefore, was how the existing power could be brought to support the maintenance of a dynamic balance among the contradictory factors affecting the structures and functions of the political system in the interests of freedom as well as national integrity, stability and economic development.

In the event, the proposal was rejected. The group never

succeeded in having direct communication with the Shah. It was informed by the queen that His Majesty had appreciated the thought and the effort, but with the people he had around him, he could not implement the idea at the time. And then a strange caveat was added: that Iran was a democracy and the prevailing two-party system, as explained in His Majesty's book, *Mission For My Country*, would remain the appropriate political frame of reference. The message was clear—the boat was not to be rocked.

Nonetheless, in 1975 the Shah presented his own adaptation of the Rastakhiz idea, containing some of the points in the original suggestion, but deviating from it in very important respects. While the original idea had been proposed basically for the purpose of national reconciliation, His Majesty's mood, reflecting the recent successes of the regime, was rather combative. Within the general nebulousness of the proposed idea, two points stood out clearly. First, the Shah identified the progress of the nation with his personal leadership and suggested that one of the reasons for the proposed change was that, while the accomplishments of the country were due to his decisions, only the majority party could share in the credit and others, just as patriotic as the majority, were left out. The new situation would allow everyone the opportunity to participate in the progress of the nation.

The second point was harsher and probably reflected his irritation at criticisms he considered unjustified in the face of the apparent progress achieved by the nation. He stated that the time had come for the Iranians to clarify their political position and promptly suggested three categories into which they might be divided. The first category contained the majority of the people who accepted the three principles of the Rastakhiz: the imperial order, the Constitution, and the principles of the Shah-People Revolution, and were desirous of actively participating in their promulgation. These were the chosen people who would hold the political offices of the state. The second were those who showed no overt enthusiasm for the new order, but did not actively oppose it. They would be free to engage in and benefit from the socioeconomic opportunities open to all Iranians; however, they should not expect equal participation in the political process. In the third category belonged the small, misguided groups who actively opposed the national progress. The system could easily crush them, but being of a benevolent character, it would allow them to leave the country and choose their preferred paradise in other lands; their passports were ready.[21]

On the organization and structure of the new system, the Shah was less clear. He spoke of it mostly as one huge party, but sometimes also as a movement. He appointed Prime Minister Hoveida as its secretary general for the first two years, during which the party's constitution, organization, by-laws, and membership were to be developed to allow for the election of new officers.

In spite of the obscure nature of the new proposal, the idea of the Rastakhiz met with considerable enthusiasm among the people. For the first time, sizeable groups of professionals and intellectuals who had never participated in politics before showed an inclination to take part in its proceedings. Much of this new burst of enthusiasm was due to the relief from the impasse created by the already ossified Iran Novin party, but, more importantly, it showed the need for political participation felt by a people fast passing beyond the confines of traditionalism. The Rastakhiz, however, proved an empty shell, not only because of the obscurantist mode of its conception, but more significantly, because of the contradictions involved in a one-party system under a powerful monarchy.

It was clear from the beginning that the reformed Communists would play a dominant role in the shaping of the Rastakhiz concepts. The Shah's unclear statements about the structure of the party had emboldened the more democratically minded to hope and agitate in favor of a movement that would allow for the gradual development of new political parties along the lines envisaged in the original proposal. Soon, however, word came that His Majesty had decided on one all-encompassing party and, therefore, insistence on the concept of a movement was futile and irrelevant. The preparation of the first draft of the concepts and organization of the party had already been entrusted to Manuchihr Azmun, a deputy prime minister who happened to have received his doctoral degree in social studies from the Karl Marx University in East Germany.[22] The result was fascinating. A former Communist had produced a perfectly fascist plan according to which each profession would be organized internally and then joined at the top through a series of command organs that would coordinate their activities. Thus, farmers, workers, teachers, students, guilds, doctors, and so on, were to be organized separately and join the party at the top in corporate form through their representatives in the party's command organs. Characteristically, the major argument in favor of the proposed plan was that of efficiency. It was argued that only in this way could the party be organized quickly and controlled under the country's leadership structure.

Opposition to the plan was vehement. It was argued that not only was the idea a hybrid of Italian and Spanish models of fascist organization and thus antithetical to the spirit of the Rastakhiz, but that it would make the country's pretensions to freedom and political participation ludicrous in the eyes of the whole world. Help was sought at the highest levels of the political order and, finally, with the aid of the queen, the proposal was rejected before it could come out for a more public discussion.

In the end, the organization of the Rastakhiz assumed the general characteristics of the Communist-type parties under totally different ideological premises, a condition that, in effect, converted the Rastakhiz into a bureaucratic phenomenon drained of political vitality. Although not directly mentioned in the text, the structure of the party reflected the concept of democratic centralism as it was based essentially on two parallel lines of communication joined at each hierarchical level. The command line was to be organized from the top downwards under the supervision of the secretary general who, elected by the party congress, appointed a hierarchy of secretaries who in turn would organize and lead the participative line at each level of the party's organization. The participative line was based on the party's primary organizations, called *kanun*, or cell, whose representatives would join together in a series of hierarchically organized councils at town, province and *ustan*, or region, levels, culminating in the party's central committee. The central committee would, in turn, elect the party's executive committee, presumably the party's highest organ, that would act in place of the central committee in between its sessions. Coordination between the government and the party was to be achieved through the political bureau under the chairmanship of the prime minister and composed of the representatives of the executive committee and a number of cabinet members selected by the prime minister. To maintain party supremacy, the executive committee's representation was to be slightly higher than the cabinet's.[23]

Every step in the process of the development of the

Rastakhiz pointed to the contradiction between the position of the ruler as king and the requirements of party politics as the mode of generation and management of power. To begin with, the very idea of an all-encompassing party appeared as a contradiction in terms. Parties, by definition, are representatives of political clusters of interest. As such, they never encompass the totality of the people. This is particularly true of revolutionary parties agitating for exclusive power. The operational efficiency of such parties depends on their policy of limiting their membership to a core of ideologically trained and committed cadres who, as the political elite of the system, are charged with the management of power and transformation of the society.

Rastakhiz, however, was decreed to include every Iranian above the age of 18 unless he or she officially refused its membership. The unstated reason dictating the comprehensive character of the party was obviously the fact that the Shah was its presumed leader; since the institution of monarchy belonged to the whole people, it followed that the whole people should belong to the party of which he was the leader. It was, therefore, coextensive with the political society and as such made no sense as a party.

On the other hand, precisely because it was not a party, party-like political organizations could have emerged from its interstices. But, as the experience of the party wings demonstrated, this also proved impossible because of the contradictions involved in the structure of power on one hand, and the conception of Rastakhiz as a single political party on the other. The experience is sufficiently revealing to bear a more thorough examination.

As mentioned before, the new party, at its inception, had generated considerable enthusiasm among the people. This interest was reflected in the parliamentary elections of the summer of 1975. On the average, three candidates for every parliamentary seat were endorsed by the executive committee of the party. The election proved a lively contest in which every candidate campaigned for his seat with a force and enthusiasm rarely witnessed in the recent history of the Iranian parliamentary elections. To assure absolute impartiality, the members of the supervisory electoral boards were selected, in equal proportion, from the ranks of the people suggested by the candidates themselves. In the end, some 60 per cent of the eligible voters participated, an impressive ratio considering the sociopolitical as well as geographic conditions of the country.

A study of the election results suggests that they were largely determined by the cumulative impact of three factors on the elected candidates: affiliation with the Iran Novin party, residence in the electoral district, and the availability of financial support. On the average, those candidates tended to be successful who had not had previous affiliation with the Iran Novin party, who had been a native of their respective electoral districts, and who had mobilized greater financial support for their candidacy.[24] The important point for this discussion is that, having all been selected by the executive committee of the Rastakhiz, they had to be presumed loyal to the regime; and having all contested and won a hard-fought election, particularly in the single-member districts in semi-urban and rural areas constituting two-thirds of all parliamentary seats, they had to be presumed to have some influence and support in their constituencies. In other words, had the regime not castrated these people politically, it could have drawn on them, as well as on others, to support it in time of need.

In the meantime, to channel discussions on policy options within the party, two wings were proposed, each under the leadership of one of the highly trusted officials of the regime. Both wings considered themselves liberal. The "progressive wing," under Jamshid Amuzigar, leaned more toward social welfare and economic equality, decentralization and political participation; while the "constructive wing," under Hushang Ansari, the powerful minister of economy, appeared to place greater emphasis on economic growth and industrialization. To discourage people from confusing wings with parties, they were dubbed the "thought basins" of the party.

Nevertheless, in spite of the relatively subdued character of the wings, the natural thrust of the political process recognized them as politically more logical than the unstructured Rastakhiz and imbued them with a vitality that went beyond the expectations of the system. The élan was particularly felt among the newly elected members of the parliament who joined the wings in the hope of giving structure to their political interests. Accordingly, about two-thirds of them joined the progressive and one-third the constructive wings. Immediately, however, the basic contradictions of the Iranian political system began to assert themselves. It was argued that if the Rastakhiz were a single party, how could it present itself with two voices? The wings, therefore, should be construed only as channels for arriving at political decisions; they should not reflect divisions in decision-making. The result was two sets of contradictory decisions about the parliament. First, that parliament representing a single party should legislate with a unanimous voice. And, second, that the wings should be represented equally in the leadership positions of the parliament, with the curious effect that the minority opinion received relatively a far greater weight than the majority opinion. The party therefore became incapable of relating meaningfully to parliamentary operations. Parliament in turn was reduced to a rubber stamp and seen as such by the people. Rather abruptly, the initial élan created by the hope of political participation gave way to despair, reinforcing the latent cynicism of the Iranian people.

Rastakhiz was obviously meant to be a mobilization party. It failed, however, because, under the Iranian kingship, it was not possible to have an effective single mobilization party. As an agent of political mobilization, the throne, represented by a powerful king, seemed anathema to the sociopolitical conditions of the country in the last quarter of the 20th century. Up to the era of the Pahlavi kingship, Iran had been a relatively homogeneous society. The Qajar shahs, the aristocracy, the clergy, the merchants and the peasants saw the world, more or less, through the same lenses. They ate the same type of food, wore the same type of dress, listened to the same type of music, and saw the same type of *ta'ziyih* (religious mourning) as a form of entertainment as well as religious cermony. The difference in their experiences related more to their relative wealth and poverty than to their *weltanschauung* and ideational orientation.

The transitional process to modernization had drastically changed this relative homogeneity of the society. There was no longer a patterned culture on the basis of which a political understanding could be reached. On the contrary, the reality of Iranian life was represented by the facts of political fragmentation and cultural heterogeneity. Necessarily, political leadership engulfed a person in fractional politics of the widest range, involving not only the traditional center, left, and right, but a whole gamut of differentially mobilized social types whose world views were determined by the interaction between the characteristics of their culture base and their sociopsychological proximity to the kinds of modern idioms that were floating in the political space.

By tradition and by law, the monarch was the symbol of the whole nation. He was the embodiment of the majesty of the state, and hence, inviolate and inviolable. His role was best suited to that of the supreme arbiter of the conflicts among his people, an umpire to call it quits when necessary, a force to maintain the integrity of the political game against the centrifugal forces effected by players who did not always acquiesce to the same rules or the same aims.

As a political leader, he became party to the game, a captain whose interests were inextricably intertwined with the victory of his team against all others. He could no longer remain untouchable and unsullied. Yet, by its very nature, the throne could not be attacked as a political office. A challenge to the throne was a challenge to the majesty, integrity and the constitution of the state. Herein lie the dilemma and the tragedy of Iranian politics under modernizing kingship. The Shah did not fail as a political leader; rather, as a political leader he simply could not have succeeded as a king.

Nevertheless, the dialectics of power relations in Iran forced the Shah toward the assumption of an increasingly greater role in the daily political life of the country. Once the sanctity of the throne was forfeited by the plunge into a political arena marked by lack of consensus, the same forces that everywhere in the developing world work for the ascendance of personal power began to shape the political destiny of the nation.

The concentration of power in the monarch's hands had two disastrous consequences for the Iranian political scene. On the one hand, it radicalized the opposition and thus gave it a political import beyond what it was meant to signify. Since the Shah was constitutionally inviolable, opposition had to be directed at the constitutionally responsible government; as the government lost its constitutional identity under the monarch's power, it became increasingly ludicrous to oppose it. Thus, policy differences tended to transmute into incontrovertible constitutional questions.

The second effect of the monarch's assumption of personal power proved more catastrophic for the future of Iran. It depoliticized the supporters of the system in a nation yearning for political participation as it underwent an intense process of social mobilization. Consequently, when the revolutionary fuse was lighted, the Shah stood alone in the face of what superficially appeared like a nation rising against him in formidable unity.

Notes
Chapter 2

1. For background information on the Communist movement in Iran see *inter alia*, Ervand Abrahamian, "Communism and Communalism in Iran: The Tudeh and the Firqah-i Dimukrat," *International Journal of Middle East Studies* 1, no. 4 (October 1970) 291–316; George Lenczowski, "The Communist Movement in Iran," *Middle East Journal* 1, no. 1 (1947) 28–40; Sepehr Zabih, *The Communist Movement in Iran* (Berkeley and Los Angeles: University of California Press, 1966).
2. Mahmud Foroughi, "Iran's Policy Towards the United States," in A. Amirie and H. A. Twitchell, eds., *Iran in the 1980s* (Tehran: Institute for International Political and Economic Studies, 1978), 335–52; see also George Lenczowski, "United States Support for Iran's Independence and Integrity, 1945–1959," *Annals of the American Academy of Political and Social Sciences* 401 (May 1972), 45–55.
3. For an analytic study of the Point Four program in Iran, see Jahangir Amuzegar, *Technical Assistance in Theory and Practice; the Case of Iran* (New York: Praeger, 1966).
4. It is only with the publication of Gabriel Almond and James Coleman's *The Politics of the Developing Areas* (Princeton: Princeton University Press, 1960) that new vistas begin to appear in the study of comparative politics. Still, in 1964, Leonard Binder wrote, "The one feature common to all of these attempts to define political development is the teleological emphasis. It is assumed in all these cases that we know what political development, as a terminal stage, looks like." "National Integration and Political Development," *American Political Science Review* 58 (September 1964), 622. For an outstanding review of the movements in the field during the 1940s and 1950s see Harry Eckstein, "A Perspective on Comparative Politics," in Harry Eckstein and David Apter, eds., *Comparative Politics* (New York: The Free Press of Glencoe, 1963).
5. POSDCORB stands for planning, organization, staffing, directing,

coordinating, reporting and budgeting. See Gulick & Urnick, *Papers on the Sciences of Administration* (New York: Institute of Public Administration, 1937).
6. For a theoretical analysis of the relationship between development administration and political development see the author's "A Theoretical Model for the Analysis of the Relationship Between Political Development and Public Bureaucracies in Transitional Systems," Ph.D. dissertation, University of Colorado, 1967, chaps. 6 and 8. Iran's Fifth Development Plan summarizes the administrative objectives of the government in the following terms:

"—to avoid administrative congestion and centralization in the capital by gradually limiting administrative personnel to those with staff responsibilities and distributing other government personnel among the provinces in accordance with the volume of executive duties and local needs, while at the same time assigning greater authority to those in charge of provincial and urban district departments;

—to raise levels of administrative and technical skills among government employees;

—to evaluate the work of civil servants and enforce a system of incentives and penalties;

—to extend the proper use of electronic data processing in government agencies as an aid to decision-making, good management and faster service to the public;

—with regard to salaries and allowances of civil servants, to recommend the payment of equal pay for equal work and the gradual establishment of a reasonable relationship between maximum and minimum salaries, while also providing for adjustments in the salaries and allowances of civil servants in line with increases in per capita national income;

—to provide for the welfare of civil servants, particularly through the establishment of consumer and housing cooperatives;

—to revise the civil service code with a view to abolishing the present tendency for people to seek academic qualifications solely for the purpose of obtaining administrative employment or promotion. . . . ;

—in the case of public enterprises, first, to lay particular stress on the establishment of short-term management courses for senior personnel, and second, to ensure that all such enterprises use modern accounting systems and publish their balance sheets, statements of profit and loss and annual reports regularly." *Summary of Fifth Development Plan*, 5–6.
7. Theodor W. Adorno, et al., *The Authoritarian Personality* (New York: Harper, 1950).

8. See Introduction, note 2.
9. For a study of these characteristics among the Iranian elite see Marvin Zonis, *The Political Elite of Iran* (Princeton, NJ: Princeton University Press, 1971), 199–298.
10. Karl Wittfogel, *Oriental Despotism* (New Haven, CT: Yale University Press, 1957), 161.
11. S. H. Udy, Jr., "The Comparative Analysis of Organizations," in James G. March, *Handbook of Organizations* (Chicago: Rand McNally, 1965), 688–91.
12. In Persian usage, particularly in Tehran, *Bala-yi shahr*, meaning upper city, distinguishes the city's more opulent districts. In Tehran, the term refers to the northern section of the city which is also situated at higher elevation.
13. See chapter 1 above.
14. Compare the prevailing conditions in these fields under the Second and Fifth Development Plans. Electricity output, for example, rose from 200 million kwh in 1948, to 400 million kwh in 1960, to 9100 million kwh in 1972 and to 14000 kwh in 1974/75. According to the unrevised Fifth Plan, the annual consumption of electric power was to grow at an annual rate of 21 per cent from 9100 million kwh in 1351 (1972) to 23,790 million kwh in 1356 (1978). See *Summary of Fifth Development Plan*, 74–9; and Charles Issawi, "The Iranian Economy, 1925–1975," in Lenczowki, *Iran Under the Pahlavis*, 134, 136. The revised Fifth Plan foresaw a rise in the rate of annual average consumption of 31 per cent a year and a total increase to 32,000 million kwh in 1978. See Kayhan Research Associates, *A Guide to Iran's Fifth Plan 1973–1978* (Tehran, n.d.), 87–90.
15. See chapter 8, below.
16. The contemporary labor union movement in Poland gives a possible example of actualized union power in a Communist country.
17. As the deputy minister responsible for elections, the author was present at the meeting.
18. The author was associated with the group between 1970 and 1973.
19. The idea is contained in Article 39 of the Supplementary Fundamental Law specifying the royal oath of office and supported by a number of other powers, including the power to dissolve one or both houses of parliament stipulated by Article 48 of the Fundamental Law.
20. Article 2 of the Supplementary Fundamental Law.
21. *Kayhan*, March 8, 1975.
22. Manuchihr Azmun later played an important role in the Sharif-Imami cabinet. He was summarily tried and shot by the Khomeini regime.
23. See *Asasnamih-i Muvaqat-i Hizb-i Rastakhiz-i Millat-i Iran* (The

Provisional Constitution of the Resurgence Party of the Iranian Nation) (Tehran: Kayhan Publishing House, 1976).
24. *Barrisi-yi Natayij-i Intikhabat-i Rastakhiz* (Analysis of the Results of the Rastakhiz Elections) (Tehran: unpublished document of the Ministry of the Interior, 1975).

3 | The Shattering Of The Image

There is a thread of almost diabolical logic in the sequence of events between the creation of the Imperial Commission in November 1976 (see below) and the Shah's departure from Iran in January 1979. That logic represents an aspect of the relationship between personal power and systemic capability. By the fall of 1976, the Iranian political system had lost its capability to respond efficiently to the requirements of the Iranian infrastructure, including its human-resource base. Structural changes, as mentioned before, required the promulgation of two interrelated steps: political decentralization and political participation. Both steps were directly dependent on the dynamics of power relations within and around the system. In fact, power relations internal to the system tended to agitate in favor of the affirmation of the royal power, while environmental pressures also pushed the system toward greater centralization and concentration. Thus, precisely at the time when systemic efficiency demanded decentralization and distribution of power, the objective forces defining the limit and character of power worked in the opposite direction. Caught in the middle, the Shah himself was probably both a perpetrator and a victim of these contradictory pressures.

Basically, the disparity between the manifold increase in the Iranian income and the limited absorptive capacity of the economic infrastructure proved beyond the capabilities of the central government to cope with. The government's immediate response to the resulting waste and inflation was to use force. Accordingly, on September 9, 1975, price stabilization and a campaign against profiteering were announced as the 14th principle of the Shah-People Revolution.

The man immediately responsible for handling inflation and profiteering was Firaydun Mahdavi, the minister of commerce—a man of exceptional administrative ability and considerable political ambition. The minister of commerce was in charge of government policy with respect to foreign purchases and imports, and, as the highest government official dealing with the country's wholesale and retail operations, he also oversaw the guild organizations which performed the distributive functions of the economy. With the formation of the Rastakhiz party in 1975, Mahdavi was also appointed as the party's deputy secretary general, with far-reaching authority in matters pertaining to both function and organization. He, in turn, proposed to use the commerce ministry as a springboard to whip up activity and enthusiasm for the party. Accordingly, as the all-encompassing party, the Rastakhiz undertook to oversee and control prices and profiteering through the use of members mainly drawn from the universities and high schools.

The results were disastrous. The inflationary spiral due to the discrepancy between the relative scarcity of goods and services, and the growth in purchasing power could not be curbed by fiat. Instead, it tended to corrupt the younger people who were acting as joint inspectors for the party and the ministry, and to create dissatisfaction among the bazaaris and the shopkeepers. In the meantime, the government's indiscriminate shopping abroad had established numerous bottlenecks in practically every aspect of the economy. The waste was phenomenal, exacerbating inflation, unmet development schedules, and corruption.

By the fall of 1976, Mahdavi had been dismissed from his duties and had become a prime scapegoat for the economic and political ills of the country. Government policy began to gear itself to the requirements of a cooling period of the economy, while steps were taken to assess the managerial shortcomings of the government.[1] In retrospect, it is not difficult to see how a series of strategic political mistakes, resulting from the characteristics of the political system itself, helped prepare the way for the fall

THE SHATTERING OF THE IMAGE

of the regime. This section will discuss the options taken by the Iranian government in terms of the theoretical meaning of each of the following intervening periods: the Imperial Commission, the Amuzigar government, the Sharif-Imami cabinet, the Azhari cabinet, and the Bakhtiar government.

The Imperial Commission was established under the chairmanship of the chief of the Imperial Bureau in November 1976 to look into the reasons for recent power shortages and the ministries' inability to meet their developmental schedules. It was, in fact, a device to show the people that the monarch's role was far more extended than that of the chief executive, and that, in his capacity as custodian of the national interest, he was both willing and able to hold the bureaucracy responsible for its shortcomings. The result was a singularly devastating public indictment of the Iranian government, through a schedule of hearings in which the Imperial Commission sat as prosecutor, judge, and jury, while ministers, their deputies and other civil servants were called upon to explain why the schedules of production were not met.

The desired effect of separating the Shah and the bureaucracy was never achieved, however. On the contrary, the fact of the interrelationship between the Shah and the government became even more imbedded in the public mind. If all the credits belonged to the Shah, so did all the failures.[2] Within the bureaucracy itself, the hearings, broadcast in their entirety on prime-time television, produced a sense of gloom and desperation, and of disgust with what appeared to be a hypocritical move to find scapegoats in order to foil a nebulous threat the nature of which was still unclear.

Within the cabinet, the preponderant feeling among the ministers responsible for more general questions of public policy was that the system was no longer capable of carrying out its defined mission and would not be able to do so unless certain structural changes were introduced. The ministers of both the plan ('Abdul Majid Majidi) and the interior, (Jamshid Amuzigar), for example, agitated for decentralization and participation. Others vacillated, and faced with political, social and economic pressures, tended to cling to their powers and prerogatives. As a result, what was essentially a systemic problem concerning the decisionmaking structures, continued to be interpreted as problems in administrative inefficiency and corruption.

The appointment of Jamshid Amuzigar as prime minister in August 1977 was guided by the same logic. Amuzigar was known as a man of moral integrity and organizational capability. Over the years, he had gained a reputation for quick wit, sharp tongue, and tough leadership. His brilliant performance as the Iranian representative to OPEC had brought him international respect. But, unlike his predecessor, Amir 'Abbas Hoveida, who was naturally a public and gregarious man, Amuzigar was temperamentally withdrawn, selective, and happiest in limited company. More by temperament than by logic, he fell in line with the false interpretation of Iranian problems as basically moral and managerial. Accordingly, he set out to correct these with a hitherto unequalled enthusiasm.

Amuzigar's method was that of government by example. Since he could not possibly have control over everything related to the government, he concentrated on areas in which he did have control. He proposed and insisted on absolute frugality and the observance of spartan principles in government, especially in matters pertaining to housekeeping and expenditures. He succeeded in lowering the inflationary trend considerably, particularly in the areas related to land speculation and housing. His budget introduced greater balance between urban and rural expenditures, between high and low technology, between the rich and the poor. In short, under ordinary circumstances, the balance sheet of his one year in office, as he himself argued, was deserving of compliment.[3]

But the year between August 1977 and August 1978 was not an ordinary year. It was a period in which ten years of anti-Shah activity and propaganda culminated in a dramatic transformation of the character of the opposition movement from an essentially leftist-modernist to a religious-traditionalist one.[4] The bulk of the demonstrations against the regime, of course, occurred after the Amuzigar premiership. However, most of the opposition's strategic and tactical plans concerning logistics, lines of communication, agitation, propaganda, and methods of operation were drawn and put into effect during his tenure in office.

The patterns of the division of labor in the Iranian political system placed much of the responsibility to fight and respond to antiregime agitation outside the purview of the prime minister's office. The division of responsibility had been relatively successful in the past because of the nature and characteristics of the regime's active opponents. Since the anti-Shah riot in Berlin on June 2, 1967, and the active association of various groups of Iranian students with radical European movements, including the Baader-Meinhoff group, the immediate threat to the Iranian system had been identified as basically limited to terroristic activities such as those undertaken by the Marxist-Leninist and Islamic Marxist groups. None of them, however, was seen as presenting a real danger to the regime. They were viewed as surrogates in Iran for the general international forces opposing the Shah. They had not seemed particularly successful inside Iran except as providers of evidence of SAVAK brutality to relevant international organizations. As the 1971 "Siyahkal incident"[5] had shown, they appeared to command greater sympathy among the middle-class intelligentsia than among the urban or rural masses.

In 1977, the anti-Shah movement began to reflect a new strategy. It began to concentrate on the most traditional elements of Iranian society through the intermediary of religion. It became potentially a mass phenomenon. The Iranian security organizations may be faulted for their ineptitude in dealing with this strategic change during its early stages. Once the move had been made, they were no longer equipped to cope with its new dimensions. Since it had become politically encompassing, it required a total political response.

Amuzigar, however, was inclined to translate political issues into moral, economic and managerial questions. Accordingly, during his premiership, his office remained rather distant from the prevailing political turmoil. There was little understanding of the need to elicit a grass-roots counterresponse to the gathering storm. The short-run effects of his economic policy were antithetical to political stability. By combatting inflation through policies designed to lower land and housing prices, he not only alienated much of the traditional business community which had considerable investments in speculative land, and the bankers whose collaterals were about to become worthless, but also, by bringing the construction business to a near halt, he released a formidable force of unemployed migrants to be used by the revolutionaries. In addition, the curtailment of the flow of government subsidies made the clergy more responsive to antiregime instigation. The Rastakhiz deputies in the Majlis, having been cut off from practically all political influence, lost what influence they had in their constituencies. Consequently, when needed, their support of the system became politically meaningless. The same may be said about the lot of the party in this fateful year. Failing to effect a meaningful relationship with the government, the Rastakhiz as a party became a meaningless adjunct of the public bureaucracy. Stifled in their logical development, the party wings became reduced to lifeless gatherings for the esoteric discussion of practically irrelevant issues.

There can be no intimation, of course, that all of this was Amuzigar's fault. His predicament, however, points to a curious characteristic of the Iranian political system. We have already touched on Amuzigar's qualities as a man. He was morally upright, technically superior, and administratively efficient. He was a skillful dialectician, capable of mastering intricate, fine points and abstract relations in rather involved theoretical and technical problems. Altogether, he was certainly as impressive as any of his peers around the world. Nevertheless, within the framework of the Iranian political system, he became politically impotent, and, consequently, in his year as prime minister, administratively dysfunctional. Had he been alone among the Iranian politicians to find himself in this situation, the phenomenon could be attributed to his political temperament. In fact, he represented the best of the Iranian governing elite.

It is always tempting to find the causes of this debilitating deformity in the special properties of the Shah's personality. This explanation, however, is patently simplistic. A political system, after all, is never the result solely of the creative abilities of one man. It comes into being and gradually assumes its characteristics as a result of interrelationships among individuals within a matrix of interfacing economic, social and cultural forces. Personalities are important, but the Shah of Iran had neither the galvanizing charisma of a Hitler, nor the ruthless cunning of a Stalin. In retrospect, it appears that he was malleable enough to have reflected an image inculcated in him by the needs and requirements of an evolving system of which he was an important part.

The problem, however, is more involved. In the introduction and the first two chapters of this book, we have emphasized power's propensity to concentrate at the top in the earlier stages of rapid socioeconomic development. The process of concentration and personalization of power has its subjective corollary in a parallel process of image building. By the time centralized power has performed its function the image becomes an essential part of the prevailing political culture. The Iranian political elite helped establish that image. When the socioeconomic base had sufficiently changed to render the image inappropriate to the satisfaction of its rapidly evolving needs, the image had become so ingrained that it did not admit modification. Thus, a curious phenomenon resulted. While everyone inside and outside the country looked to the Shah as the power's ingrained image to take care of the impending disaster, the image stood helpless because the reality of his power resided, as it always had, in the perceptions which had created it. It was therefore not only the Shah who had become paralyzed; it was the regime which could no longer reflect itself in his image. In this sense, not only Amuzigar, but all others who were involved in Iranian politics during the last years of the Shah's rule may be faulted. Iran could not have been built into the economic showcase it had become without their help and involvement. On the other hand, had they been politically more aware and courageous perhaps they would have made a difference in the pattern of the unfolding disaster.

Dialectically, the most significant event of the Amuzigar period was the gradual transformation of the manifest character of the anti-Shah movement from secular to religious. The change was reflected in the opposition's recognition of the potential power of religious organization, ideology, and cadre under more liberal circumstances and was consummated by the establishment of a series of communication patterns relevant to revolutionary action based on religious institutions.

The strategy and tactics utilized in this transformation appear to have been based on the Marxist-Communist experience and geared to the special properties of the Shia sect. It must be kept in mind that until rather late in the game the anti-Shah movement remained essentially urban, unconnected with organized public or private enterprises, and based mainly in the universities and mosques. The content of its communications was organized to correspond with the division between propaganda and agitation used in Marxist strategy. Tactically, it never confronted the system wholly in one place, but attacked it in quick strikes in a variety of places aiming at one or two real or imaginary casualties to use as martyrs. It utilized the time-honored practice of mourning on the seventh and the 40th day of the death or martyrdom. Unlike the avowed Marxists who had never succeeded in living Mao's parable of the fish and the water, the new revolutionaries in religious garb could easily disappear among the surrounding masses.

Within the radical religious movement, two distinct and sometimes contradictory modes of approach could be discerned in ideological terms. The Islamic movement based in the university derived its ideological substance from the works of Dr. 'Ali Shari'ati on the meaning of Shiism as a revolutionary force for human dignity and progress. Essentially, instead of deriving the sanctity of *imamat* from the fact of the imams' descendance from the Prophet's family, Shari'ati stressed the historical validity of Shiism as a movement in support of the meek and the righteous and against the oppression of the rulers. He argued that Shiism had been bastardized during the Safavid reign, becoming an arm of the secular power as the official religion of the state. Since then, it had tended to play the opposite role as a reactionary force, supporting the status quo and the powers that be. Thus, to regain its lost dignity, it had to ask anew the kinds of questions that constituted the basic issues of the dawn of Islam, and approach their solution in the manner of 'Ali, by fixing its moral gaze on what was right and wrong in social, economic, cultural and political relations. "Alawite" Shiism, i.e. the Shiism of 'Ali, therefore, had been and could be again something quite different from what was, in fact, experienced as the legacy of the Safavids: a religion of blind faith designed to maintain the oppressive character of the society.[6]

This new interpretation of Shiism was received by some sectors of educated Iranian youth as a breath of fresh air in what appeared to them as the depressing climate of a closed, bipolar space in which the human psyche had to choose between the ignominy of religious superstition as traditional culture, and the opprobrium of a culturally meaningless and abusive technology as modernism. Needless to say, the official clerical hierarchy was not particularly pleased with Shari'ati's interpretation of Shiism and his description of the role hitherto played by its clerical mandarins.

The new interpretation rarely received an audience among the masses. It was mostly confined to the university and some intellectual societies. Through these media, it gradually seeped out into an increasingly wider circle of the middle-class intelligentsia. Much in the manner of a discussion of Marx by people who have never read an original work by Marx, the latter tended to discuss Shari'ati as a possible panacea for the cultural impasse in Iranian society. Later, when Shari'ati had been quite lost in the Khomeini avalanche, the same intellectuals tended to speak of Khomeini as if he were another Shari'ati, again without ever having read any of the latter's relevant works. The result was that, in the summer of 1978, among at least portions of the Iranian intelligentsia, religion had been bestowed with a kind of respectability it had not enjoyed for many years.

In the ordinary mosques of the realm, the Shia ideology operated at a different level. It stressed the sinfulness of the system, erected the vision of Shimr's* infamy against the courage and innocence of Hussein, raised the imagery of the Pharaoh's helplessness against the will of God, and insisted that the true religion was being sold out to the foreign devils. It also suggested that every man, woman and child was entitled to his or her share of the oil income and intimated that every family was due—the amount changing depending on the generosity of the speaker of the pulpit—some $15 to $45 a day which all would receive as soon as the system was overthrown.

The religious organizational network proved an inimitable structure for revolutionary action. Its effectiveness is brought home when it is compared and contrasted with the problems faced by futuristic ideological revolutions. Such revolutionary activities would have to develop an esoteric ideology, find ways of communicating the ideology to other elites and masses, organize cells in which adherents would gather, establish channels of communication capable of eluding the police, and find people who believe strongly enough in the cause to welcome danger and accept death. All of this was, in fact, ready-made in Iran, as *it is potentially in other Muslim countries*. What was needed was a responsive political atmosphere on the one hand, and the ability

---

*Shimr Ibn Zil Jawshan was one of Hussein's main adversaries at the Battle of Karbala. He was instrumental in Hussein's death and the subsequent severance of his head and is the principal villain of the 'Ashura passion play. (See Rahnima, Zayn al-Abedin, *Zindigani-yi Imam Hussein* (The Life of Imam Hussein) (Tehran, Amir Kabir, 1358.) 323–94.

to transform the religious establishment into a revolutionary force, armed with doctrine, strategy and tactics, on the other.

Obviously, the process of transformation could not have been effected overnight. It took place over a period of time in which greater awareness of the threat and a more sagacious counterpolicy could have altered the end results. Instead, the government remained essentially aloof and substantially ignorant of the extent and the depth of the transformation. The Shah, himself, after certain initial attacks, assumed a largely dejected mood, waiting for the crisis somehow to disappear. In the meantime, the regime's responses were haphazard, basically defensive, and often irrelevant.

The first serious signs indicating the growing momentum of the anti-Shah movement appeared in 1977 through the intermediary of various political factions testing the validity of the Shah's liberalization policies. These groups belonged mostly to the liberal intellectual circles in the universities, legal associations, segments of the National Front, and sometimes to the more serious and politically powerful groups with established links to the clergy, as exemplified by Engineer Mehdi Bazargan's Rally for Freedom. The activities of such groups were essential for the success of the Khomeini movement. As the main domestic political leaders representing various international human rights organizations, they became an umbrella protecting political groups that entertained vastly different notions of human rights. Since the Shah's system sought to prove its commitment to the precepts of human rights and the liberalization of political space under constant belligerent foreign and domestic scrutiny, such liberal groups, in effect, were instrumental in helping totalitarian antisystem activists escape the system's counteraction by persistently representing them as opposition movements within the nation's constitutional framework. Ironically, most of them were later victimized by the Khomeini regime. Their right to the revolution was totally denied. Many of them went underground, to jail, or into exile.

By the end of 1977, it had become increasingly apparent that religion was to be the main base of attack against the system. Somewhat buoyed by President Carter's lavish praise on the eve of 1978 in Tehran, the Shah decided on a more aggressive posture vis-a-vis his opponents. Accordingly, an article in the January 7, 1978, issue of the evening daily newspaper *Ittila'at* deprecated

THE SHATTERING OF THE IMAGE

Khomeini as a man and a religious leader in terms that could only be judged as the sign of the system's determination to declare an all-out war on religious extremism. The next day, on the occasion of Women's Day, in a markedly belligerent speech, the Shah characterized Khomeini's ideology as sexual apartheid and vowed that he would not allow such ignominy to befall the nation. In a none too subtle reference to his own achievements and his opponent's insignificance, he ended his speech with an idiom of which the literal meaning was "the dog barks, but the moon keeps on shining."[7] As he spoke, the first serious clash occurred between the military forces and students at the Qum theological seminary, protesting the *Ittila'at* article. From then on, the cycles of the seventh and 40th day mourning became the rule of the protest, eventually engulfing the whole of the country.

As it turned out, January 26, 1978, was the last day during the reign of the Pahlavi dynasty in which a large crowd came to cheer the Shah's achievements. From that date, representing the 15th anniversary of the White Revolution, the Iranian streets belonged to the opposition, even though serious students of power agree that, in the early months of 1978, the Shah could still have brought out substantial numbers of people and given them tactical and strategic support through the military.

The Amuzigar cabinet resigned on August 27, 1978. Until the last month of his premiership, the system operated as if nothing extraordinary was happening. The government had not admitted publicly that it was faced with a serious problem. Antisystem activities were routinely described as the work of a few saboteurs who had been imported from the other side of the border.

The opposition, however, had gradually perfected its organization, method of operation, and pattern of communication, at least in conceptual terms. Strategically, it had to demonstrate to the people that the Shah's system was really not as strong as everybody believed and that the Shah himself was not sacrosanct, rather, that he was a paper tiger on whose brow the divine glory no longer shone. If this much could be imparted to the people, it would turn the whole idea of the revolution into a self-fulfilling prophecy. Destroy the myth of authority and power and what is left is a pitiful figure with a rusted sword that once shone in the luminosity of the myth.

The myth and the sword, however, are intertwined. The myth gives the sword its brilliance; it is also nourished by the sword. Thus, power resides in the barrel of a gun but emerges only when there is a will to use it. The question in the minds of many Iranians was how to withstand and cope with the awesome might of the Shah's military force. Would the Shah be willing and able to wield that force? Would he remain in control of the force? For those whose familiarity with Iran had penetrated the veil of adverse propaganda which had depicted the Shah as a ruthless tyrant, the answer to the question concerning his will had to be in the negative. The military, however, would probably remain loyal to the Shah.

Here, necessarily, facts and conjectures mingle. The fact is that the Shah's aversion to the use of force was well known to his friends. In the summer of 1952, during the mass demonstrations and riots that toppled the Qavam government and reinstated Mossadiq, he had almost paralyzed his generals by his constant admonishment to refrain from bloodshed.[8] In the famous CIA operation of 1953, he simply left, instead of staying and fighting. Ten years later, in 1963, during the first of the Khomeini assaults, his friend Asadollah 'Alam had to assume total responsibility and effective power to quell the uprising.[9] Characteristically, rather early in the holocaust of 1978, he declared categorically that he would leave Iran rather than use his military might offensively.

The first phase in the process of breaking the myth was to show that the Shah's system was not able to cope with its most rudimentary governmental responsibilities. Accordingly, certain institutions that could be meaningfully related to Islamic injunctions—banks, liquor stores, moviehouses, restaurants—were selected and systematically attacked around the country. The operation closely followed tested guerilla methods. Like the effect of a swarm of bees stinging a large animal from all sides, it exasperated and humiliated the regime.

By the middle of August, acts of sabotage and riots had spread to a large number of Iranian cities. On August 11, 1978, the city of Isfahan was placed under martial law after a number of public and private places, including part of the famous Shah 'Abbas Hotel, were destroyed by fire. On August 13, a traditional restaurant in Tehran frequented by foreigners was bombed. More than 40 people, including foreigners, were injured, some seriously. Finally, on August 19, the 25th anniversary of the Shah's return to Iran, some 28 cinemas, the figure presumably corresponding to the 28th of Murdad in the Persian calendar, were bombed, of which the one in Abadan, Cinema Rex, proved a major tragedy. Close to 400 people, mostly women and children, perished in this brutal act of terrorism. What ensued could only be a testimony to the depths to which government credibility had descended.

The government naturally characterized the event as the "great terror," and accused the opposition of having perpetrated the tragedy. The opposition, for its part, began an extensive propaganda campaign accusing SAVAK of having committed the act in order to incriminate the opposition. In spite of the efforts of the Khomeini regime to whitewash the case, it is now reasonably clear that the fire was a result of the routine operations of the revolutionary activists. No culprit, however, was identified under the Shah's regime. According to the responsible officials, it was safer to keep the matter as quiet as possible because the government was suffering from a credibility gap, and, therefore, whatever they said would have been ridiculed by opponents as the last gasp of a moribund criminal.

Amuzigar and his government resigned a few days after the Abadan holocaust, on August 27. The man chosen to succeed him was a former prime minister, Ja'far Sharif-Imami. At the time, Sharif-Imami was the president of the Senate, the deputy president of the Pahlavi Foundation, and the grandmaster of Freemasonry in Iran. He was in fact the very symbol of the Shah's system. He had a reputation for being corrupt. Specifically, he was reputed to draw salaries from 50 different sources. His family, however, was supposed to have close ties with the Isfahan clergy. He also kept a nebulous relationship with the National Front through a family relationship with 'Abdollah Mu'azzami, one of the most respected members of the front under Mossadiq.

The selection of Sharif-Imami was symptomatic of the system's confusion about its predicament. The monarch had come to face the moment of truth. In reality, he had only two choices: either he must don his military uniform and charge against his enemies in the name of honor, nation and history, accepting the full consequences of the decision; or he must take his chances and allow a man or a group of men, who could forge an independent following of their own, to take the reins of government and act as a political buffer between the Iranian monarchy, symbolizing a historically significant reality, and the people's anger, representing a fleeting moment in the painful process of sociopolitical development. By following either path, he would probably have stopped Khomeini and bought himself and the country a breathing spell to rearrange the future political policy and structure. Instead, he opted for the worst possible alternative: piecemeal and gradual appeasement.

The Sharif-Imami cabinet was rather extraordinary in its composition. It consisted mainly of members who had the reputation of belonging either to Freemasonry* or to SAVAK. Needless to say, both organizations were extremely unpopular with the Iranian middle-class intelligentsia. Nevertheless, the new cabinet was dubbed the "government of national reconciliation." The new prime minister announced that the time had come to heal the bleeding wounds of the nation. His government would guarantee the basic freedoms bestowed on the nation by the Constitution. He would direct his government to look into the cases of all political prisoners and free everyone except those who had committed nonpolitical crimes. Political cases were no longer to be heard in military tribunals. The Rastakhiz would no longer be considered the only political party in the nation; other parties could be established and could prepare for the next year's elections.

To appease the clergy, the new government abolished the imperial calendar and reinstated the Prophet's flight to Medina as the base of the solar calendar, closed all the casinos, ordered the Ministry of Information and Tourism to prevent the publication and distribution of all written material offensive to religion, and vowed to consult eminent clergy on all important legislation. To underline the new democratic circumstances, Sharif-Imami announced that neither he, nor any member of his cabinet, would ever again hide behind the throne. They would consult the parliament on all matters and would serve as long as they enjoyed its confidence. Rather curiously, he announced to the Majlis that he was no longer the old Sharif-Imami, suggesting perhaps a mood of atonement for past mistakes.

Sharif-Imami's first major encounter with the opposition occurred a week after he took office on 'id al-fitr at the end of Ramadan on September 4. The government had promised open

---

*For a history of Freemasonry in Iran, See Isma'il Ra'in, *Faramushkhanih Va Framasuniri dar Iran*, 3 Vols., (Tehran: 1968).

politics; the opposition organized a march and public prayers in order to test the government's will and ability to stand by its promises. The government had exacted some assurances from the organizers in Tehran that participants would refrain from insulting "the national symbols," *muqaddasat-i-milli*, a euphemism for the Crown. In return, the troops and the security elements were ordered not to interfere with the marchers. In the event, most of the marchers complied with the agreement. Some strategically located detachments, however, produced large-sized portraits of Khomeini, chanted anti-Shah slogans, and called for the establishment of an Islamic political system. There were some tense moments between the troops and the demonstrators. The day in Tehran ended without bloodshed, but it did produce several ominous consequences.

The size of the crowd was beyond anyone's expectations. No doubt, at least part of it was innocently religious. Most marchers, however, appeared to be quite conscious of the political dimension of the demonstration. Psychologically, the phenomenon devastated the Shah. All through his life he had been told, and he believed, that he was loved by his people. Now, for the first time, he was struck by the possibility that he may have been misled by the people around him. He felt dejected and betrayed.

The marchers' discipline was also extremely impressive, demonstrating considerable organizational and leadership capability. It meant the existence of a formidable number of trained cadres with the ability to produce, control, and lead the crowd at will against tactical and strategic targets. The crowd responded perfectly to cues, as for example in their slogans or the presentation of flowers to the military and the police. Naturally, both the government and the military became edgy and apprehensive, particularly because the visible religious leaders within the country, such as Ayatollah Shari'atmadari, did not seem to be in control of the protest movement.

In a preemptive move, the government forbade demonstrations in Tehran without police permit. The move was aimed at September 7, the seventh day of the martydom of three men killed in Tehran in the clashes of the previous weekend. On September 8, 1978, however, having been informed that a large crowd would gather at the Zhalih Square, the government announced an impromptu, and, since many had already gathered in the square, in effect, a post facto martial law, ordering the demonstrators to disperse. The ensuing clash resulted in the death of nearly 150 people in a day that has since become famous in the annals of the Iranian Revolution as Black Friday.

This tragedy exacerbated the inherent contradictions of the Sharif-Imami government. He had committed his government to a policy of national reconciliation, but, within only ten days after he had taken office, an unprecedented number of people had died on the first day of the promulgation of martial law. The Rastakhiz Majlis, representing the epitome of the Shah's power, now was called upon to criticize a period that had fathered its very existence. In a manner reminiscent of the Imperial Commission, the government and the new opposition benches blasted away at practically every aspect of the policies of the past 15 years. In the spirit of the new democracy, all of this was directly broadcast through the national radio and television networks. Everyone within and outside the government was busily producing lists of "culprits" deserving to be tried, imprisoned, and even executed as sacrificial offerings to soothe the rage that had suddenly awakened within a hitherto seemingly peaceful society. And all of this was presided over by perhaps the most identifiable member of the Shah's establishment.

The Iranian Revolution, like most other revolutions, was based on two interacting axes. One axis was represented by a general sense of dissatisfaction with the system's policies; the other, by different groups of revolutionaries bent on the destruction of the system. The second would take advantage of the first, but would not be guided by it. On the contrary, its most important revolutionary task was to feed and lead it. Appeasement, of course, is the process in which a threatened regime, in a mood of reconciliation informed by a sense of guilt, addresses itself to the first axis—general dissatisfaction—in the hope of mollifying and taming the second axis, the revolutionaries. The process has never worked in the past; it is unlikely to work in the future.

The Shah's regime fell into this trap. To justify its position theoretically, it began to develop the idea of the distinction between revolution and rebellion, the demand for change and the act of violence. The idea was toyed with all through the Sharif-Imami government and was finally made officially explicit on November 6, in the Shah's declaration to the people that he had heard the voice of the revolution and accepted and pledged himself to satisfy its demands as soon as the rebellion ceased.

The Iranian Revolution demonstrated that unless launched from a position of absolute strength, this approach is doomed to failure. The system, in effect, admitted its guilt, provided the necessary public channels for its critics, tied its own hands and nourished its enemies.

The dialectical meaning of the Sharif-Imami government for the revolutionary process was to pave the way for the opposing forces to move to the second phase of the revolution, that is: to begin to attack the system from within its own ranks. The tragic incidence of Black Friday furnished the opposition with new ammunition. That the forces of revolution were in no mood for reconciliation was shown by their premeditated effort to exaggerate the number of casualties. The number of dead was placed anywhere from 1,000 to 10,000. Since it was not possible to kill so many in so short a time by ordinary means, it was suggested that the mass murder had occurred by waves of helicopter aerial attacks. Since it was neither morally conceivable nor strategically desirable for the people to believe that Iranian soldiers could slaughter their brethren with such vehemence, the word was out that the government had hired specially trained Israelis to perform the task. Obviously, no reconciliation could be contemplated with such a fiendish regime. Accordingly, measures were taken to intensify the attacks on the government.

In September and October, while riots, acts of terrorism and arson increased, a large number of government agencies embarked on a series of countersystem strikes that finally crippled the government. The strikes began ostensibly as demands for higher wages and benefits to enable the employees to cope with inflation. The government encouraged the move in the hope of converting what was obviously a political phenomenon into an economic issue. Under the revolutionary pressure, such strikes quickly spread to almost all of the government organizations and, following an established procedure, changed in character from economic to political in predetermined periods. The new demands almost invariably required the abolition of martial law, abrogation of SAVAK, dissolution of the parliament, unconditional freedom for political prisoners, and the return of all exiles. By the end of the Sharif-Imami government, such strikes had brought the government's extractive and distributive functions to a stop. The government could no longer guarantee the proper functioning of the oil industry, the banking system, or the communication system.

Schools played a major role in harassing the security and martial law forces. Iran is a very old nation and a very young society. Approximately 50 per cent of her population is below the age of 16.[10] Youth inundated the city and its fringes. High schools and even elementary schools were skillfully used to keep the soldiers off balance. Children aged ten to 16 organized themselves in groups of 20 to 30 in numerous parts of the city, shouting antisystem slogans; stopping traffic; sometimes attacking and burning banks, cinemas, liquor stores and other establishments presumably obnoxious to religion, obstructing the paths of grotesquely huge Chieftain tanks with cars, tires and other obstacles, shouting obscenities at the soldiers; and dispersing only to gather again in a nearby street or alley. In the provinces, children were often instrumental in forcing their parents into the mold of the revolution.[11]

Routinely, each group of youngsters responded to signals given by an older man who stood unnoticed among the onlookers outside the group. The purpose was to engage the military, for whom the encounter was always a harrowing experience. Big men in military fatigues appeared either ludicrous being harassed by children, or sadistic attacking children.

In the evenings, the same children invaded the roofs of the city at appointed hours and kept up a remarkably effective cacophony of cries of *Allah-u-Akbar*, (God is great) and *Bih-gu marg bar Shah*, (say Death to the Shah), synchronized with prearranged power blackouts. The process was carried out with devastating effect, giving the impression that the whole city cried with supernatural unity.

By the end of October, the Sharif-Imami cabinet had become helpless against attacks from inside and outside the system. Acts of sabotage had become routine and commonplace. Within the cabinet, rifts among the so-called idea men—Hushang Nahavandi, Manuchihr Azmun, Muhammad Bahiri, Manuchihr Ganji—had created an untenable situation in which the unity and effectiveness of the cabinet as a collegiate body had been seriously hampered.

The authority of the Sharif-Imami government was undermined also by the Shah's overt efforts to find a substitute more acceptable to the opposition. The process dragged on because candidates were either unacceptable to the Shah or were deemed incapable of relating meaningfully to the revolution. The ideal man would presumably possess the following qualifications: he would believe strongly in the Constitution; he would not have occupied a high governmental position in the past 15 years; he would have a reputation for political independence; he would have bases of support in the bazaar and among the clergy; and he would be familiar with foreign policy.[12]

A man who fitted these qualifications in early September was 'Ali Amini. Amini was an old and experienced politician with established ties to the commercial as well as religious circles. He was known to be on good terms with the Americans. As the minister of finance in the first post-Mossadiq government, he had successfully negotiated the terms of the National Iranian Oil Company Consortium Agreement which started anew the flow of Iranian oil to world markets. As prime minister in 1961–62, the last in office with a flair for independence from the Crown, he had gained a reputation for being his own man. But the most imporant point about Amini was that he was ready to accept responsibility when most others were not.

In September 1978, however, Amini was not acceptable to the Shah. The royal family was deeply distrustful of Amini, and considered him dangerous in spite of the fact that it treated some members of his family, including his son, as favored protégés. His Majesty was particularly offended by Amini's reputed suggestion that he should retire to the Island of Kish in the Persian Gulf. He thought that Amini was a congenital pessimist who would denigrate whatever had been built in all these years in Iran, and who would not hesitate to endear himself to the Shah's opponents by denouncing everything and everybody, including the Crown.[13]

The Shah's assessment of Amini's position suggests that his suspicions were at least in part due to a misapprehension of facts resulting from lack of direct communication. Amini's basic position, for example, was that the Shah should move to the background, not involve himself directly in the affairs of the nation, and lend his support totally to his prime minister. He had not asked, however, to be given control of the armed forces against the constitutional injunction. As an experienced politician, he recognized that the armed forces disposed of their own power, which could not be handed to one man or another. Nevertheless, he insisted that as prime minister in such a turbulent period he was entitled to the assurance that he would not be undermined by unauthorized military action. He could be so assured only if he could trust the man in charge. He had in mind, and suggested, General Firaydun Jam, an old friend and relative of the royal family and a former chairman of the Supreme Commander's Staff.[14] Though at the time Jam was not on the best of relations with the royal ramily, he was trusted and respected by them and by a large sector of the military community.

None of this was, in principle, unacceptable to the Shah. The very fact that he sought a nonmilitary alternative to Sharif-Imami suggested that he felt the need for someone who could stand on his own and act as a buffer between him and surrounding anger. General Jam was later asked, indeed urged to accept the position, but to no avail. The irony of it all was that early in November, when it had become too late, the Shah spoke of Amini as a true statesman who loved his country and understood power.[15] Amini and a number of other venerable men who had been kept away during the last years of success had by then moved in to advize in time of trouble. Obviously, the earlier distrust on both sides had been in large part a result of lack of communication.

Late in October, a major effort was launched to induce the leaders of the National Front to join a coalition government. Some leading members, including Shapur Bakhtiar, had urged the Front's executive committee to accept the offer. The Front leader, Karim Sanjabi, however, decided to go to Paris, ostensibly to convince Khomeini of the correctness of the decision to join a coalition government. As it turned out, Khomeini was in no mood to "discuss" the matter with Sanjabi. He told him in no uncertain terms what his position was, as he had told others before, and as he would tell emissaries in the future. After the meeting, Sanjabi announced, in effect, his acceptance of "the Imam's line," and suggested the Front would not enter a coalition government under the Shah's regime. Immediately afterward, on November 6, 1978, the Shah announced the formation of a military government.

The composition of the military government surprised both the regime's friends and its enemies. The expectation was that it would act decisively to quell the riots and establish order. On the eve of November 5, after substantial damage by unopposed groups of rioters rampaging through the streets of Tehran and burning down selectively a number of buildings and offices in their path, the news from the inner circles of the court and the

THE SHATTERING OF THE IMAGE

military strongly suggested the Shah would establish a military junta, outside of the constitutional order, for the strict purpose of brutal and selective attack on the opposition in the political and economic sectors of greater strategic significance for the country. The idea was to show Khomeini as well as the secular elements of the opposition that the system was determined to fight to the end, that it still had both the power and the will to do so, and that, true to its promises, it was also willing to continue its policy of liberalization provided the sanctity of the constitutional framework was respected. According to the rumors, the junta was to be headed by General Gholam 'Ali Oveisi, the military governor of Tehran and commander of the imperial ground forces, and was to include the commanders of the military branches who would jointly undertake to confront and crush the rebellion.[16]

Instead, General Gholam Reza Azhari, the benign and genial chairman of the Supreme Commander's Staff, was elected to head a cabinet of nine military and 12 civilian members. The Majlis was retained because of the constitutional requirement of holding elections within 90 days of its dissolution. Most of the military members of the cabinet were replaced by civilians as soon as the new prime minister could persuade them to join the new cabinet.

The Azhari cabinet proved to be superconciliatory. It began by arresting the former officials of the regime, including former prime minister Hoveida and the former chief of SAVAK, General Nasiri. It promised to stop corruption by looking into the affairs of the royal family and the Pahlavi Foundation and to speed up liberalization by freeing more political prisoners and striving to arrive at an understanding with the striking newspapers. Azhari himself appealed to the clergy by reaffirming his faith in religion and its leaders. He insisted that what the military really wanted was to return to the barracks. In short, the top ranking officer of the Imperial Armed Forces began his short and unhappy career as prime minister by begging the opposition for understanding.

Still, the first days of the Azhari cabinet were relatively quiet. The idea of a military government had awed most of the people. Many went back to work. Even the opposition cadres quieted down to reassess the new situation.

In a short time, however, it became apparent that the new government differed from the previous cabinet only in the fact that the prime minister wore a military uniform. Demonstrations began anew. Strikes resumed. The government proved helpless in dealing with the oil industry, the banking system, customs, and power, areas that directly affected the economic and political vitality of the system.

Nevertheless, the Azhari government carried the nation through the month of Muharram and its most dramatic period—the two days of *tasu'a* and *'ashura*—days nine and ten of the month in which had been born Shiism's greatest epic of martyrdom. To Iranians, the martyrdom of Hussein, grandson of the Prophet, son of 'Ali, and husband of Shahbanu (daughter of the last Sassanian emperor, Yazdgird), was the quintessence of human tragedy, depicting man at his most sublime, knowingly and willfully accepting death so that truth and justice might prevail.

Traditionally, the passion of Hussein was celebrated in a communal manifestation of mourning in which young and old together, in frenzied passion, engaged in different forms of self-flagellation to atone for their sins in memory of the majesty of the death of the "Lord of the Martyrs."

Hussein had welcomed death at the hands of the Umayyad Yazid Ibn Mu'awiyya who, in Shia folklore, represented a usurper king given to baseness of character, immersed in riches and debauchery, and forgetful of Islam and its sublime injunctions. Hussein, on the other hand, represented all that was good, pure, unsullied. Here were the seeds of the essential Manichean duality of good and evil grafted on to a dichotomized version of kingship and religion. The similarity to the prevailing political controversy was too glaring not to cause concern. In fact, predictions of the future largely posited these two days as some sort of historical divide. If the regime could survive them relatively unscathed, and especially without much bloodshed, then it would have passed the peak of the Khomeini assault.

The main showdown was expected to take place in Tehran. For days there had been a debate as to whether or not mourning ceremonies should be permitted. In the end, it was decided to allow demonstrations against a guarantee that the demonstrators would refrain from acts of rioting, destruction and arson, and confine themselves to religious procession. The first day passed as planned. On the *'ashura*, the day of martyrdom, slogans became exclusively political. But the day ended relatively peacefully in Tehran.

THE SHATTERING OF THE IMAGE

In terms of prior expectations, the *'ashura* should have been considered a success for the regime. Nothing resembling the previous gory predictions had happened. There were, however, two characteristics in the opposition's demonstration that further immobilized the system: the discipline and the variety of the participating social types. The phenomenal discipline of the marchers indicated an organizational capability that went far beyond the prior levels of assessment. More impressive were the class affiliations of the participants. Obviously, the Iranian revolution had been transformed from a revolt essentially of the poor of the urban fringes, organized and led by professional agitators in the name of Islam, to a movement encompassing a large portion of the professional middle class. Sensing the essential plasticity of the Sharif-Imami cabinet, the bureaucratic segment of the middle class had effectively paralyzed the operations of the political system by stopping the operations of the bureaucracy and now, having been assured that the military, in practice, had neither a loud bark nor a sharp bite, it had moved onto the streets. Curiously, the revolution never deeply penetrated the ranks of labor or the peasantry until the last days, when power had effectively changed hands.

The historical function of the Azhari government was to complete the breakdown of the regime's inner structure begun during the Sharif-Imami cabinet. The system lost its capability for decision-making and implementation during the Sharif-Imami period. General Azhari shattered hopes that the government would regain those capacities by showing that the dreaded force behind the throne was chimerical, since the will to use it simply did not exist.

The fact that the Iranian armed forces remained loyal to the Shah is a point of interest for the comparative study of the relationship between the military and politics in developing countries. The Shah is often faulted for not having allowed the development and maturation of an esprit de corps resembling that of the legendary German general staff among his ranking military officers. The underlying suggestion is that had such a feeling been allowed to emerge, the military would have acted independently to safeguard the interests of the Iranian nation.

The logic of the statement is difficult to sustain on two counts. First, it is not at all certain that a highly motivated, well-organized military will always act in the interest of the nation as that interest is interpreted by the partisans of social democracy. After all, the German prototype placed itself totally at the disposal of the Nazi dictator. Secondly, a strong military with an independent political opinion is likely to become the dominant political force under conditions of cultural diversity and institutional weakness. This is certainly the case in most, if not all, of the developing countries.

In Iran, the military's relationship to politics was minimal because it had become institutionalized in connnection with the Crown. This mode of institutionalization had allowed the system to develop its goal-specification and goal-implementation functions largely free of military influence. The military's interests were, of course, well taken care of through the mediation of the Crown. No doubt, if the liberalization process had succeeded, interests opposed to the special privileges of the military would have asserted themselves. The ensuing clash also could have been contained only through the mediation of the Crown. In other words, under more liberal circumstances, the military could have learned to accept and look after its legitimate interests within a framework of civilian supremacy only if its relationship with the civilian government were to be mitigated by the characteristics of its institutional setting within the Iranian constitutional frame of reference. This is so because the constitutional precepts regarding the Shah's role as commander in chief corresponded, in this case, with the reality of the evolving military norms, mores, and values,[17] including the military's loyalty to the Shah. This also suggests a set of possibilities for the future, which will be addressed in the conclusion of this study.

In the event, the military's apparent inadequacies had made the formation of a coalition government increasingly urgent. Attention was now focussed mainly on the National Front. Sanjabi, however, refused to cooperate. The Shah turned to Dr. Gholam Hussein Sadiqi, a venerable professor at Tehran University, Mossadiq's old friend and a former minister of the interior, a man deeply respected by the intellectual community. Sadiqi agreed on the grounds of national duty, tried valiantly to form a cabinet, but failed and finally gave up because his old associates in the Front not only refused to give him aid, but warned him publicly against the undertaking. The result was loss of ten precious days for the monarchy and the affirmation of the opposition's claim that the system was isolated and that its perpetuation now depended totally on the politically inefficacious support of the armed forces.

The Shah turned to Shapur Bakhtiar toward the end of December. Among all members of the Front, Bakhtiar proved superior in both courage and sagacity. Early in the summer, he had urged his colleagues to prepare themselves to take up the mantle of government. He had seen the unfolding political events as the harbinger of possible transition to a democratic form of government within the framework of the constitution, but also replete with extreme danger for the future of the nation. Failing to persuade his colleagues, he had made independent approaches to the court as early as September, through the intermediary of a select number of people, including the former prime minister, Jamshid Amuzigar. His efforts, however, had come to naught for several reasons.

As mentioned before, early in the fall of 1978 the Shah was still emotionally unprepared to entertain the notion of having the National Front as a partner in government. The memory of Mossadiq lingering in his mind, he suspected that the aim of the Front leaders was to force him out of the country and eventually make him abandon the throne.[18] He was determined, therefore, to try all other possible avenues before turning to the Front.

Once that point had been reached, another problem presented itself, The Front's leadership had devolved on Sanjabi. Bakhtiar did not belong to the top rank of the Front leadership; the highest position he had held during the Mossadiq premiership was that of vice-minister of labor, a relatively important office for a young man but not high enough to place him among the top leadership. He was, therefore, not treated as a serious contender for the office of prime minister in the turbulent months of the fall of 1978, until the list of the so-called older and more recognized leaders had been exhausted.

By the time he asked Bakhtiar to form a government, the Shah had apparently decided to leave the country.[19] He remained until the new government had received the required votes of confidence from both houses of parliament, ordered his military commanders to take their directions from General Fardust, and ordered Fardust to cooperate with Bakhtiar. On January 16, 1979, the Shah and the Shahbanu left Iran for Egypt. For the Shah, it was his last day on Iranian soil.

Bakhtiar placed himself squarely in Mossadiq's tradition. He was abandoned by all others who had a claim to that tradition. He promised to respect the parliament; abolish SAVAK; free the political prisoners; allow maximum freedom of the press, political assembly, and organization; and to wage an indefatigable war against those who spoke of the *khalq-ha* (peoples) of Iran. Supported by the Shah's army, he created an aura of power, rekindled a new hope of salvation, and indeed, brought a breath of fresh air to the heat of suffocating gloom. In his acceptance speech, he compared himself to a bird of tempest, unafraid of the storm; a wave that would not flee from the sea's anger. Events proved him wrong.

Khomeini arrived in Tehran on February 1, 1979, to a tumultuous welcome. He went directly to Bihisht Zahra, Tehran's main cemetery, where he denounced the West, as well as the Soviet Union, and called for revolutionary vigilance until a true Islamic government had been established upon the earth. Later, he named Medhi Bazargan as his prime minister. He denounced the Regency Council as illegal, refused to receive Bakhtiar as prime minister, and announced the formation of a Revolutionary Council, whose members remained unknown to the public.

On the evening of February 9, a prerecorded film of Khomeini's arrival was shown on prime-time television. A few skirmishes occurred among the air force technical students. On Feburary 10, the martial law administrator of Tehran announced that the city was placed under curfew from 4:00 PM to 12 noon the next day. In the streets, as people tried to reach their homes before the hour of the curfew, strategically situated children announced the locations where weapons would be distributed. Late that night, at the air force technical base at Farah-Abad in southeast Tehran, a battle started in which elements of *mujahidin-i khalq* and *fada'iyan-i khalq* also joined. The curfew was never totally successful.

On the morning of Sunday, February 11, quite unexpectedly, the chairman of the supreme commander's staff announced over the radio that the Iranian armed forces would henceforth remain neutral in the raging controversy. The announcement was the death knell not only for the Iranian monarchy but also for the elite of the Iranian military establishment.

The decision to make the announcement was apparently made without Bakhtiar's prior knowledge. He managed, however, to escape from his office in the prevailing turmoil. In a rather unexpected turn of events, most of Tehran's military bases fell to the revolutionary contingents, and their supply of arms was distributed to organized bands of popular fighters, as well as to other individuals who happened to be present at the depots. The prisons were opened. Many high-ranking officials of the regime who had been jailed in the past few months to appease the opposition escaped. Some were recaptured as they were moving out of the prisons. A few, including former prime minister Amir 'Abbas Hoveida and former minister of health Shuja'iddin Sheikhul-Islamzadih, turned themselves in. For the moment, the 2500 years of Iranian monarchy had reached its end.

Notes
Chapter 3

1. See the text of the Shah's interview with the editor of the daily newspaper, *Kayhan*, October 26, 1976.
2. Marvin Zonis, "He Took All the Credit, Now He Gets All the Blame," *New York Times*, January 14, 1979.
3. *Karnamih-i Yik-salih-i dawlat* (The Year's Balance Sheet [of the Amuzigar Government] (Tehran: August 1978).
4. For a provocative analysis of the conspiratorial and terroristic roots of the Iranian Revolution see Edourd Sablier, *Iran: La Poudrière* (Paris: Editions Robert Laffont, 1980).
5. In the spring of 1971, a detachment of the Marxist-Leninist *Saziman-i Chirik-ha-yi Fada'i-yi Khalq* (The Organization of the People's Devoted Guerrillas) attacked a number of gendarmerie garrisons in Siyahkal, in the Mazandaran jungles. They were captured or killed by the security forces, reportedly with the active help of the local population.
6. See particularly, 'Ali Shari'ati, *Shi'ih-yi Safavi va Shi'ih-'i 'Alavi* (Tehran: n.d.).
7. The monarch's combative statements in defense of women were rather surprising in view of his previous stern warnings to the Women's Organization not to make new demands nor make any statement that might provoke the clergy.
8. From conversations with Generals Mahdiquli 'Alavi-Muqaddam, Ahmad Vusuq, and 'Abdollah Hidayat, at the time commanders of the national police and gendarmerie, and chief of the armed forces staff, respectively; and with friends and relatives of the author's father.
9. Personal conversation with the late Mr. 'Alam's close friends.
10. Iran Statistical Center, *Preliminary Results of the 1975 Census* (Tehran: 1976).
11. The consensus among some 150 secretaries of the provincial committees responsible for the campaign against illiteracy. Much of the information in this study on popular and governmental re-

THE SHATTERING OF THE IMAGE

     sponses during the fall and winter of 1978–79 is based on the author's personal observations, contact with government officials, and the reports of the members of the National Committee for World Literacy program, of which the author was secretary general. The secretaries and other members of the committee were constantly in touch with the lowest strata of Iranian society in all of the small towns and most of the villages.
12. These ideas were contained in a memorandum submitted to the Shah by a group of loyal advisers in late September 1978.
13. Personal audience with His Majesty, Niyavaran Palace, October 6, 1978.
14. From several conversations with Dr. 'Ali Amini, September and October 1978.
15. An audience with His Majesty, early November 1978.
16. On November 5, the Shah apparently still thought that a civilian government was feasible. He had consulted Amini, 'Abdullah Intizam, and other members of their group. They advised him that only a military government might succeed in confronting the perpetrated chaos. (Conversation with Dr. Amini, November 5, 1978.)
17. See Chapter 4, below.
18. Personal audience with His Majesty, October 6, 1978.
19. A distinct impression of the author from numerous meetings with Her Majesty the Shahbanu in November and December 1978.

4 | The Dilemma of the Military

The role of the military was considered to be pivotal in all calculations concerning the future of the Shah's regime. The regime's supporters and opponents, both inside and outside Iran, believed that their success or failure depended largely on the attitude of the armed forces. The Iranian army was considered to be extremely powerful and fiercely loyal to the Shah. As mentioned in the last chapter, throughout the revolution two persistent questions remained on the minds of those who followed closely the contest between the Shah and Khomeini: a) did the regime possess the will to use its military might; and b) would the military remain to the end united and loyal to the Shah? It has been suggested that those who were intimately familiar with both the Shah and the military believed that the armed forces would probably remain loyal to the Shah, but their power would scarcely be used, since the will to use it was lacking. In the end, the Iranian military gave up under the pressure of the Khomeini assault. The regime's last defenses were overrun, the Bakhtiar government was dissolved, and Muhammad Reza Shah's reign came to an end.

This turn of events surprised practically everyone, including Khomeini. The supporters of the regime began to look for traitors and found them in characteristic positions: friends and close associates who had played the roles historically and archetypally assigned to Judas and Brutus. The most intriguing role was said to have been played by General Hussein Fardust, the Shah's childhood friend and close confidant of many years. Fardust is supposed to have been chosen by Khomeini to organize and lead his secret service organization, SAVAMA, by reorienting and utilizing the salvageable elements of the SAVAK. He is supposed to have masterminded the assasination of the Shah's nephew, Prince Shariyar Shafiq, an able and dedicated commander in the Imperial Iranian Navy, as well as many other successful and unsuccessful attempts on the lives of former Iranian officials. None of the Iranians who accuse Fardust can produce solid evidence of his culpability; the fact that he appears to be alive when lesser officers have been killed by the Khomeini regime has generally been taken as evidence enough. The kindest opinion of Fardust was expressed by the Shah himself who found it extremely difficult to believe that his friend would betray him.

The same kind of opinion has been expressed about the Shah's last chief of staff, General 'Abbas Qarabaghi. General Qarabaghi is supposed to have masterminded, under Fardust's tutelage, the disintegration of the Iranian army, as well as the assassination of a number of Iranian general officers, including Generals 'Abdollah Badri'i, the regime's last commander of ground forces, and Biglari, the deputy commander of the Imperial Guard. Qarabaghi is supposed to have been identified by the late prime minister Hoveida as one of the hooded judges in his brief trial. Again, there is no reliable evidence that this has in fact happened, or that Hoveida was ever questioned by masked interrogators.[1] General Robert Huyser, Jimmy Carter's envoy to the Iranian military, strongly suggests that Qarabaghi was something of an opposition mole in the Iranian army.[2] The Shah writes that based on what Qarabaghi had done, he has to conclude that he betrayed him and the Iranian army.[3] Here again the only real evidence against Qarabaghi seems to be the fact that he is alive, when lesser officers have been caught and killed by the Khomeini regime.

It is not our intention to probe into the guilt or innocence of the Iranian high ranking military officers. Since there is really no hard evidence to the contrary, we shall base our discussion on the assumption of innocence. This assumption is important, because instead of engaging in a senseless search for traitors and culprits, it allows us to look into the general condition of the Iranian armed

THE DILEMMA OF THE MILITARY

forces toward the end of the Shah's regime, from which in fact a satisfactory account of Iranian military behavior can be drawn without recourse to unfounded and largely unprovable presuppositions of malfeasance.

There is not much information on the pattern of behavior of the Iranian army during the revolution. The information that exists is also unhappily tainted with a considerable amount of prejudice, emanating in part from the acerbity of the experience and in part from the confusion that reigned among the decision makers and in the decision-making process both within and outside Iran. There are, however, a number of sources that taken together give a relatively clear and balanced picture of what generally happened inside the Iranian armed forces during these months. Of these, the most valuable to date is General Qarabaghi's book, recently published in Persian in France.[4] The book leaves many questions unanswered, but its greatest virtue is that it is a reasonable account that agrees with much that is known of the prevailing political and psychological conditions of the time, written by a man who held the most pivotal military position in Iran and who was privy to the most relevant information pertaining to the relationship between the military and its politicocultural environment. Furthermore, in most cases it is possible to corroborate his statements by referring to other witnesses who were present at the time and who survived the revolution. The book is a detailed and sometimes day-by-day account of the decisions made and conversations held by the Shah, Prime Minister Bakhtiar, and the top military officers. We have therefore taken it as our sourcebook, accepting only those statements that have been either verified by other participants, or witnessed by the writer himself, or otherwise appear reasonable in the face of existing evidence. The information in the book has been particularly balanced against the material presented in the Shah's *Answer to History*, Shapur Bakhtiar's *Ma Fidelité* and *37 Days After 37 Years*,[5] General Huyser's statements on his trip to Iran, Ambassador Sullivan's *Mission to Iran*,[6] relevant material in the Carter,[7] Brzezinski,[8] and Vance[9] memoirs, as well as writings of other American and European participants and observers, and a number of Iranian generals and knowledgeable civilians who have been sounded on the reliability of the statements made in the Qarabaghi book.

The central conclusion that may be derived from

Qarabaghi's account of the military's experience of the revolution is that by the time he was appointed chief of the Supreme Commander's Staff on December 4, 1978, the revolutionary process had led to a substantial lowering of military morale, to a relatively high desertion rate among conscripts, and to significant problems of leadership and control. The situation deteriorated progressively, so that by Sunday, February 11, 1979, when the Imperial Iranian Army's High Council declared the military's neutrality, the army's command system had already broken down, its communications interrupted, and its high-ranking officers demoralized to the extent that many of them felt hopeless against the march of events and concluded that the Shah would not return, that both Bakhtiar and Bazargan were jockeying for position within a largely secular or Islamic republic, and that therefore a declaration of neutrality would not only be the only practical thing to do, but also under the circumstances, given the two existing political options, that such a declaration would not be inimical to their oath of loyalty to the Shah and the Constitution, nor contrary to the orders that the Shah had given before leaving Iran. Qarabaghi's position corresponds to the opinions expressed by Sullivan and Huyser to their respective superiors. A number of Iranian generals present in the last High Council meeting justify their signatures on the document by saying that they expected a coup d'etat to be effected that same night and thought that the declaration was for the purpose of lulling the enemy, but they also aver, in the same breath, that by the morning of February 11, everything had been lost.[10] They tend to fault Qarabaghi for not having taken command of the situation and acted sooner, when there was still time. Qarabaghi, on the other hand, recapitulates painstakingly what may be presumed to be the gist of the statements made by the participating generals in which apparently a difference of opinion was produced between those who favored an outright commitment to the Khomeini revolution, and those generals who favored a declaration of neutrality. There was no statement at this meeting in favor of a coup d'etat and/or continued resistance.[11] Quite obviously, however, it was presumed that the armed forces would maintain their integrity, largely under the command of the existing general officer corps, if not specifically the individual commanding officers.

This presumption, of course, testifies to the political naivete of the Iranian generals, but this kind of make-believe was not unique to the military. Not only did the bulk of the Iranian middle class mistake the Khomeini phenomenon for a reform movement, but the misunderstanding was apparently shared by those organizations and personalities that acted as fronts for the fundamentalist attack.[12] It was essentially through the operations of these fronts, epitomized by Bazargan and his Freedom Movement, that the deceit retained its tenacity. Bazargan appeared genuinely to believe in the advisability of retaining the structure and the personnel of the armed forces, and conveyed this belief to the officers who came in contact with him and his followers. Indeed, after he became prime minister, many of the high-ranking officers were reappointed to their posts; some lasted only a few hours, others a few days or weeks. Bazargan himself had an unhappy tenure as a prime minister whose function was to provide the clerics with a breathing spell to become politically and administratively organized.[13]

The behavior of the military was affected by a number of factors of which the most important was the Iranian military culture. The events of the last months of the Shah's regime achieved their particular significance in relation to this cultural perspective. They may be discussed in terms of four basic subjects: tactical options in the face of the prevailing political atmosphere, the Shah's departure, the Huyser mission, and the inadequacy of the time span in which the military was expected to change itself from an essentially apolitical organization accustomed to taking orders, into a political force capable of making independent political decisions. The rest of this chapter will address each of these questions in the light of the prevailing military culture.

The Iranian military was the creation of the Pahlavi dynasty.[14] The relationship between the military and the Shah, therefore, transcended the constitutional provisions which vested the Crown as commander in chief with supreme authority over the military. Both Reza Shah and Muhammad Reza Shah became personally the nation's major advocates of military strength. They very nearly acted as a lobby for the military interest. At the same time, they became a buffer that separated the military from its domestic political environment. Indeed, there were only two periods during the Pahlavi era when the Iranian officer corps played a politically significant role. The first included the years between the coup d'etat of 1921 and Reza Shah's ascent to the throne in 1925,[15] when the military acted as the main force that catapulted him into power. After the coronation, Reza Shah retained the command of the newly organized armed forces, not only as their titular commander in chief, but, more importantly, also as their actual commanding officer. The loyalty that evolved in the years before World War II toward the Pahlavi kingship played an extremely important role in providing support to the young Muhammad Reza Shah after the Allied occupation of the country and Reza Shah's deportation.

In the second period, between 1941 and 1953, the military's involvement in politics also resulted in a lack of political stability and a prevalence of conditions in which a variety of forces in fact challenged the legitimacy of the Crown. Many of these forces tried to penetrate the ranks of the military. Some, like the Tudeh party's military organization, met with considerable success. The bulk of the armed forces, however, remained loyal to the Crown and the person of Muhammad Reza Shah. In 1953, they played a pivotal role in the fall of Mossadiq and return of the Shah to power.[16]

The Iranian military's postwar organization, process, weapons systems, and strategic and tactical thinking were largely defined and developed under United States tutelage, in terms of material support, training, and advice.[17] This linkage also involved the idea of professionalism, which required the cadre to respect the lines of command within a nonpolitical framework. Given the characteristics of the Iranian political system, the result was the strengthening of the ties between the armed forces and the Shah. In spite of a fundamental difference in the levels of sophistication of the Iranian armed forces during the reigns of Reza Shah and Muhammad Reza Shah, from the 1950s on the relationship between the latter and the military began increasingly to resemble that which his father had had. By 1963, a whole class of commanding officers, many with family and political ties that went back to the pre-Pahlavi period, were retired, some in disgrace. The new command corps were mostly of the same age as the Shah, or younger. They were far better trained than the older officers, and they were taught to be uniquely devoted to the person of the Shah. As the Shah's conception of the role of Iran in the politics of the region evolved to encompass increasingly larger perimeters of action, the military's outlook also changed to accommodate the new responsibilities. The successes of the

White Revolution years made a locally inspired challenge to the Shah's authority seem an unlikely prospect. Indeed, in spite of the fact that there existed, at least in theory, an elaborate counterinsurgency program, in effect the Iranian military never seriously prepared itself for such an eventuality. Even less probable seemed what actually began to happen in 1978: a condition in which the military would be called upon to face a protracted assault by large groups of Iranians under circumstances where it would have to endure persistent insult to all the symbols it had been taught to venerate, while it would not be permitted to defend itself.

The organization and lines of command of the armed forces were such that lateral communication between commanders of the same rank was rather difficult. This is not to say that these commanders did not associate with each other. In fact, in Iran as in many other countries, the military for the most part resembled a relatively closed caste, where members tended to stick together in leisure as well as in work. But the lines of official communication were essentially vertical, with minimum horizontal linkage.

The Iranian armed forces were composed of the Imperial Iranian Army (*artish-i shahanshahi*) which included the ground forces, the air force, and the navy; the Imperial Guard (*gard-i shahanshahi*); and the organizations of state gendarmerie and police. While the gendarmerie and police were formally under the authority of the minister of the interior, both structurally and functionally they were tied to the military in terms of regulations and facilities governing personnel, command, planning, weaponry, and logistics. Essentially, they operated as the other constituent military organizations.[18]

Budgetary provision and military procurement were the province of the Ministry of War. Although a member of cabinet and constitutionally responsible for military affairs, the minister of war had no command functions with respect to military organization and operations. General planning and coordination were the responsibility of the Supreme Commander's Staff and its chairman, who was in practice the monarch's military chief of staff. Under ordinary circumstances the line of command bypassed him and led directly to the Shah as supreme commander. Thus, the commanders of ground, air, and sea forces, the commander of the Imperial Guard, the commander of the gendarmerie, and the chief of the state police each reported directly to the king, and received orders from him. In matters of general applicability, the Shah's orders were transmitted to all commanding officers through the intermediary of the supreme commander's headquarters.[19] The direct liaison, however, was considered a matter of honor for both the organization and the commander. General Samadiyanpur, the chief of police, feigned illness and asked to be retired when early during the Azhari government it was decided that the police and gendarmerie would henceforth report to the minister of interior. General Ahmad Muhaqiqi, commander of the gendarmerie, believed that the idea was a ruse to neutralize the gendarmerie as a fighting force.[20]

For the Iranian military the Shah was not only a symbol, but also the essence of the country's national independence and integrity. The cadet's military oath, sworn on both the Quran and the flag, equated the two in the material reality of the Shah as at once the personification of the nation, and the commander to whom loyalty was perpetually due. Ordinarily, therefore, the Shah could not be separated from other revered national values, as they were thought to be inherent in his person. This mode of thinking was stressed and consistently reemphasized through a variety of systems of reward and punishment. On the one hand, the idea of the Shah as the embodiment of military loyalty was so widespread that for most members of the military it had become a compelling fact of life; on the other hand, alleged networks of intelligence and counterintelligence reputed to cross-check every officer's attitude and behavior made it prudent to shun ideas that would possibly suggest disloyalty. The result was that for the most part the Iranian military universe received its light from the Shah. Without him, bearings were lost, command structures were debilitated, and decisions were left unmade.

However, the military organization and its personnel were also a cross-section of the society. While the officer corps was drawn largely from the middle and lower middle classes, the bulk of the army, the NCOs and conscripts, belonged mostly to the lower classes from both rural and urban areas. Most of them were profoundly religious, and therefore susceptible to religious propaganda. Indeed, the army had traditionally encouraged devotion to religion as a reliable hedge against leftist propaganda. While there is no systematic data to support this contention, most knowledgeable Iranians would argue that in relative terms the

THE DILEMMA OF THE MILITARY

armed forces contained more religious elements than most other state organizations.

This force, insulated from the contradictions of domestic politics for nearly a quarter of a century, was called upon to face a revolutionary movement whose strategy and tactics vis-a-vis the military were almost flawless. When still weak, the opposition never attacked the military. Rather, it appealed to its national and religious sentiments. It proclaimed the military as its brother, offered it flowers, and beseeched it not to kill its brothers. Slowly, as it became evident that the Shah would not order the armed forces into offensive action, exhortations were coupled with terror and studied acts of violence. Military personnel were not merely killed; they were maimed, dismembered, hung from trees. Their wives and children were attacked, and often effectively ostracized from their community.

As the system began to imprison former friends and release former enemies, the line between right and wrong became progressively blurred, at least for the conscripts and younger officers. Their commanders, under orders from above, forced them to stand motionless as demonstrators insulted the very symbols they had sworn to protect and preserve with their blood. They were not allowed to fight, nor to withdraw. As their frustration increased, instances of independent revenge also increased, and in a few cities commissioned and noncommissioned officers began to threaten bazaars or attack revolutionaries on their own. In most cases, however, they were immediately called to task by their superiors, reprimanded, transferred, and sometimes courtmartialed. The longer they endured, the larger became the crowd, the less meaningful their actions, the less the possibility of redemption without passing through a devastating bloodbath. The military government behaved exactly the same as the civilian: Tanks in the streets still recoiled when their routes were barred by cars and other such obstacles; leaders of the revolution, publicly known and publicly active, were left free and in control of the means of communication, sources of energy, banks, and customs; the Shah and government, seemingly incapable of any decision, appealed to the clergy and others whose aim was to overthrow them. The clergy, on the contrary, became more adamant as the system revealed its inherent weakness. If in the beginning they pleaded with the military, now, slowly, they began to order and threaten. The end was presented as inevitable, and the army was beginning to feel increasingly isolated from the environment the protection of which was presumably its raison d'etre.[21]

By the end of 1978, the army had lost its capacity to continue the policy of resisting without striking back. But it still could have achieved superiority by concerted swift action. Indeed, many Iranian generals kept pressing the Shah for such a decision.[22] However, even then, military success would not necessarily lead to a meaningful political solution, and, at any rate, required unified action born out of wholehearted commitment. The Shah, as we have seen, had early in the upheaval decided that he would not use force. His logic, apparently, was that he was the king. In a passage in *Answer to History* he clearly states that his generals had often urged him "to use force in order to reestablish law and order in the streets," and wonders whether stronger action on his part could have saved his throne and his country. "I know today," says he, "that had I then ordered my troops to shoot, the price in blood would have been a hundred times less severe than that which my people have paid since the establishment of the so-called Islamic Republic. But even that fact does not resolve my dilemma—a sovereign may not save his throne by shedding his countrymen's blood. A dictator can, for he acts in the name of an ideology and believes it must triumph no matter what the cost. But a sovereign is not a dictator. He cannot break the alliance that exists between him and his people. A dictator has nothing to bestow for power resides in him alone. A sovereign is given a crown and must bequeath it to the next generation. This was my intention."[23]

If the Shah would not order his officers to act, would the Iranian officer corps be capable of initiating action independently? The easy answer based on the benefit of hindsight would be no. However, there were many complicating factors that need to be taken into account. Given the prevailing military culture and the characteristics of the opposition's strategy, the cumulative effect of the Shah's departure, Bakhtiar's investiture, and the Huyser mission was to make action, even by the hardiest of generals, extremely difficult. Nevertheless, there existed an impulse for strong action, but without adequate planning and provisions. The reasons, as we shall see, were twofold: loyalty to the Shah did not allow the top military officers to collaborate on any scheme without his express order as long as he was in Iran, and the time available for making plans and provisions after he had left was not sufficient. As a result, the idea of a military coup d'etat never moved beyond the level of talk. As General Huyser states, the Iranian ground forces were seriously short of fuel. But they were not able to unload an American supplied tanker from Bahrain against the striking dock workers, and did not seem to have any plans to take over the control of the oil installations in the country.[24]

The Shah's decision to leave Iran was a great shock to the officer corps. According to General Qarabaghi, the matter of the Shah's departure was discussed in the Supreme Commander's Crisis Committee, established for the purpose of achieving coordination between the three forces, and it was decided that the generals would seek suitable occasion to plead with the Shah to reverse his decision. In spite of their efforts, however, the Shah's decision remained unchanged. There were too many factors in favor of his trip. He himself had become weary of remaining in Iran. Bakhtiar would accept office apparently on condition that the Shah would leave the country for a rest. The Guadeloupe meeting of Carter, Giscard d'Estaing, Schmidt, and Callaghan had resulted in suggestions that he should leave.[25] Certainly, the American ambassador reminded the Shah of this necessity often enough. The Shah states that in his meeting with Ambassador Sullivan and General Huyser, his visitors' main interest was to know the day and hour of his departure.[26] Sullivan argues that in fact the Shah was happy to leave; Huyser suggests that Sullivan hated the Shah, and pressed his departure. As the appointment of Bakhtiar was predicated upon his departure, it may be that the final push was provided by a former British foreign secretary. The Shah writes, "I finally decided to name Bakhtiar prime minister after my meeting with Lord George Brown, once foreign secretary in Britian's Labor government. We were old friends. He took my hand and pleaded with me to leave the country. Just take a two-month vacation, he said. Then he strongly endorsed Bakhtiar. On December 29, Shahpur Bakhtiar was asked to form a civilian government."[27]

The Shah had assumed a seemingly ambivalent attitude toward the military in the last days of his stay in Iran. Qarabaghi maintains that he seemed indifferent to matters in which he had always shown keen interest. One such area of traditional interest was the question of military appointments.[28] The Shah initiated

General Badri'i's appointment as the commander of the ground forces while also keeping him as overall supervisor of his previous command, the Imperial Guard, of which the day-to-day management was now entrusted to its deputy commander, General Biglari. Beyond this, according to Qarabaghi, the Shah did not pay much attention to other cases. Still, he insisted that the generals keep their regular schedules of audience even though there were no specific issues to discuss.

The Shah ordered his generals to obey and support the Bakhtiar government. The precise manner in which he gave this order is a matter of controversy. But the points of controversy are extremely important for the explanation of the military command's subsequent behavior. The process was initiated by Bakhtiar, who thought a demonstration of military loyalty to him was of paramount importance since the Shah had appointed General Qarabaghi as chief of staff without consulting him. Bakhtiar put the matter to the Shah in the following terms: "Sire, I would like to ask you a favor, to have the representatives of the armed forces to come and reaffirm in my presence that they take their orders from the government and government only. I give the orders and I expect to be obeyed, since I have been invested by you and have the Parliament's confidence. . . ."[29]

The Shah convened a meeting of the army commanders and Bakhtiar on January 13, 1979, three days before his departure. Present in the meeting were Prime Minister Bakhtiar; General Qarabaghi, chief of the Supreme Commander's Staff; General Hasan Tufaniyan, deputy minister of war and head of the Military Industries Organization; Lieutenant General Badri'i, commander of the ground forces and acting head of the Imperial Guard; Lieutenant General Amir-Hussein Rabi'i, commander of the air force; and Admiral Kamal al-Din Habibollahi, commander of the navy. According to Bakhtiar, whose knowledge of military ranks in the Iranian army appears less than perfect (he speaks of a five-star general, presumably Tufaniyan, when the Iranian armed forces' highest rank was four stars), the Shah told his generals: "As you well know, Mr. Bakhtiar has accepted to form a cabinet under very difficult circumstances. As I have decided to go abroad, you should know that you take your orders from him. If there are questions that relate specifically to my office, he has the possibility to convene the Regency Council which will relay the question to me and will communicate the answer to you. But, for all matters that pertain to government, it is Mr. Bakhtiar who will decide."[30] In his *37 Days After 37 Years,* Bakhtiar maintains that the Shah told his officers if there were matters of military importance such as "issuing a 'farman' or promotion or retirement of general officers, or the like . . . you will refer to the Prime Minister through the minister of war,"[31] a contention that Qarabaghi denies as "an absolute lie."[32]

Qarabaghi's version of the meeting is considerably different. It agrees with Bakhtiar's concerning the Shah's statement that he was tired and needed to go abroad for medical reasons. But, according to Qarabaghi, the Shah states: "Since Mr. Prime Minister has formed a cabinet that supports the Constitution, the Imperial Army has the duty to support the legally instituted government."[33] On behalf of himself and the generals Qarabaghi responds: "The duties and the mission of the army are clear. We all are and shall remain loyal to the oath we have taken to protect the Constitution."[34]

Contrary to Bakhtiar's intent and subsequent understanding, Qarabaghi states that the form of the meeting and what was said in it suggested unquestionably that the Shah wanted them to believe that nothing had changed as far as the military was concerned. He cites the following as evidence.[35]

1) General Tufaniyan, who had been deputy minister of war for many years, asked the Shah to allow him to retire now that General Ja'far Shaffaqat (who was not present and who, as noted earlier, had no command function) had been appointed minister of war. The Shah answered, " 'You have nothing to do with the War Minister,' and told him to continue with his work";

2) The absence of the minister of war meant that the Shah wanted to emphasize that as in the past he was not allowed to interfere in the affairs of the armed forces;

3) The presence of the commanders of the three forces individually was meant to convey to everyone that they were independent and were to carry out exclusively the Shah's orders.

The difference in nuance between Bakhtiar's and Qarabaghi's rendition of the meeting is both important and understandable. Bakhtiar, obviously, did not wish to press for specifics. He recollected Mossadiq's experience, and at any rate, recognizing that his government's life depended on the military's support, actively sought its good will. Thus, it was to his advantage to select from all that the Shah had said that which would support his position, namely, that the Shah had ordered his officers to obey him. On the other hand, the Shah's emphasis on the Constitution is not only corroborated by another participant in the meeting, but agrees with the general tenor of the Shah's statements at the time. The reason, of course, is that the future of the monarchy in Iran depended on the survival of the Constitution. The difference between the two positions could lead to different interpretations of vital consequence. If the order was to obey Bakhtiar, it would be very difficult to engage in any kind of planning and decision making without his participation. If on the other hand, the army was directed to support the government on constitutional grounds, then, under the prevailing circumstances, the interpretation of the relationship between the government and the Constitution had to be made independently. Assuming the ability to act, the military would yield its support to the government, contingent on its understanding of the government's motives and functions.

On this last point, other conversations between the Shah and his chief of staff are also revealing. On a number of occasions the general had asked his commander-in-chief to clarify what was to be done if unexpected events occurred. The Shah, as mentioned before, had remained generally noncommittal. But according to Qarabaghi: "After what had transpired between us in our last meeting, he now started to pace the room and dictated a number of orders the summary of which was the following: 'You know very well what the conditions of our armed forces were after *Shahrivar 1320* [the date of the Allied invasion of Iran according to the Iranian calendar], how much effort has gone into their development and perfection, and finally what status they have achieved today. You all have a share in this. This army is necessary for the preservation of the country's independence. Try to prevent factional divisions from developing in it and no matter what the price, protect and preserve the [integrity] of the armed forces.' . . . I asked again . . . if after Your Majesty's departure unexpected events, contrary to the Constitution, occurred, what must we do? After a moment of silent reflection, as he continued pacing the room he said, 'we do not know what will happen. Do whatever that you and other commanders deem appropriate.' "[36]

The Shah seemed to favor a collegiate decision-making process in the military after his departure. A number of factors point in this direction. First, it would be far more difficult for a group of officers whose honors and loyalties were at stake to betray him and the country, than for one individual. Secondly, if the future of monarchy depended on the preservation of the integrity of the army, then cooperation and concerted action on the part of the officer corps would be the only possible option that could prove effective. At any rate, his alleged reluctance to give his chief of staff a traditional *farman* or decree enabling him to make decisions in his absence suggests the same point. Qarabaghi even failed to establish how he, or other officers, could contact the Shah in the future.

Evidently, the Shah intended for his generals to have a degree of independence in making appropriate decisions as they faced their uncertain future. Whether this expectation was reasonable remains a moot point. The fact is that no other alternative existed. Once the Shah had left, it became incumbent on the military to make their choices on their own. The choice, however, was never made until such time as it had become practically impossible to do anything but surrender. Bakhtiar's government was never in full control. He exuded personal courage, but his cabinet could rarely enter their ministries. The Khomeini movement achieved increasing momentum, while Khomeini became progressively less inclined to compromise. Once he entered Iran, it was difficult to see how it was possible to contain him short of a phenomenal bloodbath. Throughout the whole process, the Iranian high command was caught between its own inexperience in independent action, its growing uncertainty about the Bakhtiar regime, and increasing confusion concerning the purpose and meaning of Huyser's mission.

The Huyser mission is an intriguing episode in the history of the Iranian revolution. Huyser maintains that his mission was to protect the integrity of the Iranian army and encourage it to support Bakhtiar's constitutional government.[37] There is no reason to doubt his word, as it has been consistently affirmed by practically every knowledgeable American, and has been corroborated by the Iranian military. The Shah, on the other hand, stated that Huyser had come to Iran to neutralize the Iranian army.[38] Ironically, he was also right. To pressure the Iranian armed forces to support Bakhtiar's government was tantamount to neutralizing it until such time that it could not even defend itself.

Bakhtiar had sought the office of prime minister on the erroneous assumption that once liberal demands were satisfied, reasons for opposition would no longer exist.[39] In due course of time, those opposed to the Shah's excesses would realize that the torch had been passed to a new genre of Iranian statemen, and would therefore rally to it. In fact, his government was the logical culmination of the Shah's famous "I have heard the voice of your revolution"[40] speech and therefore suffered from the same analytic shortcomings that governed that statement. As both his behavior and his program showed, his quarrel was basically with the Shah and his regime which, of course, included the military.

Bakhtiar's behavior irked the army officers. He made a point of appearing indifferent, if not insulting, to matters that constituted the core of the military's cultural values. At the apex was his treatment of the Shah, always correct, but manifestly without zeal or respect. He referred to the 1953 events that led to the fall of Mossadiq as a coup d'etat, while the military had traditionally viewed them as manifestations of the Iranian national will. He insisted on sitting under Mossadiq's picture, which meant spurning the Shah's. Though viscerally against religious government, he nevertheless seemed to do his utmost to accommodate Khomeini, short of resigning his office. And finally, as his program showed, he seemed to think that the army's discipline was incorruptible, and would persist under all circumstances. Hence, one could freely choose policies and demand loyalty from the military rank and file.

His program also stressed the same points. It concentrated on the dissolution of SAVAK, speedy trial of "ransackers and aggressors against the nation's rights" in existing courts and in specially convened national courts with extraordinary powers, appointment of a committee to look into the affairs of SAVAK employees and agents, freedom for all political prisoners, political rehabilitation of all political prisoners since 1953, payment of reasonable damages to those imprisoned for more than one year, payment of damages to the minor dependents of those who lost their lives in the so-called security prisons, abrogation of martial law and seeking cooperation of the exalted 'ulama, official declaration of those recently killed in political activities as "martyrs" by passing a bill through the Majlis, payment of damages to the families of the martyrs, and establishment of a basis for close cooperation between the government and the clergy so that the exalted ayatollahs would supervise correct execution of affairs.[41]

This position, of course, was the natural outcome of Bakhtiar's appointment to the premiership. It was, therefore, a consequence of events rather than a real choice open to him. Had he not believed as he did, he probably would not have sought the challenge. This necessity, however, could only exacerbate the tension between the military and his government. All the more so, because quite obviously his support came only from those who supported the Shah not merely as a symbol of an institution, but his person, as *shahanshah ariyamihr*. In other words, it came largely from the military and those associated with it. This fact was particularly demonstrated in a pro-constitution march of January 25, 1979, where the bulk of demonstrators were die-hard royalists.

It was in this political atmosphere that General Huyser was to discharge his mission in Iran. He arrived in Tehran on January 3, 1979, in spite of strenuous objections raised by his immediate superior, General Alexander Haig. Haig's objection was based on the opinion that Iran's case had become hopeless, and that, therefore, Huyser's mission was more in the nature of a ploy to destroy Huyser. Huyser, on the other hand, had recommended himself to General Jones, chairman of the Joint Chiefs of Staff, in response to the latter's inquiry about knowledgeable American three- and four-star generals to look into the Iranian situation.[42] Huyser, having suggested himself, was consequently unable easily to withdraw. He arrived in Iran in the cockpit of a 747 cargo plane transporting supplies to the United States military mission.[43]

The first days Huyser was in Iran, policy disputes and contradictory views in the Carter administration about Iranian options reached a high point. The basic problem pertained to the assessment of the nature of the Khomeini claim. Thus, President Carter believed that in the early days of January 1979 it was possible for "Bakhtiar to succeed in establishing a cabinet under the existing provision of the Iranian constitution. Although Bakhtiar was never supported by Khomeini, I thought there was a chance for their relationship to improve. Bakhtiar had demonstrated a degree of independence and forcefulness, and apparently had the confidence of some of the dissident groups in Iran. Ambassador Sullivan, however, was recommending that we oppose the plans of the Shah, insist on his immediate departure, and try to form some kind of friendship or alliance with Khomeini. I rejected this recommendation because the Shah, Bakhtiar, and the Iranian military leaders needed consistent American support. Reports in the Washington press, however, indicated deviations within the State Department from my policy of backing the Shah while he struggled to establish a successor government."[44]

Carter then continues: "Because Sullivan seemed unable to provide us with adequate reports from the military, which was a crucial source of information and advice, Secretary Brown and I concluded that we needed a strong and competent American representative in Tehran to keep me informed about the military's needs. One of his responsibilities would be to strengthen the resolve of the military leaders and encourage them to remain in Iran in order to maintain stability even if the Shah should decide to leave. I ordered General Robert Huyser, Deputy Commander of the United States forces in Europe, to carry out this assignment in Iran."[45]

Ambassador Sullivan had for some time believed that the Shah's fall was inevitable. The day Huyser arrived in Iran, January 3, he sent a personal message to Secretary of State Cyrus Vance, for his "eyes only," stating that for the United States "the moment of truth" had arrived. According to Secretary Vance, "He reported that all the moderate elements in and out of government agreed that the Shah must leave the country at once. He said, however, that a group of military officers were urging the Shah to forget Bakhtiar and apply the iron fist . . . I agreed with Sullivan's conclusion that American interests, as well as those of Iran, require that the Shah leave immediately."[46]

Sullivan's strategy involved direct negotiation between the United States and Khomeini. The idea of such a move presupposed the Shah's departure from the throne, for otherwise no negotiations would bear fruit. The basic flaw not only in Sullivan's logic, but also in the perceptions of almost all American leaders, was their assessment of Khomeini and his cohorts. The Khomeini alternative was seen as simply a religiously inclined government, basically anti-Soviet, perhaps not as friendly to the United States as the Shah's regime, but potentially open to negotiation on the important issues. A worse alternative was considered to be continued chaos, a sure invitation to Soviet intrigues. Thus, Brzezinski, undoubtedly the most hawkish of President Carter's

THE DILEMMA OF THE MILITARY

advisers, thought that "the formation of the Bakhtiar government meant that the Shah's regime was finished," and accepted it with relative equanimity. "The question now was whether the new regime, still relatively moderate if anti-Shah, could endure, given the collapse of the old political order and in the face of religiously aroused masses and radicalized urban youth. The strategy on which the group in Washington did agree was to make every effort to keep the Iranian military intact as the Shah prepared to leave . . . But while agreeing on the importance of keeping the Iranian military in readiness—and that was the point of departure for the Huyser mission—our group differed as to the ultimate purpose of the exercise . . . To Vance, [Warren] Christopher (who in Vance's frequent absence played a leading role during this stage), and Mondale, the purpose of the Huyser mission was to help preserve a post-Shah civilian government in power. I agreed, and I publicly stressed firm U.S. support for the Bakhtiar government, but I also stressed that Huyser should prepare the Iranian military for a coup in the likely event that Bakhtiar should fail. Brown, Duncan, and Schlesinger concurred, and Huyser's instructions specifically contained such a provision."[47]

The prevailing uncertainty in the Carter administration was reflected in the Huyser mission. Ambassador Sullivan's description of his symbiotic life with Huyser is instructive in this respect. Huyser had moved in with the Sullivans. "After dinner," Sullivan writes, "we would stroll across the compound to the chancery and take up our positions at the two secure telephone circuits to Washington. On one line I would speak to Undersecretary of State David Newsom or Assistant Secretary Harold Saunders. On the other, Huyser would speak with the chairman of the Joint Chiefs of Staff, David Jones, or with Secretary of Defense Harold Brown. We would then compare notes after our conversations to try to sort out what Washington was attempting to convey to us. There were times when we felt we must have been talking to two different cities."[48]

Reflecting their respective lines of command, Huyser and Sullivan agree that their views concerning Iran were radically opposed. Unlike Sullivan, Huyser believed personally that the Shah should not leave Iran. But apparently neither his orders nor the prevailing atmosphere permitted him seriously to convey this feeling to Iranian generals. The generals had threatened if the Shah insisted on leaving, they would either leave with him, or if they were forced to stay, they would execute a military coup d'etat. Huyser's orders, however, were to direct the generals to transfer their loyalty to the civilian government. He thought that in spite of the reverses and morale problems sustained during the revolution, the Iranian army was still the most capable and awesome regional force. By the same token, he reasoned, if the army could take over in a coup d'etat, why should it not be able to use its power to support the Bakhtiar government?[49]

Once in Iran, Huyser began a round of talks with Iranian generals, first with Tufaniyan and Rabi'i, and then also with Badri'i, Habibollahi, and Qarabaghi. From the very beginning, it seems, his relationship with Qarabaghi was strained, perhaps because of cultural barriers. Qarabaghi was French educated, did not speak English, and his conversation with Huyser had to be mediated by Admiral Habibollahi, who acted as interpreter. Huyser apparently developed an antipathy for Qarabaghi, thinking him to have better relations with Sullivan, to be ambivalent in his political posture, and after Qarabaghi's attempt to resign, believing that he had decided no longer to cooperate. Huyser has gone so far as to suggest, apparently on the evidence of hearsay, that after the Shah's departure Qarabaghi proposed surrender in a tumultuous meeting of the military High Council. In response, General Badri'i, commander of the ground forces, pulled his gun and threatened to execute him, while the air force's Rabi'i said that he would personally kill Qarabaghi on the spot and sit in his place. To all this, according to Huyser, Qarabaghi had answered that he had been just joking![50]

Qarabaghi, on the other hand, unravels a series of events and arguments which purportedly led the generals to believe that the Americans had decided that the Shah's regime was no longer viable, and that they were taking steps, through Bakhtiar and Bazargan, to replace the monarchical system with some form of republic based on Khomeini's conditions.

From the viewpoint of the Iranian military, the contacts between the Iranian armed forces and the American advisory group in relation to the political turmoil in Iran were based on two interrelated agreements. First, the purchases by Iranian government of highly advanced American weapon systems stipulated the right of the United States government to supervise the protection of highly secret and classified parts from falling into unfriendly hands. The American advisory mission, including

Huyser, therefore, spent a great part of its time ascertaining the security of these systems. Second, Iran and the United States had signed a bilateral treaty according to which the United States undertook to protect Iran's national independence and territorial integrity against external and internal Communist threat. According to intelligence estimates of the G2 section of the Supreme Commander's Staff, which, according to Qarabaghi, were normally coordinated with information secured by the advisory group, as well as statements made by the Shah, the prime minister, and other responsible sources, it had been determined that the antisystem riots were led by international communism, mediated by "Islamic Marxists." Since many of the opposition groups were armed, their activities were construed as Communist armed insurrection against the Iranian government, and therefore, based on the bilateral treaty, a joint international Communist threat against the vital interests of Iran and the United States.[51]

According to Qarabaghi, since everyone believed that the riots were Communist instigated, both Huyser and General Philip C. Gast, the MAAG chief, were initially of the opinion that they should be resisted. They declared their support of the Bakhtiar government and stated that the logical way to reestablish peace and order in the country was for the army to support the constitutional government. When the generals went over their conversations with the advisory group, they concluded that their suggestions were the same as the Shah's orders, namely, "since the Prime Minister and his cabinet support the Constitution, the Imperial army is duty bound to support this legal government." But Qarabaghi adds: "When in our subsequent discussions, General Huyser said that 'the government of the United States no longer supports His Majesty! And, in order to establish calm in the country, it is necessary that His Majesty comply with the wishes of the people and travel abroad,' we realized why Mr. Bakhtiar's premiership was conditioned on His Majesty's departure. And also that this trip was not temporary since General Huyser adds that 'not only the United States but West European governments also no longer support His Majesty.' In fact, the upshot of Huyser's statements and Bakhtiar's conditions for accepting the premiership, were the same as what the opposition and revolutionaries shouted for days and nights in their marches and demonstrations, namely, 'His Majesty's exit from the country!' "[52]

The generals' doubts and trepidations were not altogether unfounded. On November 9 Sullivan had sent a message suggesting to the State Department to start "thinking the unthinkable." What would the United States do if the Shah was shown to be unable to rule? In mid-November, State Department advisers were urging "a clearer policy to protect US interests," and some of them "were beginning to doubt that the Shah could remain even as a figurehead in a parliamentary democracy. They judged the likely outcome of the crisis to be either a military junta with the Shah as a symbol of legitimacy or a military coup without him. An alternative was a civilian government, supported by the military, in an Islamic republic. A final possibility was a complete collapse and resulting chaos. Most believed that we [US] should immediately position ourselves to adjust to an Iran without the Shah. In addition, echoing arguments urged with increasing force by Sullivan, they suggested that if the Shah could not bring himself to deal with the moderate opposition, we should seek an accommodation between the military, as the strongest pro-Western force, and the Islamic clergy, as the dominant political force in the country."[53]

In early December, at Secretary Blumenthal's suggestion, George Ball, former undersecretary of state, was invited by President Carter to study the Iranian situation and make a prompt recommendation on a US course of action. Naturally, Ball drew heavily on the State Department staff for information. Secretary Vance was confident "he would offer realistic, sensible advice." Ball's recommendation was that the US should try to convince the Shah to "make a dramatic public announcement that he was turning over power to a civilian government, retaining only his position as head of armed forces."[54] Ball's participation sharpened the differences among the American decision makers, and according to Brzezinski it delayed "basic choices by wasting some two weeks, and his subsequent willingness to discuss what transpired within the White House and the State Department with members of the press spiced the perception of an Administration profoundly split on the Iranian issue."[55]

As Ambassador Sullivan pressed the necessity of establishing contact with Khomeini, Carter and the French, British, and German leaders met in Guadeloupe. There, apparently, Carter found "little support for the Shah among the other three leaders.

THE DILEMMA OF THE MILITARY

They all thought civilian government would have to be established, and were unanimous in saying that the Shah ought to leave as soon as possible."[56] Sullivan continued to insist that he should arrange for direct American contact with Khomeini. When Carter decided to ask the French to act as intermediary, "Sullivan apparently lost control of himself, and on January 10 sent Vance a cable bordering on insolence." Realizing that since he had changed his mind about supporting the Shah Sullivan had carried out his directives "halfheartedly, if at all", the president "told the Secretary of State to get Sullivan out of Iran, but Cy insisted that it would be a mistake to put a new man in the country . . . " Carter reluctantly agreed, but from then on he "relied primarily on General Huyser, who remained cool and competent. He sought to maintain as wide a range of contacts as possible around Tehran during these last days of the Shah's reign," and as far as Carter could tell, "he always sent back balanced views."[57]

The Iranian generals tried to change the Shah's mind about his impending trip, but to no avail. On the questions of the armed forces' support of the Bakhtiar government and the reestablishment of peace and order in the country, they concluded that the task became practicable only if it were possible to prevent Khomeini's return to Iran, to prevent the dissemination of Khomeini's cassettes and other means of propaganda, and to quiet what were considered to be antiregime broadcasts by the BBC. These matters were conveyed to Huyser who said he did not think that the US government could do anything about the BBC, but that he would speak to the president on possible ways to prevent Khomeini's return.[58] Carter apparently received the message. Realizing that Khomeini's return would likely cause the downfall of Bakhtiar, he asked "the Saudis, Egyptians, Moroccans, Jordanians, and several other Moslem countries to give their support to the new government and encourage Khomeini to stay out of Iran."[59] This activity, of course, did not solve the generals' predicament!

According to Qarabaghi, in one of the meetings about the manner of dealing with Khomeini's possible plans to return to Iran, Huyser suggested that Qarabaghi meet with Engineer Bazargan and Dr. Beheshti, as representatives of Khomeini and the opposition front. "And without waiting for my answer, he immediately asked General Gast to bring us their telephone numbers. General Gast left the office and returned with several telephone numbers which he placed on the desk. General Huyser said, 'These are Dr. Minachi's telephone numbers. He will arrange for them to meet you at your convenience'."[60]

The generals were astounded. Qarabaghi reported the matter to the Shah, who also indicated his surprise. "This is strange!" exclaimed the Shah. "Does anybody know what they want?" And then he asked Qarabaghi what he intended to do. Qarabaghi reacted with the usual "whatever His Majesty orders" response, but urged further, he stated that he did not think such a meeting would bear any fruit.[61]

This was a tense period not only in Iran, but also in the United States. Iran experts in the State Department had succeeded in imposing the view that the Shah was the problem and that once he departed "the National Front would run the country while Khomeini returned as a venerable sage."[62] A few days before the Shah's departure on January 16, Huyser sent a long cable to Washington in which he outlined a number of probable courses of events that might unfold in Iran. According to Brzezinski he considered a military coup as an absolutely last resort. "Huyser indicated that the sequence of events might involve a successful Bakhtiar government, a Bakhtiar government that is successful for a while, but eventually fails, another civilian government more acceptable to Khomeini, and even 'this alternative could repeat itself under certain circumstances,' followed only then by a coup."[63] And two days before that, on January 10, Secretary of Defense Harold Brown reported to the president that "in Huyser's view it would be useful for the religious and the military to get together."[64]

These events support Qarabaghi's story. Quite palpably, Huyser was moving toward the Sullivan position, which made the generals understandably nervous as they not only distrusted but according to Huyser, also hated Sullivan. A number of generals had come to doubt the sincerity of the American statements. General Tufaniyan, for example, had apparently begun to feel that American promises of support had turned vacuous: "On one hand they speak of support, and on the other, Mr. Eric Von Marbod is consistently pressuring me about payments for our contracts and demands unpaid installments, which is impossible [to meet] at this time. General Huyser, also, says that the Iranian government should officially ask for any assistance it needs, but this also does not appear very serious, since, for example, in the matter of fuel for the forces, which we have asked for some time, he refers to a tanker they have brought to the Persian Gulf, and not only persistently asks for money, but also insists that we should unload it immediately. Given the strikes on the docks and the political condition in the oil company, this is practically impossible. If they really wanted to help us, they would supply us with fuel by air route, as they did for the air force. You see, gentlemen, American support of the Iranian army is nothing but a lot of hot air."[65]

Nevertheless, given the decision to support the Shah's departure, only two alternatives were left: either to accept Khomeini, or to execute a coup. In spite of the fact that the Sullivan position had the trappings of a self-fulfilling prophecy, in some ways it was more sensible than Huyser's at this stage. His brilliant military career notwithstanding, Huyser was singularly wrong in his assessment of the prevailing state of discipline in the Iranian armed forces. He assumed that he had all the time in the world at his disposal. He seemed to regard the position of the Iranian military more in terms of an army at war with a foreign adversary than one engaged in a morally debilitating and confusing civil war. [Four years after the revolution, he still believed that with enough money, 15 generals of his choice, and American public support, he could conquer Iran with the help of the Iranian army, provided no questions were asked about the number of casualities!][66] On January 23, Huyser and Sullivan sent a joint request asking Washington to change their instructions to "permit the possibility of a coalition between the military and religious elements."[67]

By this time the morale in the military had descended to a new low. Three days after the Shah's departure, Qarabaghi reviewed the personnel in the supreme commander's headquarters and found them in extremely bad form. General 'Ali-Muhammad Khajih-Nuri, chief of operations, explained that the morale problem was not confined to the command headquarters, but rather extended to the whole of military personnel. The reason was primarily the effect of the opposition's psychological warfare in the last few months. The situation in the headquarters was worse, only because those who worked there were better informed than others. They knew of the guerrillas' vicious attacks on the officers, NCO's and their families, without any reaction or meaningful decision by the government.[68]

THE DILEMMA OF THE MILITARY

The possibility of Khomeini's arrival in Iran, of course, exacerbated the situation. Within the military, four options were apparently being studied to deal with that eventuality: 1) assassinating Khomeini in Paris; 2) shooting down Khomeini's jet; 3) forcing Khomeini's jet to land in Qishm Island in the Persian Gulf; and 4) assigning the military to protect Khomeini if he in fact entered Tehran.[69] Obviously, unless the army took power into its own hands, these options could be executed only with the government's approval. Bakhtiar, however, was toying with the idea of finding some kind of modus vivendi with Khomeini. Qarabaghi argues that he decided to bring the issue of Khomeini to a head by resigning his office.[70] Whatever the real reason, the decision shocked his colleagues as it would be another mortal blow to the army's morale. Huyser, in fact, states that when Qarabaghi decided to resign he realized that he no longer intended to cooperate with other generals. In the event, nothing came out of Qarabaghi's decision as he was maneuvered by Bakhtiar into taking back his resignation. Bakhtiar asked the general to meet him in his office to discuss his resignation. He then asked Sullivan to see him at about the same time, apparently without informing him of the occasion. According to Sullivan, Qarabaghi "was obviously astounded" to see him there, but was finally persuaded to take back his resignation. True to form, Sullivan was about the only person who "personally agreed with Qarabaghi's position."[71]

Of the four options discussed with respect to Khomeini's return to Iran, the Bakhtiar government and the military decided on the last, namely, to undertake to protect Khomeini. Once Khomeini arrived in Tehran, it was only a matter of time before the Bakhtiar government would fall. The "unthinkable" had become a matter of immediate probability. Huyser frantically began to secure permission to return to the United States. Sullivan pleaded with the State Department, urging Huyser's immediate departure on the theory that his "presence was endangering the lives of the other Americans."[72] Bakhtiar tried to postpone the day of reckoning by appealing to Khomeini, holding meetings with Bazargan, showing off and bragging about the presumed might of the armed forces, and appearing upbeat to domestic and international audiences, all to no avail.

Within the military, conditions grew progressively worse. Soldiers in the streets were ordered not to raise arms against the

THE DILEMMA OF THE MILITARY

demonstrators; rather, they were encouraged to fraternize with them when the situation warranted. As a result, the number of declarations indicating military support for Khomeini increased dramatically. Pictures of soldiers receiving flowers from the rioters, accepting their embraces, and exchanging niceties began to mushroom in the daily papers. Predictably, a number of officers began to look for contacts among the opposition to hedge against unforeseen eventualities.

On the morning of February 11, 1979, General Qarabaghi assembled the military High Council to discuss the options available to the armed forces. According to Qarabaghi, not many options remained for the army. The night before, February 10, the intended curfew had almost completely failed. The army's crack troops from the Imperial Guard had sustained an inexplicable defeat at the hands of a combination of the air force's technical cadres and the revolution's armed paramilitary contingents. In the meantime, a significant number of police stations had fallen to the revolutionaries. The personnel in the gendarmerie headquarters were forced to wear civilian clothes as the building had been surrounded by armed insurrectionists.[73] Detachments called from Hamadan and Qazvin had been intercepted and, in what appeared as a militarily illogical turn of events, were stopped by a number of destroyed bridges. One by one, the generals declared that the units under their command could no longer carry out their assigned missions. Lieutenant General Hatam, Qarabaghi's deputy, summarized the debate, stating that based on the reports of the commanders of the forces the army had lost the ability to act. He suggested that since according to the prime minister the Shah would not return, and since the people had demonstrated their support of Khomeini, and since Bakhtiar also intended to establish a republic, therefore, the reasonable thing for the armed forces to do would be to remain neutral, and in the manner of the Turkish army support the people, while keeping out of partisan politics. No one apparently paid any attention to the anomalous reference to the Turkish model. After some further exchange of opinion, the group decided unanimously to declare the military's neutrality on the assumption that the monarchy was already lost, and that what it was witnessing was in reality a struggle to determine the character and composition of a future republic.[74]

A significant factor in the military's reactions to the revolutionaries was its failure to perceive the Khomeini phenomenon in historical perspective. For most people, in and out of the army, there remained a feeling that somehow the situation was controlled, and that there were "forces" that determined the future. The army, therefore, would remain intact, as it did not seem reasonable that those who had presumably masterminded the upheaval, meaning the Americans and their allies, would destroy the most important regional force for the preservation of peace and security. Here, of course, they received their clues from the West, as there too practically every faction agreed on the necessity of safeguarding the integrity and unity of the army, irrespective of its position vis-a-vis the Shah.

The spread of this feeling was facilitated by the attitudes of the liberals of both secular and religious persuasion. A case in point was Bazargan. Not only did he seem quite reasonable in his statements, but he was also persistently promoted by the United States embassy. Huyser's recommendation to Qarabaghi has already been mentioned. Qarabaghi was also approached by Bazargan through the intermediary of the SAVAK chief, General Muqaddam, and agreed to meet him, according to Qarabaghi, because of encouragement by both the members of the military Crisis Committee and Prime Minister Bakhtiar. In the course of the meeting Bazargan referred to the extremities that people had endured, and asked how long the situation was to continue. Qarabaghi stated that these were political matters and needed to be taken up with the prime minister. He then asked Bazargan whether he remembered the oath he had taken when doing military service. He himself, as others in the armed forces, intended to honor that oath. Bazargan appeared reasonable and understanding.[75]

Qarabaghi met with Bazargan once more in the afternoon of Sunday, February 11, after the armed forces had declared their neutrality. Bakhtiar was also expected to participate in the meeting, but due to the collapse of his regime, he had, quite rationally, decided to go into hiding. Qarabaghi's conversation about the necessity of respecting the integrity of the armed forces, and Bazargan's promise to do whatever he could to stop the attacks on military barracks, demonstrated a surreal atmosphere that was palpably contrary to the reality of events outside.[76] That same afternoon, General Mehdi Rahimi, the martial law administrator, and a number of other military and

THE DILEMMA OF THE MILITARY

nonmilitary officials of the regime, including former prime minister Hoveida and former SAVAK chief General Nasiri, were captured and shown on television. Rahimi's answers about the roles and duties of the soldiers under his command attested to the fact that he fully expected that the military would remain intact, even though his headquarters in the central police building had been attacked and occupied and he himself had been captured.[77] Indeed, not until the first killings did the high officials of the Shah's regime begin to recognize the truth of what had happened.

As a force accustomed to take commands, the Iranian armed forces simply did not have time enough to adapt to an atmosphere in which their survival depended on their ability to make independent decisions and to take decisive action. Under domestic and foreign pressure, they procrastinated, and in the end made a decision on the basis of a motley assortment of presuppositions that were at best only an approximation of the evolving reality. For them, reality had become increasingly elusive, as the culture that had traditionally sustained it was torn asunder. Their motto had always been "God, King, and Country." Under the circumstances, it was no longer feasible to establish a meaningful relationship between the three pillars of their faith, unless they were prepared to conquer and reshape the reality. In the end, they tried to rationalize their confusion by pretending that their decision was aimed at preserving the unity and integrity of the armed forces. They were not successful. Not only did they hand over the remnants of their institution, but many of them lost their lives to the revolutionaries, as they were forced also to surrender their God, their king, and their country.

Notes

Chapter Four

1. Opinion prevalent among military and civilian Iranians in and out of Iran.
2. General Robert Huyser's remarks to a gathering of Iranians in California, as published in *Millat-i Bidar*, Bahman 1362 (February 1984), and corroborated by a number of participants.
3. Pahlavi, *Answer*, 172.
4. General 'Abbas Qarabaghi, *Haqayiq Dar-Barih-'i Inqilab-i Iran* (Facts Concerning the Iranian Revolution) (Paris: Suhayl Publications, 1984).
5. Shapur Bakhtiar, *Ma Fidelité* (Paris: Albin Michel, 1982), and *Si-u Haft Ruz Pas Az Si-u Haft Sal* (Thirty Seven Days After Thirty Seven Years) (Radio Iran Publications, *Khurdad*, 1361).
6. William H. Sullivan, *Mission To Iran* (New York: W. W. Norton, 1981).
7. Carter, *Keeping Faith*.
8. Brzezinski, *Power And Principle*.
9. Cyrus Vance, *Hard Choices* (New York: Simon & Schuster, 1983).
10. Conversation with General Muhaqiqi, former commander of Iranian gendarmerie, May 1984.
11. Qarabaghi, *Haqayiq*, 445–7.
12. See chapter 6, below.
13. See chapter 7, below.
14. General Hasan Arfa', *Under Five Shahs* (London: Murray, 1964; Wilbur, *Riza Shah*.
15. Wilbur, *Riza Shah*, chaps. 3–7. Malik al-Shu'ara Bahar, *Tarikh-i Mukhtasar-i Ahzab-i Siyasi-yi Iran: Inqiraz-i Qajariyih* (A Short History of Iranian Political Parties: The Fall of the Qajar Dynasty) (Tehran: Pocket Books, 1357); Ervand Abrahamian, *Iran Between Two Revolutions* (Princeton: Princeton University Press, 1982), chaps. 3 and 4.
16. See chapter 1, above.
17. See chapter 5, below.

18. Qarabaghi, *Haqayiq*, 103–4.
19. Ibid.
20. Conversation with General Muhaqiqi.
21. See chapter 3, above.
22. Huyser, in *Millat-i Bidar*.
23. Pahlavi, *Answer*, 167.
24. Huyser, in *Millat-i Bidar*; Sullivan, *Mission*, 238–9.
25. Carter, *Keeping Faith*, 445.
26. Pahlavi, *Answer*, 172.
27. Ibid., 171.
28. Qarabaghi, *Haqayiq*, 197. General Rabi'i, the air force chief, had noticed the Shah's diminished interest in military hardware sometime in the summer of 1978.
29. Bakhtiar, *Ma Fidelité*, 145. Author's translation.
30. Ibid., 146.
31. *Bakhtiar, 37 Days*, 51. Author's translation.
32. Qarabaghi, *Haqayiq* 204. Author's translation.
33. Ibid., 154.
34. Ibid., 154–5.
35. Ibid., 157–8.
36. Ibid., 207, 208. Author's translation.
37. Huyser, in *Millat-i Bidar*.
38. Pahlavi, *Answer*, 172.
39. Bakhtiar, *37 Days*, 84ff.
40. See chapter 3, above.
41. From the text of the Bakhtiar program submitted to the Majlis on 21 Dey, 1357, reprinted in Bakhtiar, *37 Days*, 153–60. Author's translation.
42. Huyser, in *Millat-i Bidar*.
43. Sullivan, *Mission*, 229.
44. Carter, *Keeping Faith*, 443.
45. Ibid.
46. Vance, *Hard Choices*, 335.
47. Brzezinski, *Power and Principle*, 378–9.
48. Sullivan, *Mission*, 230.
49. Huyser, in *Millat-i Bidar*.
50. Ibid.
51. Qarabaghi, *Haqayiq*, 168–9.
52. Qarabaghi, *Heqayeq*, 170. Author's translation.
53. Vance, *Hard Choices*, 320–30.
54. Ibid.
55. Brzezinski, *Power and Principle*, 370.
56. Carter, *Keeping Faith*, 445.
57. Ibid., 446.

58. Qarabaghi, *Haqayiq*, 176.
59. Carter, *Keeping Faith*, 446–7.
60. Qarabaghi, *Haqayiq*, 178.
61. Ibid., 180.
62. Brzezinski, *Power and Principle*, 381.
63. Ibid., 382.
64. Ibid., 383.
65. Qarabaghi, *Haqayiq*, 175. On von Marbod's mission see Sullivan, *Mission*, 243.
66. Huyser, in *Millat-i Bidar*.
67. Brzezinski, *Power and Principle*, 388.
68. Qarabaghi, *Haqayiq*, 251.
69. Huyser, in *Millat-i Bidar*.
70. Qarabaghi, 244.
71. Sullivan, 243.
72. Brzezinski, *Power and Principle*, 389; Sullivan, *Mission*, 245.
73. Conversation with General Muhaqiqi, August 1984, Richmond, Va.
74. Qarabaghi, *Haqayiq*, 445–76.
75. Ibid., 285–7.
76. Ibid.
77. Interview on Iranian television, witnessed by the author, February 21, 1979.

5 | Foreign Policy: Psychological Costs of Overdependence

The privileged relationship between the United States and Iran must be the focus of analysis for any serious attempt at an explanation of the impact of international conditions on the fall of the Iranian monarchy. The historical precedents of the relationship date back to Iran's long standing desire to involve an element of third force in its international relations in order to ameliorate the brunt of Anglo-Russian pressures. In spite of Iranian efforts, however, serious involvement of the United States in Iran did not materialize until after the Second World War and then mainly as a result of the congruence of two factors: the Iranian attempt to force the Soviets to evacuate Iranian territory in 1946, and American resolve to contain Soviet expansionism as defined by the Truman Doctrine.[1]

The history of the American assumption of traditional British responsibilities in the Middle East is well-documented and needs not be repeated here. After the fall of Mossadiq in 1953, the replacement of British power in Iran by the United States reached a new height. The United States became a major partner in the Iranian Oil Consortium, a dispenser of economic assistance, and the major supplier of security and military hardware and software. Iran, in turn, began to grow into a respectable economic and military force in the area. From 1953 onwards, as a result of the Shah's increasing power, the privileged relationship between the United States and Iran became, increasingly, the privileged relationship between the Americans and the Shah, a fact of considerable significance for later events in the country.

The mutually supportive interrelation between the United States and the Shah was seen as a pillar both of American influence in the Middle East and of the Shah's power in Iran. Conversely, the presumption was that as long as this privileged interrelationship remained intact, neither American influence nor the Shah's power would decline. In fact, both the United States and the Shah publicly nurtured and encouraged this idea. Nevertheless, in spite of Carter's protestations of faith in the Shah, by the middle of 1978, the idea had begun to take root among the Iranians, including the Shah, as well as in foreign circles, that, objectively speaking, the privileged relationship had come to an end and that the United States was seeking ways to dissociate itself from the idea of the indispensability of the Shah and his policies. Given the nature of Iranian political culture, the subjective effect of this perception was phenomenal for both the Shah's supporters and his enemies. It helped to limit the Shah's options to military response which, as we have seen, he was unwilling to make, and to turn every other overture toward compromise and reconciliation into a belated attempt at appeasement. The relevant questions, therefore, revolve around the factors that helped produce this perceptual transformation.

The underlying source of conflict between the United States and Iran appeared to be a fundamental clash between two kinds of forces: one historical, the other accidental and possibly conspiratorial. The historical force related to the characteristics of political power based on a nationalistic conception of history; it was mainly a property of Iranian political development. The accidental force was the tremendous, if not profound, transmutation of the American political psyche as a result of a number of influences at the center of which stood the experiences of Vietnam and Watergate. The possible conspiratorial aspect related to the seemingly planned and coordinated attempt by a variety of liberal and leftist forces to implant in that changing psyche a distinctly anti-Shah disposition. Let us see how each of these conflicting forces affected the relationship between the United States and Iran.

A comparative study of the development of national and foreign policy postures after the Second World War suggests that as indigenous political leaders achieve greater internal power, they tend toward the assumption of a more independent posture in foreign policy, irrespective of their ideological inclinations. The experience of the Communist bloc places the above proposition in prominent relief. Having achieved power through indigenous forces, both Tito and Mao insisted on independence from Moscow. In later phases, the same tendency was demonstrated by such ideologically diverse leaders as Dubcek of Czechoslovakia and Ceaucescu of Romania. Conversely, the East German leadership, geographically and politically in a more precarious position, has tended to follow the Moscow line more closely.[2]

The same tendency may be discerned in the postwar relationship between Western Europe and the United States, even though here, on account of the different characteristics of the democratic political systems involved, the nature of dependency was more subtle. Nevertheless, even a cursory review of foreign policy postures of France and Germany before and after 1960 demonstrates the point.

In the Third World, nationalist leaders like Nassir, Nehru, Sukarno, Nkrumah, and others, made a point of following a foreign policy independent of the two blocks under the ideological umbrella of nonalignment, although real or imagined international threats at times may have pushed them toward closer cooperation with the United States or the Soviet Union.

In Iran, also, the impulse toward an independent foreign policy can be recognized in the latter years of Reza Shah's reign, and, in a more emphatic manner, during the Mossadiq era in the early 1950s. In both cases, the driving motive was nationalism, and its manifestation was made possible by the political system's perception of its own strength derived trom indigenous forces.

Moves toward independence have important psychological impacts on the international scene. Objectively, an independent foreign policy may aim at precisely what it purports to achieve: independence from the two superpowers. Subjectively, it always tends to be couched in an aura of antagonism toward one superpower or the other, given the bipolar character of the immediate postwar international scene. Thus, Titoism was seen as anti-Sovietism mainly because of Stalin's attitude toward the move. In the same vein, De Gaulle's insistence on developing an independent *force de frappe* was regarded as a manifestation of anti-Americanism, chiefly as a result of the American reaction.

Examples can be multiplied from evidence of the Third World struggle for independence.

Since American assistance was a factor in the Shah's return to power in 1953, it was natural for Iranian foreign policy to follow the American line closely. Iran joined the Baghdad Pact in 1955 and later, when Iraq withdrew as a result of the coup d'etat of 1958, she remained the pivotal link in the Central Treaty Organization, constituting a geographic bridge joining NATO and SEATO through Turkey and Pakistan. In the 20 years between 1958 and 1978, both the internal strength of the Iranian political system and the international political and military equations changed significantly. These changes, in turn, introduced new elements of stress into the relationship between the United States and Iran, in spite of regular official proclamations to the contrary.

As Iran's economic and military conditions improved, and the Shah's grasp on political power solidified, Iran gradually moved from being a passive recipient of economic and military aid to becoming an active participant in the formulation and development of regional strategic policy. To be sure, the change in the Iranian role was consonant with the Nixon Doctrine and the United States' position on the security of the Persian Gulf region as stated in the National Security Memorandum of August 1972, prepared in anticipation of British withdrawal, and explained by Assistant Secretary of State Joseph Sisco before the Subcommittee on the Near East of the House Committee on Foreign Affairs.[3] According to Sisco, Iran and Saudi Arabia had been singled out as the recipients of increasing American military and political support not only for the sake of their own strength and security, but also for keeping peace in the region. But even though this position was consistently reiterated by official spokesmen for the United States, including both presidents Ford and Carter, its clarity became increasingly dimmed for the Iranian government, as a result of internal turmoil in the United States political system in the post-Watergate era.

To achieve the required stature for her new role, Iran had to assume a more balanced political posture within the framework of the emerging multipolar international scene. This more "even-handed" policy was subsumed under the general rubric of "independent national policy" and positive nationalism,[4] although the fact of Soviet contiguity and the Shah's ideological inclinations placed Iran basically in the Western camp. The following, however, point to the thrust of the new posture.

One of the basic principles of the Shah's foreign policy was to respect, and to the extent that it did not contradict the fundamental requirements of national security, to satisfy basic Soviet interests in Iran. Since the Shah perceived the Soviet state system as inherently expansionist, Iranian national security requirements demanded that Soviet interests in Iran be defined and satisfied primarily in economic terms.[5]

Consequently, in January 1966, an agreement was signed between Tehran and Moscow whereby, in return for Soviet cooperation and technical assistance in industrial domains and Soviet export of industrial machinery and equipment to Iran, Iran would undertake to export to the Soviet Union substantial quantities of natural gas. The agreement allowed the Soviet Union as well as a number of other Eastern European countries to become significant partners in the economic development of Iran. Over the years, the agreement called for some 147 large-scale industrial undertakings in Iran by the Soviet Union, of which the most important were the Isfahan steel mill, the machinery plant in Arak, a 1400 MW power station in Ahvaz, and an 800 MW station in Isfahan. On the commercial level, Iran-Soviet exchanges had exceeded 700 million roubles in 1977, making the Soviet Union the sixth ranking commercial partner of Iran after the United States, West Germany, Japan, the United Kingdom, and France.[6] The Shah's regime obviously subscribed to the policy of maintaining normal relationships with countries with different social systems. Consequently, Soviet relations with the Shah, if not close, remained officially correct until 1978.

Iran's position in Southwest Asia hinged on the premise that superpower involvement exacerbated regional conflicts, polarizing them on a world scale within a political framework which was beyond the ability of regional states to manage effectively and logically. Iran's position recognized the inevitability of the superpower presence, which resulted from commercial, technological, diplomatic and ideological issues, and envisaged accommodating to it in terms of economic assurances, including the flow of oil, and political guarantees, including the absence of superpower military bases. In fact, the Shah's promise to Moscow in 1962 not to allow the establishment of American bases on Iranian territory had been instrumental in bringing about a détente between the Soviet Union and Iran and accelerating the tempo of economic and commercial relations between the two countries. It was also congruent with President Nixon's subsequent policy of selective retrenchment, based on the assumption by friendly states of security responsibilities in their own region, a fact that had supplied the Shah's opponents with sufficient propaganda ammunition to accuse him of having converted Iran into an outpost of United States foreign and military policy.

The two major sources of threat in the area with negative spillover possibilities in the Persian Gulf region were the Arab-Israel and the Indo-Pakistani conflicts. Admittedly, Iran's leverage with the nations directly involved was limited. Nevertheless, as early as 1969 steps had been taken to circulate the idea of a Persian Gulf security system, to improve relations with regional states, and to assess the possibilities for the development of a regional dialogue on security and economic cooperation. The Indian Ocean Common Market proposal of 1974[7] and the Iranian suggestion to expand the Regional Cooperation for Development (RCD) treaty envisaging increasing cooperation among the original members—Iran, Turkey, and Pakistan—as a first step toward the possible subsequent inclusion of India, Iraq, Afghanistan and others, were parts of this effort.

Two major regional developments in this area in the early 1970s presented new opportunities for a more vigorous pursuit of these aims. The first, a tapering off of Arab radicalism signalled by the death of Egypt's President Nassir in 1970, and the ascent to power of Anwar al-Sadat, a moderate and as later events proved a courageous and visionary leader, allowed for the development of a significantly different type of relationship between Iran and the Arab Middle East. The second, the announcement of the withdrawal of the British from the Persian Gulf, presented an open and tangible space for the implementation of a regional policy.

The rise of Sadat to the Egyptian presidency had a profound effect on the regional alliance systems as well as on the nature of radicalism in the Arab countries of the region. Sadat's anti-Soviet posture largely abated Iran's fear of Soviet encirclement through the intermediary of the Ba'thist regimes in Iraq and Syria aided by Nassir's Egypt. The rapprochement between Egypt and Saudi Arabia and the drastic change of relationship from enmity to close friendship between Iran and Egypt transformed the position of the Arab radicals from one of aggressiveness to an essentially defensive posture. That situation, in turn, enhanced Iran's dominant position in the Persian Gulf, freeing it to occupy the strategically important islands of Abu Musa and the two Tunbs at the northern entrance to the Strait of Hormuz in 1971 in spite of Arab objections, as well as to offer military assistance to help quell the Dhofar insurgency in Oman at the request of Sultan Qabus in 1973. Iran's solidarity with Egypt was demonstrated by the Shah's extension of logistical assistance, including fuel, to Sadat's forces in the 1973 war with Israel and later through substantial financial and economic aid.[8]

In the meantime, ways were sought through a variety of diplomatic channels to normalize relations with Iraq. The roots of the controversy between the two neighbors stemmed from both ideological and national interests. The fall of the Hashimite dynasty in 1958 and the pursuant radicalization of the Iraqi governments, first under Abdul Karim Qasim and later under successive Ba'thist regimes, transformed the once cordial relationship between Iran and Iraq into one of contention and controversy. Iraq aimed at the radicalization of the area and subversion of the traditional regimes; Iran, on the other hand, favored the status quo and helped to maintain traditional systems of government. Iraq had assumed an anti-Western political posture and looked increasingly to the Soviet Union for weaponry and military assistance, whereas Iran had associated itself closely with the West and, in particular, with the United States. Iraq considered itself the potential leader of the Arab countries of the Persian Gulf region and, therefore, aimed at the arabization of the Gulf; Iran's plans involved a non-ethnic system of security and economic cooperation in which she would play a leading role by virtue of geography, population, and technoeconomic capability. For the two countries directly involved, the issues were real and emanated from conflicting perceptions of their respective ideological and national interests. The economic and strategic significance of the Persian Gulf for the international community, however, often disposed others to view these controversial postures as no more than roles played by client states on behalf of the two superpowers.

The intangible points of contention converged on two palpable issues confronting the two nations: the Shatt al-Arab and the Kurdish problems. The first, the result of a British-imposed treaty of 1937 that placed the waterway under Iraqi sovereignty without drawing a median line to give Iran control over waters adjoining Iranian soil, and which Iran had long rejected as contrary both to normal rules governing international maritime relations and Iranian national interest, erupted from time to time, and in early 1960 created a serious crisis with the possibility of developing into full-fledged naval warfare. In the end, military confrontation was avoided, and, as a rule, Iranian vessels travelled along the waterway flying the Iranian flag. The dispute was ended by the Algiers Agreement of March 1975, in which the deepest channel in the Shatt al-Arab, known as the *Thalweg* line, was designated as the boundary between the two countries.[9]

The Kurdish issue was potentially far more volatile. Iran had supported Mullah Mustafa Barizani's insurrection against the Baghdad government, mainly in order to keep Iraqi forces under pressure in the Kurdish area of the north and thus prevent them from threatening the Iranian border to the south. Obviously, Iran could find no satisfaction in the establishment of an autonomous Kurdish state in northern Iraq. Such a state would act as a magnet for the Iranian as well as Turkish Kurds and present a potentially disruptive force in relationships between the Iranian Kurdish population and the central government. It was thus to the advantage of both Iran and Iraq to settle the issue. This dispute also was "settled" within the framework of the Algiers Agreement, effected through the good offices of President Houari Boumediene of Algeria. A full amnesty was offered the Kurdish rebels; Kurds who had taken refuge in Iranian territory as a result of the 1974 Iraqi offensive were allowed to go back if they so elected; and the Iranian Kurds in Iraq were permitted to choose to resettle in Iran.

The settlement between Iran and Iraq was made possible as an outgrowth of a number of factors. By the beginning of 1970, as a result of both military superiority and internal stability, Iran had achieved a relative strategic advantage. The Iraqi government had become less belligerent, as it had reexamined its military, political, and economic relationships with the Soviet Union and the prospects not only of an actual Kurdish uprising but also of a potentially exploitable Shiite-Sunni conflict within Iraq's borders. Consequently, Iraq's response to Iran's occupation of the three islands in the Persian Gulf and its involvement in the Dhofar rebellion was largely confined to anti-Iranian propaganda among the Arab littoral states and was thus less vehement than might otherwise have been expected.

Iran, for its part, had made a number of overtures to the Iraqi government, if not directly at least by implication, through proposals concerning the gradual establishment of regional security and economic systems of cooperation. Iranian foreign policy, albeit within the Western frame of reference, was assuming more neutralist dimensions in both regional and global terms. The Algiers Agreement established correct, if not overly cordial, relations between the Shah and Saddam Hussein, based on mutual appreciation of their respective legitimate interests. Not surprisingly, in 1978 Saddam agreed to expel Khomeini from Iraqi territory at the request of the Iranian government.

Regarding Iran's southeastern border, Iranian foreign policy developed largely in response to the significance of a stable and unified Pakistan for the security of Iran. Instability in Pakistan threatened Iran in two ways, both of which related to the general possibility of Soviet encirclement of the country. A weakened or dismembered Pakistan would invite considerable pressure on the 750,000 Iranian Baluchis by a Soviet-dominated Baluchistan on the other side of the border. Already, in 1973, the rise of Muhammad Daoud to power in Kabul seemed to herald a new era of Soviet domination of Afghanistan. The idea of "Greater Pushtunistan" revived under Daoud meant an immediate threat to the integrity of Pakistan and from a geopolitical standpoint contained the related notion of an independent Baluchistan. The process, if allowed, could have also meant a Soviet naval presence and port facilities in the Indian Ocean and the Sea of Oman and, therefore, Soviet domination of the traffic through the Strait of Hormuz. Iran's policy, therefore, was linked to the preservation of a stable Pakistan.

As members of CENTO (Central Treaty Organization) and its offshoot RCD, (Regional Cooperation for Development) Turkey, Iran, and Pakistan were linked to the Western alliance system dominated by the United States. The lukewarm American responses to the Pakistani defeats by India in 1965 and 1971 further strengthened the Shah in his resolve not only to develop Iranian military capability, but also to play a more active role in the resolution of regional conflicts of potential consequence for Iran. He therefore initiated a series of political, military, and economic moves connected directly and indirectly with the Indo-Pakistani conflict. On the political front, he announced

Iran's unequivocal commitment to the integrity of West Pakistan. To lend credence to his position, he made a number of decisions concerning the strength of the Iranian military forces in the country's southeastern region, of which the most dramatic was the construction of a vast naval base in Chah Bahar. The efforts to establish cordial relations with China in the early 1970s may also be construed in part as a balancing move to offset the increasingly hegemonial weight of the Indo-Soviet entente in the area.

Economically, the Shah made a number of lucrative offers to India, partly to achieve greater leverage with the Indian government and partly to institute tangible bases for the Indian Ocean Common Market idea. After 1973 such proposals involved not only the establishment of mutually beneficial joint commercial and industrial ventures, but also the extension of easy credit in order to enable a financially squeezed India to purchase Iranian oil. Under the Desai government, Indian responses appeared to be basically positive, and Indo-Iranian relations in the mid-1970s showed signs of considerable improvement.

Ironically, the Shah's foreign policy in his last years seemed extremely successful in most areas except in relation with his traditional Western friends. Tensions arose in part from the Shah's increasingly greater self-assertion and in part as a result of political and economic rivalry emanating from conflicting perceptions of self-interest among the Western powers.

The palpable focal points of the controversy between the Shah and the West, however, were the two issues of oil and armaments. The Shah had played a leading role in raising the price of oil in December 1973 for two different, though in his mind, interrelated reasons. Nationally, he thought it mandatory to raise the price of oil because it was the major source of income on which the future of the Iranian economy was based. It was a depletable resource that would last for no more than a generation at the projected levels of extraction and export. It was therefore imperative for the country to build the necessary infrastructure in order to be able to survive and prosper once oil as a prime source of energy had been depleted. He referred to oil as a noble product and conceived of it as a major source of foreign exchange for generations to come, not as fuel but as the main ingredient of a projected Iranian petro-chemical industry.

In a related sense, he thought that the increase in the price of oil would in the long run be beneficial to the West as well. Since it was depletable, it was essential for the West to seek and develop other sources of energy. Given the character of the Western economy, serious and sustained effort in that direction could obtain only when the costs of alternative energy sources became competitive.[10] At the same time it was obvious that the higher price of oil would be reflected in Western exports and therefore would be paid in appreciable part by the importers of technological products, specifically the oil-producing countries themselves. If anywhere, the brunt of the pressure would have to be borne by the Third World nations which lacked oil resources.

In the event, the American press attacked him as one of the most hawkish members of OPEC, bent on the destruction of the American and Western economies. The European liberal and leftist press identified him as an American stooge, raising the price of oil in order to be able to buy bigger and more advanced American weapons. He was at once accused of squandering Iranian national wealth by catering to the economic requirements of the West, and of destroying the Western economy by pursuing the dictates of his own demented megalomania.

The same mood prevailed on the issue of armaments. Amidst controversy and vituperation, the Americans, the British, the French, and the Germans sold to the Shah what he demanded, presumably because they thought the sales were consonant with the West's economic and strategic interests. For his part, the Shah may have erred in bits and pieces in his armaments and military policy, but not in his belief in the necessity of building a regionally significant military force for Iran, nor in conceiving of it in strategic terms. As a general rule, he tended to view military requirements as dependent on political judgment. As he regarded the threat to Iranian security to be determined by geopolitical considerations, he conceived of the logic of Iran's military capabilities in geopolitical terms. It was obvious that Iran could not withstand a serious Soviet assault in isolation. It was imperative, however, to have the capability to overcome and therefore deter an attack by surrogate powers and to withstand direct Soviet assault, short of nuclear attack, long enough to allow for international action. Both contingencies could be dealt with more effectively through weapons systems with high and continuous linkage in training and technology with the United States. Contrary to the accusations of his opponents, the costly weapons on which he insisted were scarcely suitable for the suppression of internal uprisings.

As we have seen, the relationship between Iran and the West was defined primarily by the dominant position of the United States. Significant changes could not have been brought about without severe implications for this preferred relationship. Iranian moves toward greater diversity in foreign relations, therefore, implied the necessity of effecting an understanding with the United States government. However, whereas in the past US-Iran relations had been largely regulated by a relatively clear stand by American administrations, after 1973 the clarity of the American position became increasingly obscured by the prevailing turmoil in United States domestic politics. Consequently, it became progressively more difficult to make projections about future American postures with respect to general or specific issues.

In Iran, the tempo of socioeconomic development since 1963, and with it the Shah's increasing political prominence, suggested a natural tendency toward a more independent and diversified foreign policy. To the Shah, a more independent policy obviously did not signify a less friendly policy; it did imply, however, a rearrangement of the existing client relationship toward a more equal partnership. The idea appeared to have found sympathy within the Nixon administration, as exemplified by the President's cordial relationship with the Shah. Projections concerning the future Iranian role in the international scene, therefore, may be presumed to have been made in terms of two interrelated premises, namely that they had the support of the American president and that the American president could be relied upon to represent, in fact as well as in theory, the American position in foreign relations. The Shah's personal experience with American presidents, from Roosevelt to Nixon, had indeed predisposed him to see the process of formulation of the American foreign policy in these terms and to regard the president's support as a sufficient basis on which to build his relations with the United States. Indeed, his premature and diplomatically reckless intimation of support for Nixon's candidacy in 1960, and the subsequent problems he faced during the Kennedy administration, had strengthened his belief in the above premises.

These premises, however, lost much of their validity in the aftermath of Watergate. While presidential support was still forthcoming, its nature and tenacity had changed significantly. For one thing, the American presidency no longer appeared to be the focal point of American consensus on foreign policy. That consensus, initially strengthened by Nixon's landslide victory in 1972, was later weakened by the Watergate fiasco, as the popular perception of the role of the president was undergoing a painful revision. Neither President Ford nor President Carter appeared able to commit the United States to a long-range policy. Having sailed into office on the crest of a new wave of American mistrust of the executive power, Carter proved incapable of inspiring confidence in America's allies. In the Shah's case, the result was a lingering sense of doubt concerning American intentions—a disposition that apparently remained with him to the last day of his life.[11]

The Shah's response to the new political situation in the United States was essentially twofold. He tried to accomodate the new President's stand on human rights by taking steps toward the liberalization of Iranian politics and by moving toward a dovish position on the oil issue. On the other hand, sensing the dangers inherent in American vacillation, he insisted on speeding up the tempo of the modernization of the Iranian armed forces.[12] Domestic and international reactions to these two sets of moves, as we shall see, exacerbated the already existing tensions within the Iranian political system.

Since the end of the Second World War the Iranian military organization had committed itself to American weapons systems. Military weaponry and organization cannot be overly diversified without significant loss of money, materiel, and system capability. Once Iran had opted to modernize its armed forces through the intermediary of American military strategy and weapons systems, it was no longer possible to change course in midstream without incurring unacceptable financial as well as capability setbacks. Thus, even if money were available, rationality demanded the continuation of the adopted course.[13]

The American congressional and media response to the Shah's military demands, however, turned increasingly vituperative. Whatever the internal reasons for the prevailing negative mood in the United States,[14] its effect on Iranian society was to confirm the doubts about the American position vis-à-vis the Shah. Such doubts were exacerbated not only by the seemingly concerted attacks on the Shah and his regime by the American media, but also by the disparaging comments of some highly placed officials of the Carter administration. Not surprisingly, the effect of the president's lavish praise of the Shah's leadership in his famous New Year's Eve speech of 1977 in Tehran,[15] did not outlast the festivities for more than a few days.

The significance for the stability of the Iranian regime of the debate in the United States Senate and the Western media over arms is fully brought forth only if it is placed in a larger context, namely an anti-Shah movement that, by 1976, had pretty much succeeded in capturing the liberal psyche in American politics. The sources of this movement remain unclear, but its trajectory, its strategic and tactical dimensions, and finally its political effects have been and remain significant enough to warrant further analysis.

The first signs of the movement appeared in Europe, among the leftist-liberal circles, in the latter part of the 1960s. It was composed of ideologically diverse elements whose point of convergence was a concerted attack on the Iranian regime. The Shah referred to the internal component of these forces as Islamic-Marxist, suggesting an unholy alliance between the reactionary Islamic elements and foreign-based Marxist revolutionaries. He characterized the outside components as proven agents of international communism.[16] The implication was that the Islamic elements had become dupes of international communism. He argued that, while devout Muslims could not become Communists, devoted Communists could easily play the role of devout Muslims. In support of his position, he pointed to the fact that many members of the antiregime terrorist groups had been trained in Cuba, East Germany, and, for a while, even in China, as well as in Libya, Syria, and Iraq by the PLO and other related Palestinian organizations. Others have traced the origin of the anti-Shah movement to an effort by rival European interests to drive a wedge in US-Iranian relations.[17] Whatever the sources of this phenomenon, its pattern of evolution and its strategic success indicate a coordinated effort with devastating effect on the internal politics of Iran.

One of the basic consequences of this protracted psychological assault on the Iranian regime was to predispose a significant part of American opinion to view the Shah as a corrupt and oppressive tyrant who not only sucked the lifeblood out of his own people, but also emerged as a powerful megalomaniac menacing the peace of the world. The effort was particularly successful with liberals whose profound disappointment with the American involvement in Vietnam, the American presidency and CIA operations had predisposed them to accept the grotesquely exaggerated anti-Shah allegations in a uniquely indiscriminate manner. The point is not that the Shah's regime was neither oppressive nor corrupt; it is rather that the liberal perception of repression and corruption in Iran had been formed by nonfactual criteria and, therefore, had become impervious to empirically based evidence. Viewed in this light, it becomes neither accidental nor surprising that an experienced liberal politician of Edward Kennedy's stature, running for the office of president of the United States, naturally and inadvertently speaks of the Shah's "umpteen billions" without a thought about the necessity of providing evidential proof to support his implied condemnation.[18]

The process of fomenting a negative opinion of the Shah in the United States was successful partly because of the Iranian regime's misunderstanding of the bases of American politics, and partly because of the relative openness of the American public to political manipulation. The reasons for this malleability in foreign relations are socio-cultural and complex. They relate fundamentally to a historically determined penchant for self-righteous presumption of innocence. The archetypal American mind still conceives of the purpose of American politics as equality and freedom[19] and projects this image onto America's international relations. American involvement in the world, however, is naturally based on the objective interests of the United States in a world fraught with diverse and sometimes decidedly hostile forces. When the process is explained and legitimated by irrelevant values, it not only becomes hypocritical internationally and deceptive domestically, it tends to create a schizophrenic mentality. This schizophrenic tendency, in turn, renders political opinion vulnerable to displaced moral pressure and prone to political vacillation.

The atomization of the American society and the character of American politics have made the American public particularly responsive to the vagaries of the mass media. The European, for example, typically communicates with his political environment through the intermediary of his political ideology, largely defined and continuously supported by his party and its communications organs. The American is generally left alone to deal individually with complex problems of foreign and domestic policy. Given the looseness of the American party system, he depends essentially on the media, either directly or indirectly through the intermediary of his peer groups, to establish order in his political perceptions.

The media, on the other hand, are necessarily selective and typically unidirectional in their communication. They are consumer-oriented, competitive, and geared to a news culture that stresses controversy, whips up emotions, and appeals to the human sense of adventure, albeit within a defined political framework. As the American media in the 1960s and 1970s were largely dominated by a liberal frame of reference, they reflected the liberal perception of the world. That perception was particularly adept at affecting the schizophrenic aspects of the American political culture.

Informed and nourished essentially in the university, the liberal view extolled and perpetuated the myths of freedom and equality in American foreign policy when American foreign policy was (and given the economic and political requirements of the American system, had to be) determined, as noted earlier, on the basis of objectively defined American interests. It denigrated the foreign political leaders who had avowedly placed themselves on the side of American interests while it tended, subtly, to glorify or benignly ignore those who were found outside the purview of American friendship. Thus, in effect, it had become a support factor for the forces whose interests were essentially antithetical to those of the United States' friends and unwittingly a front for the weakening of American belief in American leadership. Given the influence of the liberal view on the media and public opinion, it is not surprising for the situation to have become increasingly baffling for America's friends.

The strategic mistake of the Iranian regime in its relations with the United States was its sluggishness in recognizing the imperative of confronting the anti-Iranian movement in its proper arena. Instead of addressing itself to the American conscience, it chose to pursue the traditional line of relying on profession of friendship by particular leaders. The Iranian ambassador to the United States, for example, had achieved notoriety for enjoying the favor of influential people in government and the private sector. He was far less adept at relating to the American media, universities, social organizations, and other categories of opinion makers. Nevertheless, that was essentially where the battle of the minds was fought and lost. Given the character of American politics, it was foolhardy to expect protracted American commitment, without providing for continuous popular support.

The anti-Shah movement gathered momentum in the United States during the turbulent years of Vietnam and Watergate. By 1976, it had become politically impractical for a self-respecting liberal to defend the Shah and his regime unapologetically. Those in responsible positions had to defend the American friendship with Iran, not on the basis of the virtues of the Shah's system, but on the grounds of the American national interest. The perception of the American national interest, however, had become considerably confused by the American disposition to expound it in terms of what appeared to many to be irrelevant and contradictory moral precepts. Thus, with the advent of Jimmy Carter to the presidency of the United States, the promotion of human rights became a major tenet of American foreign policy, apparently in an effort to gain moral superiority over the Soviet Union. The character of national sovereignty in the contemporary world order being what it is, most nations identified as violators of the new American principle refused to discuss the matter on the grounds that the American demand was hypocritical and amounted to undue and illegal interference in their internal affairs.[20] To demonstrate his faith in American friendship, the Shah proposed to comply, and thus by implication admitted to such violations, thereby giving new ammunition to his opponents.

The Shah's efforts to liberalize the Iranian political system could not possibly have satisfied his international critics. He conceived of liberalization as a gradual process of opening up the political space in order to allow for the participation of those people who had already accepted the legitimacy of his definition of the Iranian constitutional system. He saw those who opposed him as bent on overthrowing the Iranian constitutional system. His leftist and liberal critics, however, viewed them as types of loyal opposition. He saw the Iranian political culture as fragmented with respect to both structure and purpose. His critics were oblivious to the structural dimension and saw the controversy as revolving mainly around the manner of defining purpose. He had a vision of Iran's grandeur. His critics interpreted that vision as megalomania. He thought he was honestly trying to find a way to liberalize Iranian politics without destroying what he had constructed. His critics saw that effort as a diversionary move to confuse the issue and hold on to power. He was frustrated at what he considered a premeditated and conscious effort by the Communists to misrepresent his position to the Western liberal mind and thus raged against the liberals' malleability. His critics saw his attitude in terms of arrogance of power and delusions of grandeur.

The break in communication, therefore, was almost total as frames of reference were essentially different and contradictory. The net result was that as time went on, the Western liberal received his information about Iran basically through the intermediary of the Shah's opponents. The latter, for their part, had correctly identified repression as the Shah's Achilles' heel. Given the characteristics of the Iranian political culture, evidence of repression could be supplied continuously regardless of the regime's intentions. Guerrillas and terrorists could be imported into the country and the system's inefficiency could be relied upon to provide new examples of systemic violence. The more open the system became, the greater the possibility of manipulation and exploitation of the situation. The greater the manifestation of violence in the streets of the Iranian cities and villages, the easier and more convincing the allegations of viciousness and brutality.

To the Shah, the condition of American politics represented a threat not only to the security of Iran, but also, in a larger framework, to the world geopolitical balance that he saw eroding inexorably in favor of the Soviet Union. He thought he understood the nature of the vulnerability of American politics and was convinced that the Soviet view closely paralleled his own. Given the circumstances of nuclear parity, the Soviets would shun direct confrontation as they had since Khrushchev, and would concentrate tactically on creating vacuums in the Western sphere of influence and would exploit them in times and places that suited their strategy. To create political vacuums, they encouraged the Americans to withdraw effective power, and, as Vietnam had shown, the withdrawal of power had as much to do with confusion and loss of will as with the removal of actual military paraphernalia. The Soviets, therefore, were concentrating on tactical policies that would add to American confusion and lead to loss of will by appealing to the soft spots of American liberalism. Détente, SALT, human rights campaign, repression, corruption, identification of leftist tendencies with nationalism, creation of a sense of guilt, identification of anti-Soviet postures with fascism, were all seemingly different, but, in fact, related aspects of the same political thrust. In the Shah's own case, he saw the Soviets succeeding in creating their preferred image without ever appearing to be directly involved.

He was not impressed by the arguments about the bankruptcy of the Soviet sociopolitical system and its consequent lack of appeal. To his mind, power created its own appeal and the significance of Soviet ideology lay essentially in the manner in which it shaped Soviet long-range hegemonial and expansionist strategy. Naturally, the Chinese understood this. He was astonished by the West's apparent nonchalance concerning Soviet political inroads in the southern half of the African continent, where lie most of the world's strategic metal resources, in which only the Soviet Union was substantially self-sufficient. The change in Soviet naval policy since the early 1960s, and their development and deployment of one of the finest and most effective naval armadas along the world's strategic maritime trade routes only confirmed his suspicions. The fact that the West was totally dependent and the Soviet Union largely self-sufficient with respect to strategic resources, including fuel and metals, gave the Soviet naval capability an offensive character qualitatively different from that of the West.

The Soviets operated from an established sanctuary. The sphere of Soviet influence was no longer a matter of contention. All the rest of the world was open territory. The Soviets chose the form and style of their assault. Obviously, they were not always successful, but the strategic consequences were clear. Unless the United States and her allies awakened to the danger, the Soviet sphere of hegemony would expand until it included the areas commanding control over the sources of Western economic life. The Shah believed that in the final analysis nothing was worth a nuclear holocaust. Given the evolution of Soviet geopolitical supremacy and Soviet preponderance in conventional weapons, the West could lose without ever firing a shot. To the Soviets, he thought, détente was war by other means, in which the Soviet Union was winning.

The Shah felt that he had to address himself to the West as a friend, but he was rarely able to communicate successfully. Characteristically, his manner and speech reflected the pomp of his office. The geopolitical and historical circumstances of his country, specifically the long and vulnerable borders that both separated and joined Iran and the Soviet Union, did not allow him to speak openly of the Soviet threat. He spoke of the West's softening of fiber, of the need to tighten the belt, and of political and economic realism. The Western media, and through their influence Western opinion, interpreted his statements as those of a mind gone mad with power, of a nouveau riche man who thinks his sudden wealth gives him the right to advise and admonish the rest of the world.

The Shah considered the debates about Iran's military demands that took place in Congress and other agencies of the American government to be carried out, for the most part, within basically irrelevant frames of reference. The relevant issue, in his opinion, was the geopolitical significance of a stable and militarily strong Iran for the security and defense of the West. In public, he had to base his argument on the right of a sovereign state to determine the kind of weapon system it needed and was willing and able to pay for. In private, he suspected that the arms debate was an aspect of a complicated and sinister strategy designed by forces whose purpose was clearly to drive a wedge between Iran and the United States, to weaken his position and, if possible, to overthrow his regime.

With the weakening of the CIA in the aftermath of Watergate, the kind of tangible evidence required to impart his concern effectively had become increasingly more difficult to obtain. Frustrated by his helplessness to affect the American media and American opinion, he chose to rely on the American president by undertaking to support his human rights policy even beyond the president's requirements.

The Carter administration, however, was never able to develop a unified and comprehensive policy concerning Iran. Contrary to the Shah's expectations, instead of leading opinion it proved to be its vacillating follower. Unique in the history of the American postwar presidency, the Carter administration had, in effect, pledged itself to executive weakness and, therefore, structurally speaking, premeditated vacillation in foreign policy. Carter as president was not only unable to shape congressional opinion or impart to other opinion makers a sense of the national interest in their interpretation of the US-Iran relations, he even seemed unable to coordinate the statements of the high-ranking officials of his own administration.[21] The result was a sense of bewilderment in the Iranian government.

The psychological impact of American vacillation on both the supporters and opponents of the Shah's regime should not be underestimated. To most Iranians, the United States never behaves irrationally. Every move by the United States government is taken to mean something significant as a link in a chain of events and decisions that represent comprehensively the American perception of its own interest. To an American, this position, or rather predisposition, may seem absurd. Nevertheless, it is a crucial characteristic of Iranian political thinking on which political analysis and prediction are based.

There are different cognitive and psychohistorical reasons for this Iranian predisposition. First, there are very few Iranians who fully understand the operational mechanisms of the American political system. Second, a historically determined reverence for Western rationality as well as communist propaganda have imparted to them an anthropomorphic notion of capital. America is capitalist. Capitalists control America. America's power is therefore judiciously and consciously used to enhance the interest of capital. Capitalists are seen to act as one great Capitalist represented by the president of the United States. And third, as a psychohistorical effect of the experience of colonialism, the average Iranian thinks that nothing of much importance happens in Iran without the explicit or tacit involvement of the United States.

To the average Iranian, therefore, the United States' official vacillation on one hand, and the media's denunciation of the Shah, on the other, did not suggest a possible bungling administration; it meant a premeditated decision to withdraw support from the Shah. The only question in his mind was, why?

Logical explanations were furnished by a variety of sources, including the leftist and liberal European and American press.[22] Essentially, they stressed a set of interrelated but not necessarily empirically relevant arguments starting from the premise of the indispensability of Iran for the West and ending in the conclusion of the dispensability of the Shah. In the fall of 1978, the average middle-class Iranian with an average education tended to lean toward the following explanatory points, in various combinations:

1. The West cannot afford to lose Iran because of the country's resources as well as its strategic position.

2. The Shah has become increasingly more powerful and correspondingly less inclined to play the game according to the traditional rules. Consequently, it has become progressively more difficult for the West to control his policies. Western apprehension about the Shah's covert efforts to secure nuclear capability falls in this realm.

3. The Americans are particularly concerned about the internal contradictions of Iranian society, including corruption and repression, which may render the nation vulnerable to Soviet designs. They may be thinking of other political alternatives.

4. The Americans have always kept alternatives to give themselves the necessary latitude in their relations with the Shah. The National Front, the Rally for Freedom, different religious organizations, and political personalities, like Dr. 'Ali Amini, are relevant examples.

5. Religion is, by definition, anticommunist. Furthermore, there are 50 million Muslims in the southern provinces of the Soviet Union. A religious rally on the borders of the USSR could be used to bring pressure on the Soviet Union, possibly even to the point of changing the structure of Soviet policymaking.

6. Such a religious movement, brought about with the United States' assistance, would be expected to be a natural friend of the United States. A person of Khomeini's background, for example, obviously could not rule. Furthermore, he would not want to rule. Once the natural anticommunist forces within the Shiite community have been used to change the system while containing communism, the management of the system will be transferred to rational and knowledgeable elements.

Certain events were particularly stressed as evidence for the last point. The sudden, yet celebrated Sanjabi-Bakhtiar-Furuhar open letter to the Shah in 1977;[23] the equally sudden burst of political activity of hitherto quiescent people like Hidayat Matin-Daftari, a grandson of Mossadiq, in conjunction with nationalist—human rights—anticommunist elements like Hasan Nazih; the increasingly closer association of such American-groomed politicos in exile as Ibrahim Yazdi, Sadiq Qutbzadih, and, indirectly, Abul Hasan Bani-Sadr, with Khomeini; the obvious American courtship of Bazargan; and, most important of all, the basic anti-Shah posture of the BBC, a voice considered in Iran as the most authoritative interpreter of Western political inclinations, indicated to the more sophisticated Iranian a palpable possibility of American governmental involvement in the anti-Shah movement.[24]

The Persian psyche simply did not accept as authentic the British protestations concerning the BBC's political independence. No doubt, the relationship between the government and the mass media in Iran was partly responsible for Iranian cynicism. But other factors were also involved. For example, given the horrendous effect of the BBC on the internal politics of a great number of Third World countries, it seemed unreasonable to assume that a group of individuals who had no political responsibility would be given an unchecked power to speak, in effect, in the name of a historically great colonial power. In fact, they considered the nebulous character of the official association between the British government and the BBC as a perfect example of the legendary British shrewdness in foreign policy. British political intentions were carried out through the BBC, while the British government was left free to maneuver as demanded by circumstances, unfettered by prior commitment. Furthermore, Iranians remembered previous occasions when the BBC had followed minutely the interests of the British government. Certainly, Mossadiq's cause in the Anglo-Iranian oil dispute of the early 1950s could have been construed as enjoying at least partial historical, economic, and moral merit. The BBC, however, closely parroted the British government's line in attacking him as a theatrical buffoon geared to Communist interests and bent on the destruction of international law and order. Now, suddenly, a state radio historically considered the quintessence of colonial propaganda was transformed into the voice of "the people," informing and in many ways guiding the anti-Shah movement.

The Persian mind, of course, is essentially intuitive and conjectural in its interpretation of events. Since the end of 1977, to the Iranian mind, the Shah and Khomeini began to appear as two opponents on a field of battle. When two Iranians enter an arena of potential physical conflict, they follow certain rituals the essential purpose of which is to impress the adversary with their respective courage and ability. Much of this behavior is verbal, known in the history of Iranian heroics as *rajaz*, accompanied by certain demonstrative moves designed to achieve psychological superiority by convincing everyone concerned of one's courage and determination. The outward manifestations of the Shah's response to the Khomeini challenge, therefore, was of great psychological importance for the Iranian mind.

We have dealt with the Shah's response in some detail in previous chapters. Suffice it to say here that it only helped to justify the suspicion that he had lost the support of the United States. Very few Iranians in early 1978 really believed that the Iranian monarchy could be overthrown. The expectation was that the Shah could and would utilize his enormous power resources, essentially far superior to Khomeini's, to quell what was then considered sporadic manifestations of rebellion. It was assumed that the Shah was in a position to mobilize and demonstrate popular support for the regime through his organizational paraphernalia controlling the workers, peasants, guilds, women, and other social groups, and use both SAVAK and the military in support of the popular demonstrations to demolish Khomeini's pretensions to power.

Such actions never materialized. Instead, step by step, and in retrospect rather meekly, the Shah gave in. While the propaganda machine governing the Khomeini assault depicted him as the most ruthless leader of the century, he seemed helplessly and irrelevantly preoccupied with demonstrations of faith in keeping his promise of an open political system. The inevitable conclusion for his friends and his foes was that his options were determined and limited by other forces.

Notes
Chapter 5

1. See *inter alia*, the three volumes by Rouhollah Ramazani, *The Foreign Policy of Iran, 1500–1941* (Charlottesville: University Press of Virginia, 1966), *Iran's Foreign Policy, 1941–1973* (Charlottesville: University Press of Virginia, 1975), and *The United States and Iran; The Patterns of Influence* (New York: Praeger, 1982); Lenczowski, *Russia and the West*; Shahram Chubin and Sepehr Zabih, *The Foreign Relations of Iran* (Berkeley and Los Angeles: University of California Press, 1974), especially chapter 2.
2. Walter Laqueur touches on this subject in his discussion of polycentrism. He suggests that different levels of socio-economic development, cultural heritage, and national peculiarities are of prime importance. No doubt, such characteristics define the quality and tenor of response to hegemonial relations. But if they were the main determinants of moving toward greater independence, one would assume that the East Germans would have greater propensity to oppose the Soviets than do the Poles, Rumanians and Czechs. See Walter Laqueur, "The Schism" in Walter Laqueur and Leopold Labedz, *Polycentrism: The New Factor in International Communism* (New York: Praeger, 1962), 1–8.
3. Joseph J. Sisco, "Statement before the Subcommittee on the Near East, House Committee on Foreign Affairs, August 8, 1982," *Department of State Bulletin* 67, no. 1732 (September 4, 1972), 242–243.
4. Pahlavi, *Mission* 124 ff.
5. Nevertheless, until 1973, the Soviet Union was the second largest exporter of non-strategic arms to Iran. See Faroughi, "L'URSS et la Révolution Iranienne."
6. Ibid.
7. Pahlavi, *Answer* 198–204.
8. Al-Sadat, "Speeches and Interviews."
9. Alvin J. Cottrell, "Iran's Armed Forces Under the Pahlavi Dynasty," in Lenczowski, *Iran Under the Pahlavis*, 414.

10. The Shah made these points at every opportunity. His last references may be found in *Answer*, 97.
11. Ibid., 165.
12. The relationship between the Shah's uncertainty about the reliability of American support and his insistence on building up Iran's defense capability has been noted by a number of military analysts. The following may serve as an example:
    "There is no question that a pivotal point in the Shah's external policies came during the Pakistan-Indian conflict of 1965, long before the impact of the oil crisis. Noting that the CENTO powers, especially the United States, had not come to the aid of Pakistan, he determined that Iran had to be prepared to stage its own defense of vital national interests. And he had come to recognize that in an era of evermore contagious conflict and sophisticated weaponry defense had to be extended beyond the immediate perimeter of Iranian interests in the Persian Gulf and it had to be supported by an active diplomacy on the global scale." Alvin J. Cottrell, *Iran: Diplomacy in a Regional and Global Context* (Washington, DC: Center for Strategic and International Studies, 1975), 1–2.
13. See Shahram Chubin, "Iran's Defense and Foreign Policy," in Amirie and Twitchell *Iran in the 1980s*, 320.
14. The prevailing inconsistencies in the Carter administration's posture on arms transfer to Iran appeared to result from the clash between the president's campaign promises on one hand, and Iran's geostrategic requirements, on the other. The situation became progressively more confused by the existing range of opinion both inside and outside the administration. For an illuminating discussion see Michael Ledeen and William Lewis, *Debacle: The American Failure in Iran* (New York: Alfred A. Knopf, 1981), 80 ff. On the activities of American firms dealing in weapons systems see Barry Rubin, *Paved with Good Intentions* (New York: Oxford University Press, 1980), chap. 6.
15. Formal dinner speech at the reception in President Carter's honor in Niyavaran Palace, December 30, 1977.
16. For a detailed reference to Iranian student groups engaged in anti-Shah activity outside Iran and their political ties see *An Alliance of Reaction and Terror* (Tehran: Focus Publications, 1977).
17. "Qui Sont Les Maîtres de Khomeiny?", Supplement to *Nouvelle Solidarité*, 5, no. 20 (Wiesbaden: Dinges und Frick, n.d.).
18. In a televised interview in San Francisco after the capture of American hostages in Tehran.
19. Hans J. Morgenthau, *Purpose of American Politics* (College Park, Md.: University Press of America, 1983), 22 ff.
20. The Soviet response was essentially to increase the state pressure

on internal dissidents, further curtail Jewish emigration, and tighten its security relations with the satellite states. The response by most noncommunist states was also negative. Argentina is an example.

21. The confusion and controversy became progressively more pronounced as the Iranian upheaval unfolded in 1978. In a remarkably frank and revealing passage President Carter writes:

    "As I compared what he [General Huyser] told me with what our Ambassador in Iran had done and said, I became even more disturbed at the apparent reluctance in the State Department to carry out my directives fully and with enthusiasm. Its proper role was to advise me freely when a decision was being made, but then to carry it out and give me complete support once I had issued a directive. Cy [Secretary of State Cyrus Vance] sent one of his deputies to Iran to straighten out Sullivan or remove him, and I asked the Iranian desk officers and a few others to come to the White House.

    "I laid down the law to them as strongly as I knew how. I pointed out how difficult the Iranian questions had become, and described my procedure for making decisions. Sullivan had not been the only one who had caused me trouble. There had been a stream of news stories in Washington, seeming to originate with those who opposed my judgment that we should give our support to the Shah, to the military leaders, and later to Bakhtiar. I told them that if they could not support what I decided, their only alternative was to resign—and that if there was another outbreak of misinformation, distortions, or self-serving news leaks, I would direct the Secretary of State to discharge the official responsible for that particular desk, even if some innocent people might be punished. I simply could not live with this situation any longer, and repeated that they would have to be loyal to me or resign. And then I got up and left the room." Carter, *Keeping Faith:* 449–50. See also Sullivan, *Mission to Iran*; Brzezinsky, *Power and Principle*, chap. 10.

22. The French daily *Le Monde* may be taken as an example. Most of its articles about Iran were written by Eric Rouleau, who happened to be ideologically anti-Shah and a close friend and, some say, mentor of Bani-Sadr. Pierre Salinger calls Rouleau Bani-Sadr's favorite journalist. Pierre Salinger, *America Held Hostage: The Secret Negotiations* (Garden City, NY: Doubleday, 1981), 186.

23. This letter, dated 22 Khurdad 1356, suggested to the Shah that the only way to moral integrity and political stability was for the government to return, among other things, to the principles of the Constitution, to reject the single party, to free political prisoners,

etc. See the text in Bakhtiar, *37 Days*, 140–2.

24. Barry Rubin attributes this genre of opinion to a much more limited circle of pro-Shah elements. He argues that they misjudged America's power and intentions. In early 1978, however, by far a majority of the Iranian middle class were pro-Constitution, if not strictly pro-imperial order. By the middle of 1978 this mode of perception had become highly widespread among them. Under ordinary theoretical suppositions of nationalism, one would assume that they would be inclined to come together in defense of the system. As it turned out, the general reaction was ultimately to jump on the revolutionary bandwagon. On the other hand, Rubin is quite right when he suggests that they were wrong about the United States' power and intentions. The point, however, is not what the United States' intentions in fact were; it is rather how those intentions were projected and how they were perceived by the Shah, his supporters, and his enemies. See Rubin, *Paved with Good Intentions*, 257–60.

6 | Liberal Misperceptions: The Roots of Thanatos

One of the basic contentions of this study has been that an understanding of the Iranian Revolution, as indeed the understanding of any other phenomenon, depends to a large extent on the properties of the model used for the selection and analysis of the factors bearing on the revolution. If the model does not correspond to the realities of the object of analysis, it becomes useless as an explanatory tool and dangerous as a source of policy recommendation. The danger resides in the fact that, as soon as a model is used as a source of policy recommendation, it becomes transformed into ideology, and if it proves irrelevant to the facts of life, it becomes utopian. Utopias are enticing and valuable as points of reference, but unless they are considered in their proper perspective, they tend to confuse the issue, to obscure the relationships between realities and ideals, and to negate the usefulness of reality as a basis for the achievement of values approximating those of the utopia.

This is precisely what the application of the "libertarian model" did to Iran. The problem with the model was not that it held the ideal of political freedoms as the proper modality of the "good life," but that it confused a normative preference with existential reality by implicitly presupposing a consensual political culture that simply did not exist. Such models are ordinarily rendered irrelevant by the objective forces in society, but when they are supported by powerful international factors and absorbed in their utopian sense by a portion of strategically situated domestic elements, they are likely to produce the kind of psychological malaise manifested as *thanatos* on a social scale.[1]

The libertarian model is a powerful force affecting not only the ideologically passive, that is, those who are overtly fascinated by Western society and accept it as the model of the good life, but also the modern leftists who, on the surface at least, appear to be anti-Western. In Iran, the latter's most forceful representatives were the Fada'iyan-i Khalq and the mujahidin, mainly composed of youth, but also having their ideological kin outside of Iran, ranging from Maoists and Trotskyites and Guevarists to others who hold to the combined forms of religious and Marxist notions as bases of future revolutions. Their common denominator is their adherence to variants of utopian Marxism, their abstract concept of "mass" forged to accommodate the requirements of their ideology, and their fascination with alienated concepts of freedom and equality essentially borrowed from the libertarian model. The result is that they reject every existential model as an aberration caused by either capitalist or socialist imperialism while clinging to a notion of utopia whose historical and objective liaisons with the existing patterns of human relations are never made explicitly clear.

One of the most intriguing phenomena, the roots of which have not been studied empirically, is the covert and seemingly unconscious moral and psychological affinity existing between the liberal intellectual and the utopian leftist. Since the source of this affinity cannot be located either in a communality of factual perception or a sharing of positive values with respect to modes and contents of political action, it may be explained as a negative function of the nebulousness of their respective thought processes concerning the established political order. What happened in Iran was a dual process in which the romantic escapades of the revolutionary leftist were secretly admired by the antirevolutionary liberal who had acquiesced, willy-nilly, in drawing his share of the profit from the existing political and economic order, while the liberal's schizophrenic posture in turn acted as a moral force to weaken the system's resolve to take the necessary measures to quell the adversary because many of its members experienced an acute feeling of guilt whenever strong measures were taken.

There is, of course, a basic difference between revolutionary thought and revolutionary practice. Revolutionary thought often holds the most sublime aspects of man's hope for the future felicity of the species. Revolutionary practice, however, often descends into the most abysmal depths of human bestiality.[2] All successful revolutions of the past two centuries have exhibited this bestial characteristic. This is because, in spite of the teachings by modern masters of revolution such as Lenin and Mao, of the virtues of praxis i.e. action rising to the level of theory, unless thought descends to the level necessary to accommodate the requirements of successful action, no revolution can succeed. To succeed in revolutions is to master power, and power has its own rules. In this respect, the structure of power is more binding than the structure of thought. It demands its preferred strategy and tactics, and it imposes a propensity to sacrifice human life in order not only to break the adversary's structure of command, but also to maintain and strengthen one's own. The objective requirements of holding on to power always seem to find their justification by bending the ideology to suit their purpose. The more rigid the ideological faction in power, the greater the atrocities perpetrated in the name of virtue and truth. This is the historical lesson of the so-called great revolutions, including French Jacobinism, Russian Stalinism, German Nazism, and now the Khomeini brand of Islamic fundamentalism.

The distinction between revolutionary thought and practice in part relates to the fact that power in revolutionary thought represents a potential for good because the ideology aims at the distribution of power concentrated in the hands of one class or a ruling elite. There is always a point in the process of revolution, however, where the basic aims of freedom, equality and justice for the people can be achieved.[3] This is the point at which the ruling system has lost much of its power and, therefore, accepts the major and meaningful demands made by the revolutionary forces. The French revolutionaries, for example, had already achieved all the points they had demanded in law and ideology when they had become, in fact, capable of capturing and beheading their king. Beyond that point, the revolutionary process began to change its course and prepare for the kind of generation and concentration of power under Napoleon that had never been contemplated even by that most august of all the French kings, Louis XIV. The same may be said of the Russian Revolution and

Nicholas II. Unless one falls into the moral trap of arguing that, as heir apparent to Ivan the Terrible, Stalin represented the perpetuation of Russian political culture, and that therefore there was no escape from him, all indications are that a Kerenski-type regime would have heralded a far more humane future for the Russian people than the one allotted to them under the Communist system. It is also clear, as borne out by the events, that such a regime could not have succeeded without the twin umbrellas of the monarchy and the church as the only meaningful institutions with which the Russian masses could identify. Obviously, such a demand could not have been made of the Communists. Rather, it should have been a function of the intelligentsia to bring together the factions on whose cooperation the future felicity of the nation depended.

The same may be said about Iran. If this study treats the Iranian intellectual community harshly, it is because none of the ideologically extreme factions could have been expected to favor an intelligent and promising course for the future of the Iranian people. It fell upon this group to make the correct analysis and to promote the correct policy. Instead, they abdicated judgment and accepted a most futile panacea that represented the negation of all that could have served as the basis for the accomplishment of their presumed objectives of freedom, equality and social justice. They fell in line with the mood, organization, and slogans of the revolution, denigrating as evil whatever had been accomplished in the past 25 years. They insisted naively that once the Pahlavi regime was ousted, Iran would be blessed with a democratic system of government founded on such noble concepts as liberty, equality, and human dignity. They proclaimed proudly that, free of evil and malice, the new system would be a harbinger of a sublime morality bearing justice and charity for all. In short, the Iranian liberal intellectual became a mouthpiece for revolutionary interests rather than an analyst of the characteristics of the revolution. As such, he abandoned the distinguishing property of intellectualism.

We have chosen the term "thanatos" to describe the prevailing mood in the Iranian cities in the fall and winter of 1978, because no other concept captures quite as effectively the nonrational tendency toward self-destruction exhibited communally by otherwise vastly different social types. There were, no doubt, domestic and international reasons for the disaffection of the Iranians from their system of government.[4] But political disaffection, even when leading to revolutionary action, does not in itself explain a social phenomenon marked by widespread abdication of thought and reason by groups of intelligent and rational individuals otherwise noted for their ability to think and reason.

Now faced with the horrors of the Khomeini phenomenon, the Iranian intellectual community, mostly in exile, is trying desperately to find scapegoats for its own failure. This effort is concentrated on two main themes: the Shah's tyrannical system and Khomeini's deceptive statements. The arguments are that the Shah had proven himself an unreliable ruler who would promise anything when under pressure just as surely as he would crush the opposition once he regained power. It was therefore necessary to force him out of office. Censorship under the Shah's regime had prevented the dissemination of Khomeini's basic political ideas in Iran, making it impossible for the Iranian intellectuals to discern the considerable ideological distance that separated Khomeini from other more traditional leaders. And, finally, they had been deceived by Khomeini's pronouncements about democracy and justice and his avowed preference for the ascetic seclusion of the mosque and the school.

The argument about Khomeini's deception is patently false and requires little elaboration. It is essentially a manner of apology. In fact, the outstanding feature of the Khomeini phenomenon has been his consistency in thought and action, then as now. Certainly, from a tactical standpoint, the thrust of his attack before the revolution was naturally directed against the Shah and the alleged corruption and repression of his system. Such attacks, however, were always couched in a religious framework and derived both their legitimacy and pugnacity from their identification with a concept of fair and just government drawn from Islamic tenets and Shiite precepts. His interpretations of such precepts were also clear, as they had been set down in detail in his writings, at the center of which stood his treatise bearing on the idea of tutelary rights and duties of the *faqih*.[5] It was therefore quite legitimate for him to insist after the revolution that the whole movement was based on religious principles and that the government should be an Islamic theocracy based on these principles.

If Iran is now in the grip of total destruction, it is not because

Khomeini lied or deceived; it is rather due to the fact that his system, as it was proposed then, and as it is being instituted now, is alien to the historical realities of contemporary Iran.[6] And if the liberal intellectuals misconstrued his position, it was not because they had no recourse to facts; it was rather because of their own perceptual predisposition. Their willful ignoring of the realities led them to their own destruction, a manifestation of thanatos rather than of eros.

Much more interesting and historically significant is the set of arguments focusing on the Shah's "modernizing tyranny." They are not only prevalent today, but were used with great skill to disparage and weaken the Shah's regime. They bear closer examination.

Most liberals have adhered to some or all of the following arguments: too rapid modernization, too little participation, too much corruption, and too much repression. As can be readily observed, all of these arguments bear a certain amount of truth in spite of the exaggerated form in which they are ordinarily presented. The point, therefore, is not to challenge their veracity, since, morally speaking, even a little corruption or repression is still too much. It is rather that, contextually, as well as methodologically, they have a negative effect on analytic thought, and, therefore, on both explanation and prescription. They tend to be sociologically naive, contextually irrelevant, and historically simplistic.

Hasty modernization has been cited as an important factor in the downfall of the regime. It is not always clear what is meant by modernization. Among other things, it presumably means more schools, educational equality for boys and girls, better hygiene, more communications facilities, roads, factories, jobs, higher mobility, higher per capita income, achievement orientation, machinery and technology, higher crop yield, and rationalization in methods and procedures. One may also include such items as advanced petrochemical industries, nuclear power as a source of energy, and systems computerization. Much of this, of course, requires modern technology and with it contact with the sources that control technology.

Too rapid modernization, therefore, suggests too much contact with alien sources, too much influx of new ideas and values, and thus too rapid destruction of the traditional culture, causing a moral vacuum and widespread alienation. It erodes the social fabric and transforms the once-identifiable society into a hodgepodge of uprooted social types with no cultural identity. The clear indication is that it ought to be stopped.

This is the position taken and propagated by Khomeini and his followers. The liberal, however, does not want to stop the process of modernization. On the contrary, he is likely to complain about too little schooling, too much sloth in the process of achieving women's equality, too little progress in the development of hygiene and medical care. He is probably against nuclear energy, but not against steel mills. He has his favorite projects to promote and others to disparage. In this sense, he behaves as members of any other interest group and, as such, he has difficulty in establishing, logically and empirically, his position as that of the Iranian people and in suggesting that the Iranian people rose against the Shah because of too much modernization in some areas and too little in others.

The liberal, therefore, advances the cultural thesis. He insists that the best and the most advanced elements of Western technology should be imported, but that the purity of the national culture should also be preserved. The theory is naive and simplistic, but its appeals are self-evident. It combines notions of progress and the idea of maintaining personal and national identity. It eliminates insecurity and alienation. It promises the best of two worlds.

The argument collapses once the surface is scratched and a deeper probe is made into the nature of culture and technology. Culture is a perceptive medium through which man relates to his environment. It defines not only the manner and limits of man's values and actions, but also his facts and realities. Technology is also a manner of looking at the world.[7] One cannot deal with higher theories of physics and simultaneously believe in the flatness of the earth. Nor, on a different level, can one believe in the sanctity of the prevailing authoritarian relationships in rigidly patriarchal societies and at the same time strive to put into practice advanced notions of individual freedom. Unless culture is conceived of as being confined to such marginal aspects of human behavior as the food one eats, the clothes one wears, and the music one listens to, there is no way that notions of progress can be reconciled with the idea of petrification of culture. In fact, if there is any meaning to the concept of progress, it must involve the notion of cultural change. The kind of idea that promotes the preservation of two sets of mutually contradictory beliefs in individuals invites schizophrenia, and, as the recent history of Iran shows, it may succeed in unleashing thanatos on a national scale.

On the question of participation, the liberal is on sounder ground, but mostly for the wrong reasons. No doubt, lack of sufficient political participation was one of the major causes of the weakness of the Iranian political system. The liberal, however, stresses freedom and democracy as if they were entities that stand independently of the socioeconomic and cultural contexts in which they must be realized. In this sense, he tends to be oblivious to patterns of power distribution in the society, to the character of political values, and to the paucity of democratic institutions. He neglects to make a rigorous differentiation between structures and institutions and expects culturally rootless structures to perform functionally as institutions. His main argument stems from constitutional injunctions and is often buttressed by passionate exclamations against breaches of human rights. His mode of approach to power, however, renders him ineffective in exploiting propitious historical circumstances in favor of the promotion of democracy and, thus, places him inadvertently in the service of those whose aim is the radicalization of the society and, hence, prevention of constructive participation in a democratic setting.

In Iran, the liberal intellectuals' political demands had always centered on their contention that the Constitution must be correctly implemented, civic freedoms contained in the Constitution be respected, and the Shah be limited to reigning and not ruling.[8] Empirically, realization of these demands required not only that the Shah's power be diminished, but that power also not gravitate to other antidemocratic groups. The preservation of a democratic setting obviously could not be guaranteed by exhortations and proclamations, but rather by the establishment of systems of checks and balances that would militate against any one man or group of men wishing to concentrate power in their own hands.

In this respect, the liberal reaction to the opportunity presented in the course of the Iranian Revolution is instructive. In the middle of 1978, the Shah's power had dwindled significantly and Khomeini's power had not yet taken root. Thus, a genuine political vacuum had been created in which the liberal dream had achieved a chance of realization. The performance of the liberals, led by the National Front leader Karim Sanjabi, is well documented and needs not be recounted in detail. Basically, they argued that the Shah could not be trusted, and that once the crisis was over and he regained power, he would revert to his imperial ways, crushing the constitutional foundations of power.

The liberal position obviously stressed a crucial point. However, it neglected to take into account the central lesson derived from comparative sociopolitical studies of the Third World, namely, that it is in the nature of power to gravitate to one man and, therefore, not only the Shah but any other leader would likely be led to a dominant position unless he were prevented by the establishment of practical checks representing elements of countervailing power.[9] The point, therefore, was not what the Shah would do in the future, but rather what sort of *political and structural engineering* would render the possibility of his regaining ascendant power least likely.

On the other hand, the liberals naively expected that upon Khomeini's return they would be offered power, as it were, on a silver platter. This expectation is revealing because, in a manner reminiscent of Hitler's *Mein Kampf*, Khomeini has also written down his political beliefs in detail in his much heralded book, *The Islamic Government*. Furthermore, he had proven himself a fanatical true believer by both proclamation and action. He had been willing to die for his convictions and considered them as part of a divinely ordained mission to be implemented regardless of its human and material cost. The expectation that he would renege on this bond of fealty to the Almighty and accept the liberal version of the "good life," is not only beyond the realm of logic, but strains the limits of creative imagination.

The lesson to be derived here is that in Iran, as in most Third and Fourth World countries, the dialectical contradictions of the society did not admit of the establishment of a Western-type democracy, nor of a Western approach to questions of freedom and human rights. To maximize freedom required an ever-increasing effort to maintain a dynamic balance among the existing contradictory power structures and political demands, emphasizing the traditional moderate institutions in order to gain a breathing spell for the democratic structures to take institutional form and substance. Above all, it was only through such institutions that the means of violence might have been contained and kept out of direct political engagement.[10]

The Iranian liberal on the one hand was afraid of a politicized military, and, on the other, was in favor of policies which would inevitably force the military into political positions. Characteristically, Mossadiq, Amini, Sanjabi, and finally Bakhtiar, demanded that the armed forces be put under their command, as if it were an inanimate machine that could be controlled by anyone who held the key to its engine. They seemed not to understand that as soon as the army was severed from its institutional locus of loyalty, the Crown, it became a power unto itself, likely to dominate all other institutions. The reason behind this proclivity was, of course, the desire to benefit from the army's power; the justifying arguments, however, were couched in terms of rather misconceived analogies with the West, whose organic mode of development over the years had institutionalized the patterns of civil-military relationship within a democratic framework.

To gain an insight into the nature of repression under the Shah's regime requires not only a count of the number of people who were presumably tortured and maimed in political dungeons, and whose numbers appear to vary with the political attitude of the observer, but also an analysis of the characteristics of the Iranian polity under the Shah. A careful study of the situation, the author believes, will show that the regime was not so much debilitated by the extent of repression as it was by the existing contradictions between the limitations in the distribution of political power on one hand, and the extended freedoms in the economic, social, and cultural realms, on the other.

From the standpoint of social psychology, the experience of repression may be perceived as a function of the relationship between the expectations and demands generated by the changing cultural patterns, and the institutional and practical impediments to the satisfaction of such expectations and demands. The sources of these impediments may be social, economic, cultural, or political. The more totalitarian the political system, the greater the scope and extent of its interference in socioeconomic and cultural aspects of human existence, and, therefore, the greater the possibility of willfully creating impediments to the realization of emerging expectations. The less involved the political system, the smaller the scope of its interference in other aspects of life, and, therefore, the weaker its capacity to create political impediments to the demands for freedom and mobility. In most cases, the obstacles to the realization of human expectations may reside in the characteristics of the socioeconomic and cultural setting. Under conditions of rapid social mobilization, these characteristics are ordinarily translated into demands for political action.

Cultural fragmentation, as an endemic property of the development process, exacerbates the psychological experience of repression manifested as alienation, insecurity and cynicism. Since in a developmental context the political system is at the forefront of the developmental process, much of the psychological malaise is seen as being a consequence of the political process and affects not only those outside the political leadership, but also a significant sector of the ruling elite.[11] The experience of Iran seems to suggest that the greater the divergence and multiformity in areas of freedom and constraint, the more widespread the malaise and more vociferous its expression, even though, relatively speaking, political repression may be limited.

Iran under the Shah was basically an open society. People could choose freely their preferred mode of life on economic, social, and cultural planes. The freedom enjoyed in these realms compared favorably not only with the Communist totalitarian systems and those obtained under the present theocratic regime, but also with the conditions prevailing in many Third World countries. The economic boom had made it possible for people from many walks of life to travel abroad by hundreds of thousands every year, as foreigners came in by comparable numbers. Women were gradually achieving equality with men and increasingly participated in the kinds of behavior that had been traditionally reserved for men. Western patterns of life were freely reflected in the Iranian media and disseminated throughout the country. All this obviously irked the traditional and the puritan, and it may have been bad politics for the system to render itself vulnerable to the charge of decadence and permissiveness, but it can hardly be construed as an example of repression.

Politically, Iran was authoritarian. The monarchical system was basically Hobbesian in character, meaning a system in which the political leaders conceived of the polity as having precedence over the society and did not accept challenges to their leadership, but, unless challenged, left others substantially free to do as they pleased. The system was vulnerable to the charge of totalitarianism because, potentially, it seemed to reserve the right to interfere in all aspects of human social existence; in practice, it had neither the inclination nor the political paraphernalia to do so. Power appeared to be concentrated at the top; in reality, it was exercised by the executive arm of the government, the civil bureaucracy. The bureaucracy, however, could not exercise power except in a negative sense, that is, by withholding the service it was expected to render; it distinctly lacked the capacity to mobilize the people in support of political goals. It thus became a source of frustration and alienation.[12]

The Iranian bureaucracy tended to project economic growth as a substitute for political participation. The policy failed because the limitations of the political system hindered the flow of constructive energy pent up in the society's human resource base and thus came into conflict with the requirements of socioeconomic development.

As the case of Iran demonstrates, once the human resource base achieves the dynamic dimensions of social mobilization, two likely patterns of effective response are left open to the political system—either a move toward totalitarianism, or the provision of channels of political participation consonant with the dialectical characteristics of the social system. Both moves satisfy the requirements of participation. The difference lies essentially in the direction and characteristics of the pattern of accumulation of systemic power. In the totalitarian case, power achieves greater concentration; violence, therefore, reaches extreme levels and tends to become an endemic and seemingly irreversible property of the system. In the other, power's propensity is toward wider distribution. As the society becomes more pluralistic and the sphere of legitimacy expands, the need for violence gradually decreases.

The Iranian regime opted for neither of these two paths. Instead, it staked its hopes on the legitimacy of the Crown and the leadership qualities of the king. Its responses were contained in a series of contradictory political acts including further bureaucratization of the political system through the establishment of the Rastakhiz Party, while at the same time attacking the bureaucracy as corrupt and inefficient; feeding the critical faculties of the people through the mass media in the hope of separating the Shah's image from that of the government and the bureaucracy, and providing a safety valve against pent-up popular indignation; and, finally, associating structured criticisms of the government with modes of "Red" (leftist) or "Black" (religious) reaction fashioned by Iran's enemies and propagated in the service of the forces bent on the destruction of the Iranian nation. The result was a series of confused and essentially irrelevant responses geared to the superficial manifestations of otherwise basic structural contradictions of the political system. From the struggle against inflation in 1975–76 and the panic about power shortages leading to the establishment of the ill-conceived Imperial Commission, to a series of disastrous decisions during the Sharif-Imami and General Azhari cabinets, the regime's responses to political crisis were structurally determined, reflecting the basic inability of the political system to come to terms with the changing conditions of its socioeconomic as well as international environment.[13]

The evidence presented by Amnesty International and other relevant international bodies suggests that in fact repression had subsided during these years, as the number of political prisoners had decreased and their treatment in prison had substantially improved.[14] The regime claimed that, strictly speaking, Iran had no political prisoners; those incarcerated were presented as bands of armed terrorists, trained and led by foreign agents against the system's constitutional foundations. While the designation of prisoners as political or otherwise may be a matter of opinion, there is ample evidence* to suggest that a significant proportion of them had been trained as saboteurs whose major aim was to present the world with evidence of SAVAK atrocity and the regime's lack of support among the people. They succeeded in part as a result of the quality and extent of international propaganda and, it now appears in the light of later events, as a result of SAVAK's ineptitude.

To most people, security organizations are a distasteful reality representing the more evil aspects of human political relations. As such, their perception of such organizations is almost always tainted with negative subjectivity. This is a salutary attitude and, one hopes, acts as a brake on undue incursion by state power into individual freedom. It does, however, make objective judgment difficult because, on the one hand, the covert nature of these organizations' operations does not allow for open

---

* Based on the author's conversations with knowledgeable former Iranian government officials now in the United States.

and adequate information, and, on the other, the ideological prejudices of those who volunteer such information renders its objective validity suspect. Thus, one is never sure whether the informant is speaking from factual evidence or colored opinion. Judgment, therefore, must be based on an assortment of events logically related to an assessment of such an organization's mode of operation.

In Iran SAVAK had the reputation of being an efficient organization. According to the regime's opponents, it was the major force that safeguarded not only the stability but the very existence of the system. That feeling was encouraged by SAVAK and, curiously enough, was shared by a substantial number of people who worked contentedly within the system.

SAVAK's reputation, however, does not seem to withstand the test of facts. One of the major functions of security organizations presumably, is to gather information in order to intercept planned offenses against the system. SAVAK, however, was rarely able to prevent antisystem clandestine action. This remained true even when the attacks were limited and sporadic. The assassination of Prime Minister Mansur, the Marble Palace attempt on the Shah's life, the assassination of General Farsiu, whose role as the head of the military tribunal that convicted the leaders of the mujahidin for terroristic acts had made him a prime target for revenge, the events at Siyahkal in which organized armed attacks were carried out against a number of gendarmerie outposts near the Caspian Sea and whose perpetrators were finally captured with the help of the local people, and the attempt to abduct the American ambassador, are only a few examples of SAVAK's failure to perform its legally ordained tasks. When dissidence assumed widespread proportions after 1977, SAVAK seemed helpless in the face of the scope and organization of the pro-Khomeini forces whose establishment must have involved considerable planning and communication.

On the other hand, SAVAK continually harassed the regime's supporters. The harassment was often no more than an intimation of its continual presence, but it was enough to arouse fear and disgust. In fact, as it turned out later, respect for SAVAK's prowess and omnipotence was much more prevalent among the system's own officials than its opponents. One of the consequences of this misapprehension was that, against all the evidence to the contrary, many high officials of the regime still thought, in the middle of 1978, that the riots were SAVAK-instigated in order to show the West the futility and the dangers of the implementation of human rights policies in Iran.

In his Panama interview with David Frost on the ABC network, as in his last book, the Shah stated that until the matter was brought to his attention through the international media, he was not aware of the extent to which SAVAK practiced torture and violence in dealing with suspects and prisoners. Once he became aware of the practice, said the Shah, he ordered it stopped. His contention about stopping the torture is corroborated by the evidence submitted by Amnesty International and other human rights groups. Of the first part of the statement, it seems logical to assume that the resort to violence could have been construed as a measure of SAVAK's ineptitude as a security organization and that, therefore, the SAVAK officers were reluctant to report such acts to the Shah. In this circumstance, it would be unreasonable to attribute to the Shah an omniscience he simply did not possess.

Much had been made of the Shah's presumed strategy of appointing people antagonistic to one another to high-security and other state positions. The argument suggests that the policy assured the Shah that the officials occupying sensitive positions were not able to join forces against him, while their mutual enmity propelled them to inform him of one another's inadequacies. It is then concluded that the Shah was, therefore, aware of everything that happened in the country.[15]

The argument is interesting in that it presupposes a monopoly of intelligence for the Shah and a level of naiveté, almost bordering on stupidity, on the part of all others. The fact is that there was a tacit understanding among the Iranian high officials not to trespass on one another's political and administrative spheres, to be mindful of one another's respective areas of influence, and generally to refrain from rocking the boat. The collective political longevity of highly influential people like 'Alam, Iqbal, Hoveida, Nasiri, Amuzigar, Ansari, and many others, is a testimony to this fact. Incorrigibly troublesome individuals like Ardishir Zahidi would face the collective ire of all others and, as in his case, were likely to be banished to areas of political activity not directly relevant to the internal affairs of the country.

The effect of this subtle collusion was to produce a colossal political illusion that all the decisions were made by the Shah personally, that he was aware of the minutiae of all the policy options, and, finally, that he was the sole and supreme arbiter of Iranian society. The illusion resulted from the outward structure of Iranian politics, the characteristics of power relationships, and the astuteness of a group of players in a game of power politics, begun and perfected since 1963. In fact, except in selected areas of foreign policy and military priorities, the decisions made by the Shah were already contained in the kind of information that was brought to him. Alternative policies, even when developed in certain sectors of the bureaucracy, as, for example, in the middle levels of the Plan Organization, were never allowed to receive an equal hearing and, at any rate, could never withstand the weight of political and economic interests resulting from the structural deformities of the system. The Shah himself was perhaps the most exalted prisoner of the regime. His freedom depended not on the adoption of a different set of policies, but solely on the introduction of structural changes based on new patterns of distribution of power. Unfortunately for him and for Iran, it is not in the nature of power to distribute itself of its own free will. Thus, as mentioned before, in the last five years of the monarchical regime, concepts of decentralization, participation, and deconcentration and distribution of power were frequently mentioned by the Shah and his subordinates as the accepted policy. In reality, however, they turned into so many hollow statements of intent, seemingly unable to be implemented.

The psychological consequences of this form of repression were far greater than the malaise associated with the operations of SAVAK. Most Iranians, after all, had only a mystified notion of SAVAK, and had never come into contact with it. The regime's radical opponents used SAVAK as a symbol of oppression, being fully aware of its powers and limitations, and knowing full well that clandestine terrorism and armed uprising against the constitutional foundations of any system would have elicited the kind of reaction that, in skillful hands, could be translated and propagated as political repression. It is a testimony to SAVAK's shortcomings and the limitations of the political system that they both succumbed to these tactics and used them as reasons to perpetuate the structural causes of their own failures.

Arguments about corruption are also made in the same simplistic vein. They are basically reflections of ideological preferences rather than socioeconomic, or even moral, analysis. The general theory holds that the political and economic elite of the regime, headed by the royal family, perceived the nation as their private property and squandered its wealth to the detriment of the people and the future prosperity of the country. The royal family is depicted as morally degenerate and ethically decadent. This decadence is then seen as seeping through the social fabric, contaminating all sectors of the society. In this mode of thinking, the idea of decadence transcends the financial realm and seeps into other manifestations of life associated with Westernization by the more traditional elements of the opposition. Thus, an ideological loop connects corruption in money matters with corruption in lifestyle and liberal thinking with traditional thinking. The effect of this synthesis in liberal circles is the superficial conclusion that the future felicity of the nation lies in the selective rejection of some of the Western ideological patterns, while retaining all of its technological offerings. In traditional conservative thinking, it leads to a wholesale rejection of the West through a fundamentalist approach to religion. In either case, it is argued, rampant corruption was the cause of both elite and mass alienation, leading to the unified opposition which finally brought down the regime.

High financial morality, of course, was not the most pronounced characteristic of Iranian economic relations. Nevertheless, it would be a grotesque exaggeration to suggest that most of the higher Iranian officials were involved in questionable financial transactions. The exorbitant allegations made by the present theocratic regime concerning the squandering of the wealth of the nation are palpably false. It is interesting to note that neither the revolutionary government nor the revolutionary tribunals in the process of condemnation and execution of their victims have succeeded in presenting solid evidence of a personal nature against the high officials of the regime. In most cases, accusations have been couched in ideological generalizations: waging war against God, destroying the nation's economy, promoting prostitution, and the like. In the more defined areas of financial transactions, most of the accusations have centered on purchases made from Western industrial firms. Dishonesty in these transactions could have occurred with the acquiescence of both sides. No successful suit, however, has ever been brought against an Iranian functionary, or against Iran's foreign trade partners in

Iranian or Western tribunals. In fact, the only such suit was brought by the Shah's regime in 1976 against two undersecretaries of the Iranian Ministry of Commerce for alleged corrupt practices involving a British firm, Tate and Lyle Sugar Company. It had to be dropped because the investigation of the company's record concluded that the allegations were untrue.[16] Accusations of this nature, however, have been echoed as verdicts of guilt by substantial portions of the Western liberal press whose judicial culture, one would assume, should favor a presumption of innocence in the absence of proof of guilt obtained through the due process of law.

From the historical standpoint, the liberal's approach to the above questions was fundamentally wrong, whereas the radical left and right making the same arguments were fundamentally correct. The reason is obvious. Both of the radical conglomerations aimed at a complete transformation of the system. For them, the truth mattered only insofar as it helped the system's breakdown. All other considerations were irrelevant.

For the liberal, on the other hand, the future depended on the cooperation of all the forces that had carried the socioeconomic infrastructure to its existing level of contradictions; he could, therefore, never totally deny the backbone of its potential power: the middle class that was largely the product as well as the producer of the old regime. The pathetic image of Bazargan, the so-called revolutionary prime minister, cast in his sporadic appearances on television during his tenure of office as the inert defender of the key elements of the ancient regime—the military, the technocrat, the bureaucrat, and even the capitalist—is a testimony to the liberal's predicament in the face of his own shortsightedness.

The political arm of the liberal opposition in Iran was the National Front. When the outward manifestations of the revolution began to increase dramatically late in the summer of 1978, the Front was still very small, its followers meager, its organization undefined. But it had the potential for being turned into a tangible political movement within the framework of the Iranian Constitution. Conversely, outside the 1906 Constitution, the National Front lost all meaning and relevance, as became apparent immediately after the fall of the monarchy. To succeed, the Front leaders had to assert themselves independently of the Khomeini movement. Furthermore, they had to remain in unequivocal support of the Constitution.

The Front leadership, however, vacillated, rarely took the initiative, never accepted any risks, and finally opted to hang on to Khomeini's coattails, hoping to emerge as the only alternative acceptable to the West. As it turned out, Sanjabi's lack of resolve turned off practically all factions, including the United States: By the time he accepted the "Imam's line" in Paris, the American embassy in Tehran had already begun to promote Bazargan.

Obviously, the Front could have acted differently. The question is, would it have made any difference? The answer necessarily falls in the realm of conjecture. The prevailing power relations early in the fall of 1978, however, suggest that it probably would.

When Amuzigar resigned in late August, the monarchy was still commanding the greatest power base of the realm. The Shah, however, had accepted the necessity of introducing significant changes in the pattern of government, even though the details of the steps to be taken were nebulous in his mind. On the other hand, Khomeini was an exiled mullah in Iraq, capable of creating sporadic disturbances, but still quite distant from assuming the characteristics of the actual force that, four months later, would overthrow the Iranian monarchy. It is now established that during these four months, Khomeini's power grew mainly as a result of the support of the sociopolitical groups that could in no way be characterized as Khomeini's natural constituency. The bureaucrat, the technocrat, the businessman, the intellectual, the city shopkeeper outside the bazaar, and other middle-class strata, had far greater affinity with secular forms of protest and government than with the Khomeini brand of religious fundamentalism. In the course of time, they were forced onto Khomeini's bandwagon because their natural leaders led them to that path by abandoning their claims to independent power and leadership outside the framework of the Khomeini movement. Nevertheless, Khomeini's potential power on the periphery had brought about a creative vacuum that could have been used to establish new modes of power relations more responsive to the emerging demands for greater political participation.

Logically, every indication pointed to the National Front as the political midwife of the systemic transformation required to respond to the needs of the new situation. The Front's position, however, should have been cultivated within the constitutional framework, stressing the preservation of the letter and spirit of the Constitution rather than opposition to the Shah. The selection of correct strategy was of utmost importance for two main reasons. First, without the Shah's support, the National Front was doomed to failure. Compared to the extremes of right or left, its appeal among the masses, that is, those who could be mobilized to fight in the streets, was minimal. Thus, without the support of security elements to hold the mobs in check, it could not have hoped to survive the rush of events. The point was palpably demonstrated during the Bakhtiar premiership, even though, admittedly, Bakhtiar's was the weakest arrangement of a Front-related government.

On the other hand, with the Crown's support, it stood a very good chance of success. Had the Front taken a unified, distinguishable, and aggressive position, it could have counted on the support of the majority of the intelligentsia, the technocrats, the bureaucrats, and the rest of the modernized middle class. The Shah's support not only would have neutralized the streets through the use of the forces of law and order, but, combined with the potential appeal of the Front leaders, it would also have mobilized the peasantry and a substantial part of urban labor as further political support.[17]

The Front, however, chose to stress its opposition to the Shah, at a time when the latter had convinced himself that the West intended to force him out of the country and was therefore suspicious of any political group that had established independent political relations with foreign countries, especially the United States. Sanjabi's behavior exacerbated the Shah's doubts. He was therefore extremely cautious in his approach to the Front's leadership. Nevertheless, he invited Sanjabi and his partners to join in a coalition government. He ordered the military to treat them with exceptional deference—so much so that many Front leaders complained that the courtesy shown them by the government was politically embarrassing. He went out of his way to accommodate as many of their demands as were compatible with his own position as the constitutional head of the country.

In the fateful year of 1978, history had thrust upon the National Front leaders an opportunity rarely granted to political actors. Many Iranians looked upon them as the potential saviors of the country. Many had hoped that they would act as true statesmen, placing the good of Iran above their personal grudges, resentments, and grievances. Instead, they acted as petty politicians, immersed in the cult of popularity, morbidly afraid, long on spite, and short on true grit. As representatives of Iranian liberalism and nationalism, they proved singularly lacking in historical vision and national courage.

The Shah's dilemma was that he had been caught in a web of events from which he could not extricate himself without resort to extreme violence. History will show, however, that, rather than yield to pressure to engage in offensive military action, he had chosen, early in the process of the revolution, to leave his country on the grounds that the Iranian throne was not to be maintained on the foundation of bloodshed and fratricide.

Given the sordid state of the Iranian nation more than six years after the Revolution, the liberal mind also ought to reflect upon a moral dilemma: To what extent is the glorification of antisystem violence, as a manifestation of human dignity, justified in the face of the uncertainty of the future results? To what extent are those who instigated the revolution, provided its dialectical precepts, mapped out its strategy, and abetted its purposes, morally responsible for those who perished and perhaps more importantly, for the plight of a nation whose march to progress has been effectively halted and may not resume for a considerable time to come?

Notes
Chapter 6

1. The term thanatos is borrowed from Freudian psychoanalysis as developed by Herbert Marcuse. Says Freud: "And now, I think, the meaning of the evolution of civilization is no longer obscure to us. It must present the struggle between Eros and Death, between the instinct of life and the instinct of destruction, as it works itself out in human species." Sigmund Freud, *Civilization and its Discontents*, trans. James Strachy, (New York: W. W. Norton and Company, 1961), 69. See also Herbert Marcuse, *Counter-revolution and Revolt* (Boston: Beacon Press, 1972).
2. Compare Marxist philosophy and the Soviet practice.
3. Bertrand de Jouvenel, *On Power, Its Nature and the History of its Growth*, trans. J. F. Huntington, (New York: Viking Press, 1949).
4. See chapters 1, 2, 3 and 5 above.
5. The essentials of Khomeini's theory of government were and are relatively easy to grasp. Without going into a discussion of the esoteric aspects of the meanings of the Quranic verses to which references are made, the following constitutes the logic of his position: 1) Sovereignty belongs to God. 2) The law is God's command, His *farman*, or decree. 3) The law has been actualized in the Quran through the Prophet's speech, and is reflected also in his *sunnah*, or practice. 4) It is of the essence of government in Islam that the ruler should be conversant with the law. 5) Only the *faqih*, one learned in Islamic *fiqh*, the body of Islamic jurisprudence including the Prophet's *sunnah* and the *hadith*, or sayings, possesses the required knowledge. 6) But knowledge alone is not enough; the governing *faqih*, or a governing body of *fuqaha(re)*, need to be just as well. Hence, government belongs to and is the duty of the just *faqih*. This corresponds to the idea that in Shiism one is either a *faqih* or a *muqallid*, that is, an emulator of a *faqih* who happens to be also a mujtahid—meaning one who has been accorded a degree of *ijtihad* (the ability to interpret the law) by an established mujtahid because 1) he has demonstrated his knowl-

edge of the law, 2) he is of highest moral integrity *(taqva)*, and 3) he knows the conditions of the time. Such a mujtahid may become a source of emulation, i.e., a *marja' taqlid*, if he chooses to become one, and if a number of laymen choose him as one. For the concept of Islamic government see Ayatollah Ruhollah Khomeini, *Vilayat-i Faqih* (Tehran: Amir Kabir, 1357), 52 ff, or Bayat, Mangol, "The Iranian Revolution of 1978–79: Fundamentalist or Modern," in *The Middle East Journal*, Vol. 37, No. 1, Winter 1983.
6. See chapter 7, below.
7. See Ellul, *The Technological Society*.
8. The best examples of the liberal position are contained in the letters addressed to the Shah by Iranian dissident Haj Sayyid Javadi and the famous Sanjabi-Bakhtiar-Furuhar open letter to the monarch in 1977. Both sets of letters had rather wide circulation in Tehran and abroad.
9. See Introduction, above.
10. For a discussion of these institutions see chapter 8, below.
11. For a discussion of these attitudes among the Iranian elite see Zonis, *Political Elites*.
12. See chapter 2, above.
13. See chapter 3, above.
14. See the *Report of Amnesty International on Iran, 1978*. London: Amnesty International. 1976, Sequal. 1978.
15. See, for example, James A. Bill, *The Politics of Iran: Groups, Classes and Modernization* (Columbus, Ohio: Charles and Merrill Publishing Company, 1972), 42–4.
16. *Financial Times*, November 14, 1977.
17. This possibility was corroborated by a consensus among the provincial and local secretaries of the National Committee for World Literacy program. See chapter 3, note 13.

7 | The Khomeini Phenomenon: A Study in Alienation

The Khomeini phenomenon may be studied within the framework of the international state system, but cannot be fully understood through it. This is because it is essentially an ideology rather than a government, a regressive revolution rather than a state. It can therefore break with impunity every rule of international conduct, reinterpret every aspect of international law, impute novel meaning to Islamic jurisprudence, and erect its own standards of value and decency.

To understand Khomeini, one may also be tempted to study Islam. This is natural but not very productive. The temptation is based on the presupposition that Islam defines Khomeini's intellectual categories as it also disposes the religious public to respond favorably to his calling. The truth is that, like all other consummate religions and ideologies, Islam also has the capacity to yield itself to broad or strict construction, progressive or regressive interpretation, humane or beastly conduct. It speaks of the necessity of change as well as the importance of respect for tradition, of beauty as well as plainness, of forgiveness as well as the value of revenge, of the virtue of *jihad* as well as the sanctity of human life. Rich in depth of scriptural pronouncement and breadth of tradition, it can support many different, and sometimes diametrically opposed, political and religious postures and behaviors.[1]

The most important quality of Khomeini's ideology is its ahistoricity. It pretends to be conceptually free of temporal and spatial limitations. In this sense, it is radically different from the ideology of other theocratic states based on Islamic fundamentalism. The latter, as demonstrated by the examples of Saudi Arabia and Pakistan, strive to adapt fundamentalist thought to modern historical conditions. They are basically conservative. Khomeini strives to do the opposite—adapt historically determined conditions to an essentially ahistorical view of the world. He is at once regressive, revolutionary, and utopian. Cumulatively, these properties portend an ominous future for the Iranian people and given the country's sensitive geopolitical situation, extreme danger for the world.

The most important quality of Khomeini as a man is that he is a true believer.[2] He believes in the absolute righteousness of his cause, in the divinity of his own mission, and in the virtue of martyrdom. Such a predisposition is dangerous in any man, regardless of the cause he espouses. Extremism in the defense of God can lead to unbounded atrocity no less than extremism in the cause of the proletariat, or in the hatred of Jews. The basic characteristic of total commitment is that it allows for total destruction with pride and impunity. Potentially, it condemns every circumstance of dialogical promise, renounces every humanistic virtue, and transmutes every effort at compromise into pale and abject surrender. Its appeal is to the darker side of the human psyche as when one may secretly admire Hitler for having almost succeeded in destroying the world. Many also admire Khomeini for doggedly pursuing his own path in the face of seemingly irrefutable logic.

The most important lesson of history is that it remains impervious to wishful thinking. It unfolds in response to the interaction of the totality of forces that assume objective reality in the course of time. Khomeini is, no doubt, such a force—and therefore historically significant.

The historical meaning of the Khomeini phenomenon is that it prolongs Iran's colonial dependence.[3] Given its developmental aspirations and geopolitical conditions, it is improbable that Iran can opt out of the world developmental process. Sooner or later, it will have to face the stark reality of its relapse into economic and technological stagnation. The responses open to it will be largely determined by the longevity of the Khomeini regime and the behavior of the forces opposed to the Islamic Republic.

Khomeini's regime is self-destructive. It is essentially a negation, one of many possible antitheses to the Pahlavi system. Without the facts and fictions of the Pahlavi era, it loses all historical meaning. In this sense, it is also an aberration. It is historically irrelevant either to the developmental consciousness or the developmental requirements of the Iranian people. It is self-destructive not because it has a demonstrable tendency to opt for wrong policies, but rather because, as an inherent property of its weltanschauung such a tendency is the sine qua non of its existence. To survive, it must negate whatever the Shah expounded. The Shah stood for the future; Khomeini must stand for the past. The Shah stood for modernism; Khomeini must emphasize traditionalism. The Shah stood for technology; Khomeini must extol primitivism and fatalism. The Shah stood for hard work and productivity; Khomeini must eulogize faith and martyrdom.[4]

This closed and vicious circle is inescapable. It not only traces the boundaries of Khomeini and his followers' sociopolitical vision, it defines the framework of their legitimacy.[5] Outside this circle, their opponents stand on much firmer ideological ground and command a far more respectable claim to the governance of the country. Thus, the greater the vehemence of the outside attack, the more rigid Khomeini's adherence to the values and mores on which his authority is based.

Beyond the ideological factor, the question also relates to the exigencies of survival. Someone in the regime will have to answer for the atrocities committed in its name. Ironically, the fear is not limited to the vulnerability of the present clerical leadership to charges of corruption, terrorism, brutality, and decimation of the country's socioeconomic infrastructure, voiced by the monarchist, democratic, or leftist forces that might succeed the Islamic Republic. Outside the present substantial clerical hegemony, even the system's former nonclerical friends like Bani-Sadr and Bazargan have found it difficult to exonerate the kind of political and judicial behavior that has been exhibited by Sadiq Khalkhali and other theocratic judges.[6]

Khalkhali, however, cannot be dismissed as an unfortunate accident. Morally and organizationally, he represents the backbone of the Islamic Republic. He survived not because he was tolerated, but because he controlled. As a leader of the

Fada'iyan-i Islam, he defined the law and commanded power. His was only the burlesque presentation of the fundamental beliefs governing the Islamic Republic's view of the world. There is no escape from this conclusion.

The Khomeini system is inextricably bound to its moral and sociopolitical commitments because such commitments are its only claim to legitimacy and the only promise of survival. On the other hand, the inherent limitations of the regime's sociopolitical and moral stance will increasingly debilitate its capacity to confront the historical forces of development resulting from Iran's objective location within the world developmental process.

The socioeconomic transformation of Iran during the past 20 years has been both profound and lasting in nature. The single most important demographic fact about Iran is the youthfulness of its population. Approximately 50 per cent of the Iranian population is below the age of 16; and 75 per cent is below the age of 30.[7] The majority of the people, therefore, have no recollection of the basically illiterate, rural, fatalistic, and socially sedentary Iranian society of only 30 years ago. According to the last census, some 50 per cent of the population is literate. Most of the literate, in turn, live in the urban areas. The rate of literacy is far higher among youth.[8] In 1978, out of a population of 35 million, 10.5 million, or slightly less than a third of the population, were in schools.[9] Most of the teachers in the elementary and high schools are far more inclined towards leftist or liberal ideologies than to religious fundamentalism, a fact that explains Khomeini's insistence on the islamization of the school system. In 1976, for the first time in Iranian history, over half the population lived in urban centers. Per capita income had surpassed $2400 by the end of 1978.

Obviously, a majority of Iranians are the product of a fragmented culture that, over the past 30 years, has evolved towards modernism and has tried to accommodate the contradictory requirements of both modern and traditional values. That effort failed in its political manifestation, or rather, the political system under the Shah failed to maintain the integrity of the society under the pressure of cultural fragmentation. However, it would be false analogy and reasoning to deduce the existence of cultural homogeneity and political legitimacy under the present theocratic regime from the political failure of the pre-Khomeini system. On the contrary, whereas the failure of the Shah's system was largely the result of the system's political inefficiency, and therefore capable of self-correction, the Khomeini system is fundamentally inimical to the modern manifestations of a complex culture whose reality can be grasped mainly in terms of change and transformation, rather than stasis and regression.

The point to be repeated here is that the Iranian revolution was basically a response to the incapacity of the political system to accommodate the nascent and explosive energy of its human resource base. Religion was the most efficient vehicle for channeling the revolutionary mood and consummating the revolutionary movement. It was neither the content nor the soul of the revolution. The Iranian people had very little knowledge of Islamic fundamentalist thought. They were even less conscious of the fine nuances of esoteric Shiism. But they could easily distinguish between Khomeini and the moderate Ayatollah Muhammad Kazim Shari'atmadari because one was obviously willing to compromise, while the other seemed adamant in his opposition. Shari'atmadari was not, and could not have been, the antithesis of the Shah's regime—Khomeini was; just as years before, Mossadiq could not have been the antithesis of the Shah's regime—the Tudeh party was. The crucial difference is that the Communist party is a historically meaningful alternative whereas obscurantist Shiism is not.

Khomeini's major political support is concentrated in the Islamic Republican party whose leadership includes the clerics who have associated themselves with his "line." This group was originally dominated by the impressive figure of Ayatollah Beheshti, who early in the process of revolution assumed control of the organizational foundation of Khomeini's support in the mosques. Beheshti's assassination in June 1981 deprived the regime of one of its most articulate and talented tacticians.[10] Assuming that Beheshti's successors will succeed in holding on to power after Khomeini's disappearance from the scene, they will have to honor their commitment to his moral and ideological premises. They possess neither the intellectual capability nor the political legitimacy required for initiating the kind of departure from the Imam's line that is necessary if the developmental requirements of Iranian society are to be accommodated.

This point is manifested by the pattern of evolution of the political forces within the Khomeini camp. A movement whose success was owed mainly to the projection of a unified front under the supreme leadership of an infallible Imam quickly turned into a breeding ground for the growth of endless conflict and ruinous factions. Even before the mass executions of the ancient regimists were completed, the Imam's charisma and persuasive powers had begun to wane in face of the intensity of the prevailing ideological and factional contradictions. As the revolution commenced to devour its children, and Khomeini was forced to take sides, logically and instinctively he fell in with his clerical supporters. Gradually, the liberal and leftist fringes of the Khomeini movement were moved out from under his protective umbrella. Predictably, the liberals accepted their lot with little struggle and only faint sounds of disenchantment, while the classical left, the Tudeh hard core, cheered the clerics on. The idealistic left, the mujahidin, minority fada'iyan, and other leftist *guruhaks* (small groups),[11] in a heroic feat of miscalculation, decided to face the regime in the open. They proved no match for Khomeini's combined forces. Their main fighting body, the mujahidin, were routed in the streets amidst a colossal popular indifference resulting from the alien nature of their ideology and the ferocity of their terroristic acts. In a short period of time they were eliminated as a significant threat inside the country. Having failed in their great assault on the heads of the regime, the mujahidin have recently changed their strategy by directing their attacks on the regime's fingertips: the *pasdars* or Guardians of the Revolution, and *kumitihs*, or Committees of the Revolution.

The popular indifference to the fate of the mujahidin, however, should not be misconstrued as a sign of popular support for the Khomeini regime. It was more an indication of a negative response to the alternative presented by the mujahidin and other leftist factions. The so-called *islam-i rastin* (the true Islam), a Pol Pot-like blend of Islam and utopian Marxism advocated by the mujahidin, frightened many Iranian socioeconomic groups even more than the Khomeini version of Islam. Many of these groups were petrified by the ferocity of the mujahidin's vengeful terror, such as the bombing of the Islamic Republican party headquarters in which some 100 leaders of the party,[12] including Beheshti and a number of his associates, were killed, and saw it as an ominous sign of things to come. Their indifference, therefore, was more in the nature of "a plague on both your houses," than an indication of support for Khomeini.[13]

Nevertheless, given the sociocultural and demographic characteristics of Iranian society, the assumption ought to be that the longer the life span of the Islamic Republic, the greater the likelihood for the establishment of a leftist system. As applied to the Khomeini regime, the argument that the Islamic Republic is a bulwark against communism is probably false; more plausibly, it paves the way for communism. Khomeini's view of the world precludes the possibility of initiating meaningful socioeconomic policies to accommodate the basic developmental needs of the society. Progressively, more people in the professions, in intellectual circles, and among the middle class will be alienated, throwing the system into greater chaos, social alienation and economic despondency. For the believer, Islam has always been a moral and psychological refuge against economic, social, and political oppression. As an oppressive system, Khomeini's totalitarian theocracy forces the people towards other psychological shelters. Given Iran's historical characteristics, including the structure of its population, the most likely refuge against Islam as an oppressive social, economic, cultural, and political presence may still prove to be the left.

Politically, the meaningful left in Iran is the Tudeh party, not in the sense of its overt organization, its name, or its known leaders, but in terms of historical experience, organizational capability, strategic and tactical prowess, and international support. It is a form of Soviet presence in Iran which grows under chaotic conditions. It draws its life from the Soviet hegemonial weight, and obtains nourishment from hate and despondency. Over the years, it has evolved many faces and has proved able to jump in political bed with strange bedfellows.[14]

The most glaring example of this latter point is the party's profession of allegiance to the Khomeini regime. On the eve of the Khomeini Revolution at the beginning of 1979, the party's first secretary, Iraj Iskandari, a traditional anti-religious Marxist ideologue, was replaced by Nuriddin Kiyanuri, the sire of a long line of high-ranking 'ulama in the Shiite hierarchy. Subsequently, in an ideological about-face, the party adopted the tactical posture of giving full and unequivocal support to Khomeini and the Islamic Republic. As a result, for more than four years it was the only leftist party that was allowed to operate relatively freely in Iran. This period of freedom was obviously a breathing spell for the party to reorganize itself and place the right people in strategic positions. The extent of its success still remains to be seen, but it is reasonable to assume that the party did not waste this golden opportunity.

Since the beginning of 1983, the Tudeh has come increasingly under the regime's attack. Many of its leaders have been incarcerated or forced to go underground or leave the country. Its first secretary was induced to confess on public television that he and his colleagues had been Soviet spies for a long time, not a great revelation in itself, but, nevertheless, a feat testifying to the regime's powers of persuasion. Immediately afterward, on May 4, 1983, the Islamic government declared the party illegal and expelled from Iran some 18 Soviet envoys on charges of interfering in the country's domestic affairs and establishing links with "mercenaries and traitors to the Republic."[15]

All this, however, does not alter the basic situation and should not be allowed to confuse the issue. As argued above, the Iranian population is young, and yearns for a panacea. The Islamic alternative has proven false, oppressive, irrational, and historically irrelevant. Unless a meaningful choice is presented to them, the apparent alternative panacea will remain the left. The left in Iran, however, is paradoxical. It will not be able or allowed to come to power without Soviet blessing, which is another way of saying that it is quite unlikely that the Soviets will tolerate a new anti-Soviet Marxist regime on their borders. Their policy, therefore, will likely be marked by caution and patience. Their best bet, as they have often said, is to allow the frustrations of the Iranian people to run their course, to place their people in strategic positions, and to bide their time until the proper opportunity presents itself.[16]

A "meaningful choice," however, is unlikely to emerge from the confines of the Khomeini regime. The hope placed initially by some Western policy makers on the so-called moderate elements of the Khomeini regime, as exemplified by the accommodative references often made to the former prime minister Mehdi Bazargan and the former president Bani-Sadr, have proved unfounded.

The liberals inside Iran, now mainly the remnants of a once flourishing *nihzat-i azadi* (the Freedom Movement) led by Bazargan, have assumed a semi-parasitic existence within certain confines of the Khomeini regime, including the Islamic Consultative Assembly. Politically, theirs is the most unfortunate fate. For years they had awaited the coming of a revolution for which they had labored to prepare the grounds. The revolution, however, turned into a Frankenstein phenomenon which used them only as midwives to deliver the monster. Their voice was quickly reduced to a fading moan, heard in sporadic intervals between long stretches of silence.[17] Their dilemma is that on one hand, they lack the courage to cut their umbilical cord to the monster they have produced, and on the other, they bear the burden of responsibility vis-a-vis the nation whose salvation they had promised. Their future appears to be as bleak as their present. They are held in contempt by the ruling clerics, they do not possess the courage or the means to transform themselves into a fighting force, and they are not trusted by the elements which may succeed in replacing the Khomeini regime.

Bani-Sadr's experience is also instructive. In spite of his superficial and deceptive victory at the polls, the former president had no systematic organizational base, and, as a result, survived only as long as he was able to secure Khomeini's support. Later, when he was ousted from office under fundamentalist pressure in the summer of 1981, he could save his life only by placing himself, in effect, under the protection of the mujahidin. The less fortunate among his colleagues, such as Sadiq Qutbzadih, once the golden boy of the Islamic Republic, were caught in the fundamentalist web, and lost their lives to the vengeance of their revolutionary brethren.

The main body of Khomeini supporters, the "fighting clergy" who hold power under the Khomeini umbrella, has itself been split into a number of warring factions. Their common denominator has been reduced to a simple but fundamental understanding that they either must hold on to power collectively, or perish individually. They therefore tend to present a more or less unified front against outsiders. Within their own ranks, however, the struggle for power appears to have become progressively more intense. While individually they move in and out of different cliques, a process which may give a superficial impression of normal politics, generically, they fall into three ideologically divergent and probably irreconcilable factions.[18]

On the extreme left are the *maktabiyun*, the ideologues. Their power is concentrated in what might be loosely called the organizations of revolutionary control: The *pasdar* corps, the *kumitihs*, the *hizbollahi* brigades, the revolutionary courts and other basic revolutionary institutions. Their policies show a palpable affinity with those of the left. Their intellectual categories appear to be Marxist, even though their vocabulary, essentially the vocabulary of the regime, employs Islamic terminology; such terms as "proletariat", "bourgeoisie", and the "masses" are rarely used, but their connotations can be easily superimposed on the regime's standard vocabulary, the *mustaz'afin, mustakbarin,* and *nas*.[19] In its essentials, their Islam resembles the mujahidin's *islam-i rastin*. Their economic concepts and politics are sometimes indistinguishable from those of the Tudeh party. They advocate nationalization in most sectors of the productive process, banking, and foreign trade. They wish to expropriate the belongings of any group that can be labelled, one way or another, as antirevolutionary. In their foreign policy they advocate a genre of nonalignment which is palpably anti-Western and pro-Soviet. Objectively, as long as they hold on to their domination of the control mechanisms of the regime, they dispose of a power base which is potentially superior to that of the other factions. Once Khomeini is out of the picture, this potential gives them a decided advantage over their rivals.

The maktabiyun are in competition with the main faction to the right which calls itself the *hujjatiah*.[20] The hujjatiyun are the protectors of the *bayda-i islam*, the Islamic essence. They are strict constructionists. They control the Guardian Council, the Islamic Republic's equivalent of a constitutional council whose task is to pronounce on the legality and Islamic quality of the laws. As such, they have intercepted many laws on nationalization and expropriation pushed through the assembly by the maktabiyun and others. They also have a number of followers among the lower mullahs in the kumitihs, in organizations like *jihad-i sazandigi*, as well as some representation in the Islamic Assembly.

The dogmatic adherence of the hujjatiyun to Islamic tenets makes them extremely severe as watchdogs and judges of the outward expressions of "Islamic morality" such as the wearing of the *hijab*, the veil, for women. Thus, even though they are more lenient on economic matters, their genre of social and cultural justice places them at odds with much that has evolved over the years in the Iranian society. Beside the question of sexual politics, their zeal manifests itself particularly in their anti-Bahaism and anticommunism.[21] Otherwise, politically they seem to be more on the side of moderation both internally and internationally.

Furthermore, the hujjatiyun's idea of *vilayat*, or tutelage, differs from Khomeini's in that they argue that since perfect Islamic government is impossible of attainment in an imperfect world, and in the absence of the Mahdi, the Twelfth Imam, insistence on clerical rule and on *vilayat-i faqih* as the direct expression of that rule, may not be logically and historically valid at this point. In short, they seem to distinguish between clerical rule and Islamic government. In this sense they are ideologically close to the traditional clergy, who now find themselves more or less estranged and isolated from the regime.

The third group may be called the maneuverers. They are compromisers who excel in peddling influence. They are the political heirs and stylistic imitators of Ayatollah Beheshti, but they are less efficient and lack his panache. They have placed themselves squarely under the Khomeini umbrella and do not seem to avow or possess a particularly distinguishable ideology, other than what might be construed at different intervals as the Imam's line. They are political manipulators and for that reason they favor a sufficiently colorless ayatollah, namely Hussein 'Ali Muntaziri, as heir to Khomeini. They now appear to have the reigns of governmental power, at least in the sense of the visible niches they occupy. Their prototype is Hujjatul-Islam Hashimi Rafsanjani, the president of the Islamic Assembly, who has proved himself a master in the art of manipulating the other factions. Men like 'Ali Khaminih-'i in the presidency and Musavi Ardabili in the office of the prime minister also represent the same genre. Their power and future survival depend largely on their success at normalizing the political process before the passing of Khomeini from the political scene. Thus, in spite of their apparent support for the Iran-Iraq war, which is partly motivated by their desire to please Khomeini, and partly in order to keep the armed forces and the Guardian Corps sufficiently occupied to prevent them from making political mischief, they tend to opt for moderation in both domestic and international politics.

The maneuverers' normalization efforts were apparently consummated in the December 1982 proclamation by Khomeini of partial political amnesty and citizens' rights. Giving strict directives to Islamic judges and revolutionary courts, the December proclamation sought to prevent the kumitihs and pasdars from entering and searching homes, arresting people, conducting interrogations, seizing property, tapping telephones, questioning employees' religious and ideological beliefs, forcing people to spy on one another, dismissing civil servants, and engaging in other acts of harassment without legal authorization.[22] Concomitantly, the regime embarked on a campaign to encourage Iranian professionals in exile, particularly physicians and others whose knowhow was in great demand, to return to the country. To many observers, these moves and other steps taken by the regime suggested that the period of revolutionary excess was at its end, and the system had begun to move toward normalcy.

Such a conclusion, however, is difficult to sustain as it is based on a Brintonian analysis of forward-looking revolutions.[23] In the Brintonian cases, normalization is possible because the revolution's values correspond to dominant values of the epoch. Regressive systems, however, can open up the political space only at their own peril. The courts, kumitihs, and pasdars constitute the regime's main organizations of control. Weakening these organizations would be tantamount to weakening the system, more so because the Khomeini "commandments" provide material evidence of excesses and atrocities routinely perpetrated by revolutionary organs as a result of the actions and decisions of Khomeini's colleagues and lieutenants. It is difficult to see how the past could be condemned without affecting these men. Furthermore, in many ways and on many occasions Khomeini himself has propagated extreme policies and sided with those who have consistently advocated radical notions. The result has been unprecedented misery, widespread persecution, and innumerable lives lost to the terror of street bombs and official firing squads. And finally, even though the pragmatists and maneuverers may have gained Khomeini's ear for the present, past experience does not support the probability that they will hold it in the future. Proclamations of partial amnesty and exhortations of Islamic justice have been witnessed many times before.[24]

At any rate, the maneuverers' future success remains doubtful, because they operate within a system which has substantially lost its legitimacy. Once the Khomeini umbrella is removed, they will find themselves naked in a politically hostile environment. They will find it difficult to appeal to the country's socioeconomic power groups because they represent a system and an ideology

KHOMEINI PHENOMENON: ALIENATION

which no longer enjoy their support. They will likely find themselves at a disadvantage against the other two factions because they do not seem to possess enough following in the regime's control organizations. Thus, even if the Islamic regime survives Khomeini, power is more likely to be captured by the ideologues of the left and right than by the maneuverers of the center.

The control system on which the Khomeini regime's power is based follows the totalitarian pattern. Its center is the local kumitih, organized around the local mosque. Its muscles are the pasdar corps and the Hizbollahi thugs. Around the axis of kumitih-pasdar-Hizbollahi are the more traditional security forces: the army, the police, and the gendarmerie. The Islamic Republican party, armed with its revolutionary Islamic ideology, is present in all of these organizations either through the memberships as in the kumitihs, or through ideological commissars in the army and the police forces. Supporting this basic system are other organizations designed mainly for control over social and economic activities both in terms of allocation of goods and services and mobilization of popular and sectoral forces in the service of the system's goals. The latter category includes such organizations as the *bunyad-i mustaz'afin* (the Foundation of the Oppressed, replacing the former Pahlavi Foundation), jihad-i sazandigi (the Constructive Foundation), the *basij* (the Organization for Popular Mobilization), and the like. The system as a whole is designed for total control and pervades every aspect of the society's existence. Armed with Islamic doctrine, it portrays a seemingly invincible structure.[25]

The facade, however, should not obscure the basic weaknesses of the system. First and foremost among these is the character of the ideology itself. Islamic fundamentalism is even more alien to the historical ethos and social consciousness of the Iranian society than pure and unadulterated Westernism. It runs counter to the basic impulses of a majority of social types in the Iranian society. It tries to undo decades of sociocultural change and establish a homogeneous society based on a set of archaic values which can no longer be imposed except through the application of a most excruciating force to maintain a facade of behavioral conformity. The results have been an unprecedented exodus of the middle classes, and a phenomenal decline in Khomeini's support among the remaining Iranians.

Consequently, the kumitihs which were initially designed as

the central pillar of the Khomeini edifice now may constitute the weakest link in the chain of the regime's organizations.[26] They have turned into a number of semi-independent structures under the leadership of mullahs who wield a great deal of arbitrary power over the populace in so far as they control the rationing process, check on who occupies the houses and apartments in the neighborhood, decide who is to be arrested, and dispense or withhold favors. Since the kumitihs are more or less independent, they often encroach on one another's turf. As a result, there is often bad blood between them and their respective pasdar groups. More importantly, this freedom of encroachment keeps the people in a constant state of terror. Even when an individual has secured a modus vivendi with his neighborhood kumitih, he is still not secure from further demands or attacks by other kumitihs. The combination of the strictness of the fundamentalist tenets of appropriate behavior and the arbitrariness of the kumitihs and pasdars creates a situation in which no individual from any social group can assess with any degree of certainty his own guilt or innocence. Consequently, the most pervasive feelings elicited by the kumitihs are fear and disgust. For the well-to-do, the antidote to this situation has been bribery; for the poor, it has been mostly acquiesence in attending the Friday prayers and the regime's meetings and demonstrations.

Thus, contrary to the purpose for which they were designed, these basic "revolutionary institutions" may be a source of destabilization of the regime. They are the most visible targets of revenge for the disenchanted populace. Under attack, they may be reasonably assumed to be the first line of the regime's defenses to break down.

The kumitihs are supported by the pasdars, but pasdars have an organizational existence independent of the kumitihs. From the very beginning the hard core of the Islamic revolutionary movement, informed by leftist experience and intelligence, insisted that the success of the revolution depended largely on the revolution's success in demolishing the security paraphernalia of the Pahlavi regime and replacing it with cadres and organizations loyal to the Islamic Republic. The armed forces, particularly the army, the urban police and the rural gendarmerie were systematically attacked, many of their ranking officers summarily tried and executed, and many of their units disbanded or assigned to new and unfamiliar areas. Concomitantly, a new force, the

Revolution's Guardians, was created from a hodgepodge of revolutionary youth who had acquired their weapons at the time of the breakdown of the army depots during the transfer of power. This new revolutionary corps was intended to perform the security functions of the new regime and in due course of time replace the regular army. The new militia or pasdar corps therefore not only acted as the armed contingent of the kumitihs, but also as the trusted arm of the regime to combat the more organized opposition in Kurdistan, Azarbaijan, Gurgan, Baluchistan, Fars and other areas, both in the cities and among the tribes. In a short period of time, the idealistic elements who had joined the corps in response to their ideological zeal either left the organization because of their disillusion, or were weaned out by the leaders due to a lack of sufficient Islamic commitment. The hard core of the *sipah-i pasdaran* now consists of elements drawn from the youth in the fringes of the cities, and the lower strata of the rural areas. They are paid much better than the regular army and in this sense resemble mercenaries.

While the pasdars have been quite successful as aids to the kumitihs and in subduing city uprisings, they have showed less promise in confronting organized resistance. In the battles against the Kurds, Baluchis, Turkomans, Qashqais and others they have had to be consistently supported by the regular army units in order to maintain their lines. However, since the beginning of the Iran-Iraq war, and in some cases even before the war, the officers and soldiers have demonstrated a definite lack of zeal for fighting their own people. As a result, most of Baluchistan, vast parts of Kurdistan and Azarbaijan, segments of Gurgan and Mazandaran, and the tribal territories of Fars and Isfahan appear substantially free of control of the central government. Nor have the pasdars been particularly successful in the war with Iraq, in spite of the fact that the regime's propaganda apparatus has tried to magnify their role and depict them as the real heroes of the war.[27]

Furthermore, the regime's emphasis on the pasdars has created political expectations the result of which is difficult to foresee. As we have seen, the corps has become an arena of political competition among the regime's various factions. This phenomenon appears to have led to the radicalization of the pasdar corps and heightened its own political ambitions. While each political faction tries to turn the pasdars into its special army, the pasdars themselves are likely to emerge as a hegemonial force within the system. However, the observable corruption among the urban pasdars, their radicalization and factional divisions, and the quality of their membership suggest that many of them may be persuaded not to fight, or to dissolve into their surroundings, in the face of a serious internal assault, supported by a semblance of mass uprising, against the regime.

The political attitude of the regular armed forces is likely to prove the most important factor affecting the future of the Islamic Republic. The Iran-Iraq war forced the Khomeini regime to gather together the remnants of the Imperial Iranian Armed Forces to combat the Iraqi assault. After some initial setbacks, and against most predictions, the Iranian military demonstrated a kind of capability which the Shah had boasted about, which his foes had ridiculed, and which now surprised friends and foes alike. In a year's time, it succeeded in driving the Iraqi armies out of Iranian territory and assuming a decidedly superior posture in both tactical prowess and technical capability. It did so in spite of constant interference by the pasdars, the Islamic commissars, and the various factions of the regime which made a deliberate and concerted effort to attribute the Iranian victories to the Islamic virtues of the pasdars and their penchant for martyrdom.

The war has helped the armed forces streamline their organization and lines of command, achieve a new esprit de corps, and a sense of pride in their profession and accomplishments. Even though it must now be assumed that the organization of the army contains elements both committed to the Khomeini regime and opposed to it, nevertheless it remains the most organized and unified structure in Iranian society. Furthermore, its historical background, its military culture, its manner of evolution into one of the finest fighting forces in the Middle East, combined with the decimation of its ranks by the Khomeini regime, suggest a proclivity to anti-Khomeiniism in its ideological and professional outlook.[28] This latter point may be one of the reasons for the regime's reluctance to end the war in spite of the obvious devastation it has caused the country and the palpable strains it has created for the economy. An army released from its primary task, that is, the protection of the nation's independence and its territorial integrity, may indeed become interested in more subtle dimensions of power.

And finally, the police and the gendarmerie have been slowly rehabilitated. Both organizations were faithful to the monarchial system and have suffered immensely under the Islamic Republic. Their new lease on life is due to a basic social need which apparently could no longer be ignored by the new regime. The prevailing conditions under the Islamic Republic have gained for them a respect among the people which was lacking before the revolution. They remain, however, under the constant scrutiny of the Islamic system. Though they have lost much in power, nevertheless, of all the military forces they have the closest contact with the people. They are unlikely to defend the system because they have least to lose and most to gain by its downfall.

Thus, in spite of its organizational facade, and its demonstrated ability to project an aura of power, the Khomeini regime is inherently weak. We have already alluded to the historical irrelevance of Khomeini in socioeconomic and cultural terms. More tangibly, one may also point to the fallacy of the arguments depicting Khomeini as a powerful figure enjoying the support of the majority of the Iranian people on geopolitical grounds.

A cursory look at the map of Iran and the distribution of the population shows that the political support for Khomeini is and has been for a long time substantially confined to the areas bordering the country's central deserts. The Azarbaijanis in the northwest, the Kurds and related tribes in the west, the Arabic-speaking minorities in the southwest and the south, the Baluchis in the southeast and the Sunnis in the east, the Turkomans in the northeast, as well as the powerful Qashqai, Luri and related tribes scattered around the country, have all demonstrated a readiness for anti-Khomeini political behavior. In addition, the Caspian provinces of Gilan and Mazandaran have been under the considerable sway of different leftist and nonreligious organizations. Numerically, they add up to half the Iranian population. Strategically speaking, even in the central areas, the Khomeini regime has alienated a substantial portion of the middle class, the intelligentsia, the professionals, and the military, to which must now be added portions of the working class and fringe elements of the cities.

Furthermore, it is quite improbable that a modus vivendi between the Shia and Sunni Iranians can be achieved within the framework of a sacerdotal power system based on the present fundamentalist Shiite creed, short of military subjugation of the Sunni minorities. The only viable framework for the coexistence of the two sects within one state is a secular political system allowing for substantial freedoms in the domains of conscience, social behavior, and political participation—the latter in order to ascertain the protection of such rights.

The Khomeini regime is, by definition, the antithesis of such a secularistic frame of reference. Not surprisingly, the Kurds, Baluchis, Turkomans and others realize the fundamental contradiction between the essence of theocracy and religious freedom. When the religion in question approaches totalitarianism in its sociocultural compass, the curtailment of freedom transcends the boundaries of religious life narrowly understood, and extends to practically all aspects of human personal and social behavior. In this sense, religious domination transmutes into sociopolitical as well as economic domination. It becomes, in fact, a manifestation of domestic colonialism.

Thus, the systemic contradictions of the Islamic Republic cut across two axes. On the ethnic plane, they forbid unity and cooperation among the Persians, Kurds, Turks, Baluchis and others; on the cultural level, they alienate and expel all groups from different ethnic backgrounds that have attained some level of ideational transformation within the framework of world socioeconomic development.

On the regional and international levels, also, the Khomeini system invites disaster. As mentioned at the beginning of this chapter, Khomeini's view of the world does not comprehend the concept of "state" within the framework of contemporary international law. He addresses the world's Muslims as if they all belong to one nation, a single *ummah*. In one sense, this is not unlike the Pope addressing his worldwide Catholic constituency. The difference is that Khomeini's call is, by definition, radically political, based on the idea of the essential injustice and sinfulness of the existing orders; it aims at and advocates the overthrow of lawfully established systems of government under modern international law. It thus at once antagonizes the existing regional powers, breaks essential rules of noninterference in the internal affairs of other countries, and forfeits recourse to the protection of the international community. This last point has been amply demonstrated by the international community's reaction to the Iran-Iraq war.[29]

The range of Khomeini's ideological assault extends over the countries bordering the Persian Gulf region.[30] Most of these states have substantial Shia minorities. In some, like Iraq and Bahrain, the majority of the population are Shiis. Consequently, they are more or less vulnerable to the Islamic Republic's revolutionary propaganda (although local nationalism seems to have been stronger than Shia solidarity in Iraq and should not be discounted elsewhere). None of these countries is either politically or militarily very stable or strong. All of them, however, are of extreme economic or geopolitical importance to the industrial West, and to the Soviet state system as well, because they either produce oil, or afford control of the oil routes.[31] Obviously, the effects of Khomeini's political posture transcend the region and extend into the basic questions of war and peace on a world scale.

Objectively, therefore, the Khomeini regime is a threat also to the fragile balance that currently obtains between the East and the West. Logically, the interest of the West in Iran and the Persian Gulf is too apparent not to be taken seriously by the Soviet Union. Given the underlying assumption that neither superpower seeks military confrontation, the present Iranian crisis must be viewed by the Kremlin as a two-faced Janus bearing both an opportunity for expansion and a threat of disaster. The reasons are inherent in the nature of the problem.

As mentioned earlier, Iran is vitally important to the West not only because of its oil resources but, more importantly, because it dominates the Persian Gulf. This basically geostrategic fact suggests that as long as Iran remains a viable political unit and maintains its recent regional superiority in terms of population and sociotechnical considerations, it will tend to control the Persian Gulf's military and trade routes regardless of the characteristics of its sociopolitical system. In the latter part of the 1970s however, the West, and in particular the United States, demonstrated a surprising lack of resolve either to define their interests or defend them credibly. The results were confusion and anxiety for both friends and enemies.

Present socioeconomic trends suggest that both the West and the Soviet state system may be heading for troubled times. The Soviet system may prove particularly vulnerable as it shows relative inability to deal concomitantly with its infrastructural, defense, and consumption requirements. Furthermore, recent manifestations of labor unrest in Poland may be symptomatic of a future fraught with difficult times and different response patterns in other satellite states. The situation, therefore, is likely to lead to remedial steps to be taken on other fronts, including expansionist military and political postures.

A power vacuum in Iran will be inviting even when a basically cautious Soviet Union may not wish to strive to fill it by treating the country as a main arena of conflict. The history of warfare is replete with circumstances in which apparent lack of resolve and preparedness to counter power has led to the expansion of aggressive power to the point where war has become inevitable. Obviously, it is imperative for the West to maintain a psychopolitical as well as economic and military presence to counter Soviet expansionist tendencies. Not so obviously, the Soviet Union may see a Western presence in this region as facilitating the maintenance of peaceful coexistence. It is possible that they see such a presence as lessening the likelihood of their being drawn into a local power vacuum and finding themselves in direct confrontation with the Americans over an area they know is vital to the latter.[32]

Thus, even though the Khomeini regime represents an invitation to communism in Iran, it is not necessarily viewed as an outright blessing by the Soviet Union. The quarry runs on too difficult a field to qualify as easy prey. The Soviet Union, therefore, may prefer to be persuaded to enter into the kind of arrangements that would leave the Iranian plateau noncommunist, but would allow the Soviet Union greater access to the area's strategic and economic resources. In fact, stipulations by some Iranian activists in exile about Iran's partition into zones of influence, or its outright dismemberment, stem from arguments along these lines. The dangers inherent in the Iranian situation are seen by them as leading to a rapprochment between the United States and the Soviet Union, aimed at the establishment of a modus vivendi in Iran. They refer to the Anglo-Russian agreement of 1907 as a possible model to be used for arriving at a consensus between the two superpowers.

Even though both the Soviet Union and the United States may possess such contingency plans, partition may not be very realistic. The dramatic transformation of Iranian society and the level of national consciousness it has attained during the past 50 years, as well as the pattern of resource distribution in the country, relegate such a possibility to the lowest levels of expectancy—to be considered practical only after a long period of chaos in which a very substantial portion of the nation's economic infrastructure and much of its nationalistic fervor would have been destroyed in a prolonged civil war. The very existence of such possibilities, however, must give Iranians pause. For the anti-Khomeini forces, looming disaster on one hand, and the Soviets' willingness to steer away from inadvertent confrontation with the West on the other, might prove the key factors in determining the optimal strategy.

Notes
Chapter 7

1. This is not meant to suggest that analyses of political aspects of Shiism do not shed light on the Iranian Revolution. Recent works by such scholars as Shahrough Akhavi and Michael Fischer have done much to bring into focus some relevant aspects of state-clergy conflict in Iran. Nevertheless, to try to explain the Iranian Revolution in terms of Shiism is likely to mislead rather than illuminate. It is an intellectual trap that ought consciously to be avoided. See *inter alia*, Michael M. J. Fischer, *Iran: From Religious Dispute to Revolution* (Cambridge: Harvard University Press, 1980); Shahrough Akhavi, *Religion and Politics in Contemporary Iran: Clergy-State Relations in the Pahlavi Period* (Albany: State University of New York Press, 1980); Ervand Abrahamian, "Iran: The Political Challenge," *Middle East Research and Information Project Reports*, no. 69 (1979). For a brief but able overview of Islam's different intellectual and psychopolitical nuances in the contemporary Islamic world see Seyyed Hossein Nasr, "Islam in the Islamic World Today, An Overview," in *Islam in the Contemporary World*, ed. Cyriac K. Pullapilly (Notre Dame, IN: Cross Roads Books, 1980), 1–19.
2. See Eric Hoffer, *The True Believer* (New York: Harper, 1951).
3. See chapter 1, above.
4. These points constitute the central themes of the Khomeini regime. They became the axis of Khomeini's attack on the liberals. In numerous speeches in support of the Islamic Republic, Khomeini scolded his secular allies for suggesting that people had revolted in order "to fill their stomachs." He thought that the kind of opinion which held that men endangered their lives in order to secure material benefits was logically untenable. People had risen and died for Islam and therefore the future political system of the country would be the "*Islamic* Republic," in his own words, "not a word more, not a word less." See Khomeini's almost daily speeches in the Tehran daily newspapers *Kayhan* and *Ittela'at*, February 1979

to April 1979.
5. Unless Khomeini and his followers stand firm on the ideas deriving from the theory of vilayat-i faqih, he will have difficulty sustaining his claim to governance. See Ruhollah al-Musavi al-Khomeini, *Hukumat-e Islami* (Islamic Government), (Tehran: Amir Kabir Publications, 1971).
6. Both *Mizan* and *Inqilab-i Islami*, newspapers representing respectively the Bazargan and Bani-Sadr points of view, have been replete with sometimes open, often veiled references to corruption, murder, and illegal executions and incarceration committed by the Islamic regime.
7. *National Iranian Census, Preliminary Report*, (Tehran, 1975).
8. Ibid.,
9. *Report of the Ministry of Education* (Tehran, 1978).
10. *New York Times*, June 28, 1981.
11. Regime's adopted terminology meaning small group.
12. The regime's report of 72 dead is an obvious play on the passion of Hussein and the martyrdom of the Shiites' third imam and his 72 companions by the Umayyad army on the 'Ashura, the tenth day of the month of Muharram. Most reports from Iran place the number of casualties at 100 or more.
13. ". . . if an opinion poll could be held, about 5 to 15 percent of Iranians would support the regime and a smaller number would back the Mujahedeen, while the overwhelming majority would say 'a plague on both your houses'." A diplomat's estimate quoted by Harry Tanner, *New York Times*, (July 13, 1982) 2.
14. For a background study of the Tudeh party see Zabih, *Communist Movement in Iran* (op cit, chap 2).
15. *Washington Post*, May 5, 1983.
16. Mr. Krushchev's distillation of Marxist wisdom concerning Iran's historical lot in his famous "rotten apple" theory of late 1950s has apparently become a part of Soviet strategic thinking on Iran almost as solidly as the Russian desire to reach the warm waters of the Persian Gulf and Indian Ocean has been a part of Iranian political wisdom during the past two centuries.
17. On the treatment of the so-called revolutionary liberals by the clerical hard liners the sources are legion. As an example see Nikki R. Keddie, *Roots of Revolution* (New Haven: Yale University Press, 1981), 262.
18. The prevailing characteristics of the Khomeini regime do not allow for precise and reliable observation on the political affiliations of clerics in leadership positions. The politics of the regime is particularly obscured by the filial relations which bind many of the high clerics together. Still, the general framework is relatively clear. For

a parallel study see Daryush Humayun, *"Jumhury-yi Islami: Khatar az Darun,"* (Islamic Republic: Danger from Within) *Iran va Jahan*, Paris, May 16–25, 1983.
19. "Mustaz'af" may be translated as oppressed or meek; "mustakbar", as oppressor, proud, powerful, dominant; "nas", as people, masses.
20. See John Kifner, "Khomeini Faction Challenged by More Conservative Group," *New York Times*, April 13, 1982.
21. Hujatiyun anti-Bahaiism predates the Islamic Republic by several decades. It was, in fact, one of the basic reasons for the organization of the group in Qum, in the first place.
22. See Shaul Bakhash, *New York Times*, February 20, 1983, Op Ed section.
23. Crane Brinton, *Anatomy of Revolution* (New York: Randam House, 1938).
24. On the average, once a year since 1979.
25. This is probably the view most prevalent in the West. For a very different assessment of the regime's power and stability see Elaine Sciolio, "Iran's Durable Revolution," *Foreign Affairs* 61, no. 4 (Spring 1983), 893–920.
26. Contrast with the following sentence: "Neighborhood committees have been consolidated and centralized under the authority of the Ministry of Interior." Ibid., 900.
27. Pasdars should not be confused with the battalions of very young boys who have been routinely recruited from villages and small towns and indoctrinated to believe that martyrdom in war is the surest guarantee of salvation. Armed with a key to paradise hung around their neck, these youngsters are sent as a first wave of attack over minefields and other dangerous terrain to clear the way for the regular army or pasdar units. Indications are that the initial zeal has subsided and it has become progressively more difficult for the regime to find volunteers.
28. Information about political preferences of the personnel of the armed forces is scanty. However, contacts between antiregime military personnel outside Iran and active elements inside tend to support the points made here.
29. That the Iraqi invasion of Iran constituted an act of aggression can scarcely be disputed. The characteristics of the Khomeini regime, however, have disposed most regional governments to side with Iraq and others to let the two countries "stew in their own juices."
30. The alleged Iranian involvement in the coup attempt in Bahrain, discovered in December 1981, is an example. See John Vinocur, "1981 Plot in Bahrain Linked to Iranians," *New York Times*, July 25, 1982.

31. Indeed, Khomeini's intransigence has stimulated some very interesting changes in the political relations among the regional states. Iraq's rapprochement with Saudi Arabia, Kuwait, Jordan and the Gulf states has helped produce a possible restructuring of the framework of international relations within the Arab world. The new Iraqi-Egyptian contacts on the supply of arms and spare parts have had the contingent effect of easing up the relationship between Egypt and the moderate Arab states and may still work toward a further isolation of such hardliners as Syria, Libya and the People's Democratic Republic of Yemen, in spite of the contrary pulls of the Lebanese situation.
32. For a concise analysis of the relationship between the Soviet Union and the Islamic Republic see Shahram Chubin, "The Soviet Union and Iran", *Foreign Affairs* 61, no. 4 (Spring 1983) 921 ff. Alvin Z. Rubinstein observes ". . . Iran is now weaker and more vulnerable than at any time since the turn of the century. In a situation of enormous complexity and unpredictability, the Kremlin's restraint is linked to its anticipation that the collapse of Khomeini's Shiite millenarianism could well bring communism to Iran, and its wish not to provoke the United States by further Soviet expansion in the area." *Soviet Policy Toward Turkey, Iran, and Afghanistan: The Dynamics of Influence* (New York: Praeger, 1982), 116.

8 | The Future: Is There a Reasonable Way Out?

This study has tried to place the Iranian events in a theoretical perspective. Before embarking on a discussion of what is to be done, it may be useful to recapitulate, in summary form, some of its relevant points.

1. The transformation of Iranian society under the Shah's regime was both profound and permanent. It produced a nation that was almost new, with new capabilities and new frustrations.

2. The developmental process in Iran transformed the society from a state of essential cultural homogeneity to a state of cultural heterogeneity. The condition of cultural heterogeneity extended not only horizontally, i.e., spatially and geographically, but also vertically in temporal and historical terms. The crossing of the two axes created numerous social types within a complicated framework of contradictory sociopsychological as well as economic interrelationships.

3. In terms of political culture, the fragmentation of Iranian society suggests that no conceivable political system there could enjoy total legitimacy. Correlatively, it suggests that no conceivable political system can govern the country without the application of a certain amount of force. However, a distinction may and ought to be made between force and terrorism.

4. Under conditions of cultural heterogeneity, the consciousness of the need for development, essentially derived from

the objective experience of colonialism (as described in the Introduction), favored the centralization of the political system and concentration of political power. The inevitability of the use of force speeded up the process.

5. In the early stages of Iranian national development, and perhaps up to about the end of the 1960s, centralized and personal power were favored by the requirements of socio-economic development. Power appeared efficient and successful. In the later stages of recent Iranian national development, perhaps from the early 1970s onward, personal power began to lose its efficiency in accommodating the new requirements of the society. It lost its efficiency because its structure could no longer cope with the evolving dialectics of its social base.

6. The Shah's regime broke down under internal and external pressure mainly as a result of its own inner contradictions. The Khomeini phenomenon was a catalyst which channeled all the contradictory forces into one concentrated assault. In spite of its appearance, it was neither a revolutionary force nor a viable alternative to the Shah's regime.

7. The Khomeini regime cannot endure because it is antithetical to the historical requirements of the Iranian society at this historical epoch. It feeds on chaos. It survives because of the dispersal of all other forces, the initial breakdown and subsequent involvement of the Iranian army in war, and the manipulation of international powers.

8. The emotional energy that has sustained the Khomeini regime is fast being exhausted. Clearly, it is reasonable to assume that Iran will be faced with a set of momentous political alternatives in the near future. The general contours of the probable scenarios are more or less given. They would still represent either the extreme left, extreme right, or possibly a moderate center, upheld by the combined efforts of a variety of forces that had been actively involved in Iranian national development during the Pahlavi era.

9. It is imperative for those concerned inside and outside Iran not to make the same mistakes they committed under the Shah. It is unrealistic to think in terms of separating the process culminating in the fall of Khomeini from the process of erecting a new, viable political system. Power develops its own momentum as well as its own rules. The two processes, therefore, must be joined in a conceptually valid frame of reference that would unite

the separate acts in a common ideological and strategic framework.

No nation on earth has ever made, or will ever make, a collective choice for all time. It is only in retrospect that the tenets of the French Revolution appear in their permanent majesty. It took France some hundred years to achieve a semblance of superiority for the republican forces. The anticommunist forces in the Soviet Union were crushed only after years of application of ruthless power, cunningly amassed by Stalin. Currently, the Chinese are undergoing a spectacular transformation after Mao's demise, the end product of which is difficult to foresee. Revolutions achieve their permanence only to the extent that they begin to correspond to the ethos of their setting. If the present world situation imposes a consciousness geared to evolutionary patterns of change based on the interrelationship between patterns of value, on one hand, and patterns of socioeconomic existence, on the other, and if the transformation of the world situation happens to be governed by forces that are beyond the effective control of any one nation, then regressive revolutions whose ethos is geared to sets of archaic values and beliefs are *ipso facto* doomed, and, in that sense, are not revolutions at all.

We have spoken of the Khomeini phenomenon not as a revolution in itself, but rather as the wrong revolutionary fuse with largely negative socioeconomic and political consequences. Nevertheless, the phenomenal explosion of Iranian society must be explained in terms of factors which can stand the test of historically valid analysis. We have tried to identify and explain these factors within the framework of the Pahlavi regime. The gist of the argument has been that, historically speaking, the regime was far more than an autocratic system of government. In its last 15 years, it was, in fact, a revolutionary force of considerable magnitude, if notions of revolution are not confined to acts of violence but are extended to encompass the socioeconomic and cultural transformations undergone over short periods of time by substantial sectors of the society. If the Shah's system was a revolutionary agent because it brought about, facilitated, or hastened infrastructural changes assumed to correspond to the expected changes effected by world historical movements, then the Khomeini phenomenon must be presumed a reaction, an aberration, as noted above, and, in that sense, doomed to failure.

All of this need not be repeated here if it did not point to a possible way out of a dilemma which has become the source of a serious emotional and intellectual feud among anti-Khomeini Iranians. Certain factions, including some supporters of the *ancien régime* as well as constitutionalists of Bakhtiar's persuasion, refuse to call the Iranian upheaval a revolution. They refer to it as *"fitnih"*, a word which, in Persian usage, through its historical association with the Mongol invasion of Iran, has come to connote ruinous and dastardly destruction. Their problem, however, is how to explain the vast political outburst of the Iranian people which led to the fall of the Shah's regime.[1]

Some others, on the other hand, insist on calling it a revolution and, to justify their position, emphasize the reality of the Iranian political explosion. Associating the revolution with its period of violence, they in turn find themselves at a loss on how to deal with Khomeini and his movement, both of which they detest. They fall, willy-nilly, into the trap of suggesting that Khomeini started out as a proper revolutionary but lost his path somewhere along the line.[2] Consequently, those who abetted his purpose at the beginning but saw its folly in the middle and therefore abandoned the clerical line, should be considered true revolutionaries. In their view, the Khomeini regime's periodic outcasts such as Bazargan, Nazih, Madani, and, presumably, Bani-Sadr, and others who at some point may fall out with the clergy-dominated regime, not only should be allowed to come into the antirevolutionary fold, but should, in fact, be actively courted. This position, in turn, has placed them in a seemingly untenable intellectual and, one would assume political, situation. They have nothing positive to say about the Shah's regime, but they profess, at least in private, that constitutional monarchy is the most suitable political system for Iran. On the other hand, they define the revolution essentially along the lines enunciated by the Khomeini movement, but they cannot tolerate either Khomeini or his movement. As a result, they are floating somewhere in the anti-Khomeini atmosphere, hoping that lack of theoretical clarity might be taken as a point of least resistance on which a majority of Iranians might converge.

The intellectual meeting ground between the two positions may be that Iran in fact did undergo a phenomenal revolution, but that the historical ethos of that revolution had very little to do with either religion in general, or with the Khomeini brand in particular. It was rather the result of the rapid changes effected by the monarchial regime. The revolution, essentially a middle-class phenomenon, was meant to be a consummation at midpoint of the Constitutional Revolution of 1905–6, which had brought about the legal framework of a democratic kingship, but not the social basis, including the economic and cultural dimensions, to sustain it. The rapid changes under the Shah's system created the socioeconomic base for the materialization of values inherent in the framework of the 1906–7 Constitution; the structure of political power, however, was not able to negotiate the necessary changes in the pattern of the distribution of power. It aborted under the pressure of the Khomeini assault. The ethos of the Constitutional revolution, however, remains intact. It relates essentially to the manner in which each individual, social type, or social class can influence and affect the process of value allocation rather than to the quantity or quality of goods and services received by each individual, social type, or social class, important as this latter phenomenon may be.

The Khomeini phenomenon, therefore, was basically an aberration of a historically necessary response to a political system which could no longer deal effectively with the emerging forces, expectations and demands of its socioeconomic environment. The incapacity of the system had very little to do with monarchy as an institution. It was, rather, a function of the form of accumulation of power that, in systemic terms, had become depressing and nongenerative. The Khomeini phenomenon, aided and abetted by a multitude of contradictory forces, was a spark that activated the frustrated, pent-up energy of the Iranian resource base into an explosive chain reaction that engulfed all the secular categories of the society and, as such explosions always do, led them along a path of destruction, characterized in this study as thanatos on a national scale. The point becomes clear as soon as it is recognized that the Pahlavi regime did not fall as a result of the street demonstrations of the Iranian déclassés, but rather by the revolt of its own cadres: the middle class, the bureaucrats, and the technocrats.[3] Not surprisingly, immediately after the collapse of the Shah's regime, the same classes realized the extent of their mistake. One by one, their members were driven into jail, exile, or underground. One by one, they began to rise against the prevailing theocracy.

The reasons for the incontrovertibility of the confrontation between the Khomeini forces and the modern sector of the

THE FUTURE: A REASONABLE WAY OUT?

Iranian society is no longer difficult to assess. They are obviously related to historically antithetical world views and are categorized as such by both Khomeini and anti-Khomeini groups. This difference in weltanschauung, however, should have been noticed before the fall of the Iranian monarchy. It was not. As we have seen, it was assumed then that, once the Shah's system fell, all social classes and all social types would tend to come together in harmonious cooperation.

Not surprisingly, the same mistake is about to be made by the same political and intellectual groups concerning the future. It is now assumed by a respectable number of Iranian liberals and leftists in exile that once the Khomeini regime is overthrown, traditional and nontraditional social types will come together in a new spirit of democratic harmony. No doubt, as the harsh reality of social confrontation in Iran becomes increasingly apparent, the number of such groups dwindles. Steadfast believers in democracy by miracle, however, tend to become basically irrelevant in the unfolding historical process except as sources of nuisance and disparagement for gradualist systems which essentially accept democratic principles but may not be able to implement them immediately. In this sense, by exacerbating the already existing cleavages among the anti-Khomeini forces, they tend to add to the Khomeini regime's longevity and force the political situation, albeit inadvertently, into an impasse where the only workable alternatives might appear to be the kinds of political systems that are structurally based on forms of concentrated and centralized power.

A radically different group of Iranians yearns for the appearance of a national hero to save the country from the forces of disastrous reaction. They foresee years of military endeavor to subdue the diverse elements that agitate for the disintegration of Iranian society and to regain the true symbols of Iranian nationalism. Their prototype is Reza Shah. They find him a true representative of a long line of savior-heroes ranging from Abu Muslim of Khurasan to Nadir Shah of Afshar.*

---

*Abu Muslim was the first Iranian to rise against Arab domination. He was instrumental in the defeat of the Umayyad and the rise of the Abbasid Caliphate. Nadir Shah was the first successor to the Safavid dynasty.

The appeal of this position lies in its structural simplicity and historical parallelism. The Iranian people are thought to be culturally habituated to following a leader. Leadership requires power. Power resides in the barrel of a gun. The natural leader, therefore, is a military figure with civil ambitions and charismatic qualities. The story is well known in the developing world.

This nostalgic yearning for a savior is irrelevant, misleading, and dangerous. It is irrelevant because there is no such savior in sight. It is misleading because it overlooks the profound transformation of the Iranian society over the past 50 years. It is dangerous because, by concentrating mainly on the idea of charismatic leadership, it plays into the hands of the historical forces that, everywhere in the developing world, push for the ascendance of one man. Thus, it falls into the trap of personal power which everywhere arrives at an impasse in the face of the historically determined changes incurred in the socioeconomic base.

The last point ought to be contemplated seriously because the thrust of Iranian politics after the chaos of the last six years, among both the domestic and exiled opposition groups, is toward order, security, and a semblance of normalcy as distant as possible from the terror of the prevailing political situation, that may be justly characterized by the Hobbesian idea of the war of every man against every man. This same thrust may be aided by the international forces whose perception of their own long-range interest might be clouded by the frustration of their efforts to maintain reasonable relations with a historically illogical political system.

The future outlook calls for even greater caution. The amorphous nature of the prevailing forces within the country, the youthfulness of their membership, their commitment to their various causes, and the availability of weapons across the country, suggest the inevitability of military action in what, in the absence of careful political preparation, may turn into a protracted civil war. Several possible outcomes are likely, none of which is in the interest of either the Iranian nation, or the noncommunist world.

A protracted civil war may result in a Lebanese-type stalemate in which ideologically opposed forces will become entrenched in different areas, each receiving military, political, and perhaps economic aid, either directly or by proxy, from one of the superpower political constellations. Such a situation will not only destroy the remnants of the country's fragile economic base; given the geopolitical characteristics of Iran, it will more likely end in the dismemberment of the nation. The result would be, of course, disastrous for Iran, but it would also be extremely dangerous for the West. It would mean a Soviet advance toward the Persian Gulf, semi-encirclement of Turkey, and immediate access to Iraq. It would result in the establishment of a new bridgehead within the framework of the Soviet strategic world design. Past Soviet efforts to establish democratic peoples' republics in Gilan, Azarbaijan, and Kurdistan may be construed as prototypes of future action. The present Soviet strategic position in Afghanistan has already rendered the Iranian east and southeast, particularly Baluchistan, vulnerable to Soviet power. Under such circumstances, the future of the Persian Gulf, and therefore the West, would look extremely precarious even when one discounts the political and psychological pitfalls of doomsday and apocalyptic theories.[4]

An alternative scenario may be constructed not on the concept of stalemate, but rather on the systematic annihilation of the organized opposition by the anti-Khomeini military-civilian forces. Such a scenario must assume considerable internal political assistance for the anti-Khomeini forces, based on a combination of contrived and spontaneous popular support. Given the character of the Khomeini regime, such an assumption is not far-fetched. The characteristics of the Khomeini forces, however, make stiff resistance inescapable. There will be serious fighting, but once the hopelessness of the defenders' position becomes clear, they will tend to go underground. Their resistance would then become clandestine, selective, tactical, and political. Thus, even if apparent military and political positions were secured by the anti-Khomeini forces, violence would continue for some time.

The prevailing political circumstances will preclude the possibility of establishing a democratic frame of reference. Power will gravitate to the military leaders. Lack of meaningful political institutions will create a situation in which it will be extremely difficult to predict the future turn of events. The military leadership will not only have to fight its avowed enemies, but also its apparent allies, whose ideological inclinations are basically antithetical to the acceptance of a military regime as the normal form of government. The ruling elite, of course, will commit itself to the precepts of human rights, political and civil freedoms, and free elections to be introduced once the security of the nation is assured and political circumstances are propitious. The dateline for the establishment of a democratic form of government, however, will have to be perpetually postponed because the proposals concerning the change of the system or the change of leaders do not simply signify a different set of accepted rules or a different group of elected functionaries charged with the performance of the affairs of the state; they pertain essentially to questions of life and death. The combined forces of power's tendency to concentrate under the pressure of the political environment and the fear of an uncontrollable future would make it almost impossible for the leaders to quit. This is the central lesson of revolutionary politics in the developing countries.[5]

Such a situation, however, as we have seen, will undoubtedly come into conflict with the political requirements of socioeconomic development. The warrior-hero scenario will inevitably lead the nation into the kind of impasse it experienced under the Shah's "splendid" leadership. The difference is that, lacking any meaningful institutional frame of reference, it will entail substantially greater violence. It will retard the development of meaningful participatory institutions. In due course of time, it will alienate all the social types that constitute the backbone of its developmental process. Men who might have hailed the initial moves of the savior-heroes will begin to attribute to them the most unlikely and heinous crimes. Countries that might have assisted their initial endeavors will begin to develop doubts and second thoughts, and under the pressure of their own political forces, begin to disown and disparage them. Increased insecurity will bring forth increased violence. A vicious circle will develop that can be broken only by the forced overthrow of the political system whose ruling elite will justly claim that it is the legal and legitimate government of the nation. The country will find itself in the grips of another revolutionary process, this time dotted with a series of coups d'états in which the Communists will present an ever-growing threat. Given the contradictions in Iranian society, the system will tend to become a temporal bridge between chaos and totalitarianism.

The above scenario is the likeliest alternative which the Iranian nation faces. It is likely to happen because the existing forces inside and outside the country will work in its direction. The catastrophe of the present theocratic chaos, the natural demand for security, the need for military action, and the thrust of whatever international forces assist in the transformation of the Iranian political system, will all favor the establishment of a centralized system in which power will tend to become concentrated in the hands of whoever will play the role of the leader.

Ironically, the democratic forces will also aid the process of the concentration of power by confusing a normative preference for freedom and popular participation with the sociopolitical realities of a nation in the throes of disintegration. If the past is any indication of the future, they are likely to be rendered irrelevant by the irrelevance of their stand, thereby paving the way for the centralization and concentration of power.

A more reasonable scenario may be based on an objective analysis of the forces of a more permanent nature in the Iranian society. It will not be deceived by the prevailing slogans of the last six years. Rather, it will try to bring together the fundamental institutions of Iranian society and utilize them as support for a relatively stable foundation on which a political edifice, capable of handling the contradictory requirements of socioeconomic development and political give-and-take, could be erected. It will address itself to Iranian history, draw on its elemental features, and relate them to the exigencies of the society's cultural transformation within the framework of a turbulent world order.

Such a scenario will have to entail at least three dimensions: a value dimension positing a preferred picture of the future; an existential dimension analyzing the characteristics of the present Iranian society in their relationship to their world setting; and a strategic dimension delineating the path to be taken from the present to the future. The three dimensions must be viewed as parts of a unified conceptual framework. Dangers arise when one or the other is left out, taken for granted, or misconstrued.

Efforts at prescribing preferred pictures of the future are often criticized as aspects of the imposition of one's own preference and will on a nation. It is argued that one must turn to the "people" in order to find out what the people's preferences are. The problem is, however, that under conditions of cultural fragmentation, the people are rarely in a position to indicate their preferences with any degree of precision or permanence. They react to the existing stimuli within the limitations of the existing political forces and political circumstances. The Iranian people, for example, went to the polls and voted overwhelmingly for the establishment of the present Islamic Republic. The turnout was remarkable, even when one allows for the expected manipulation of the votes by the mullahs. By the same token, the people may be expected to vote differently under a different set of political stimuli. Thus, under nondemocratic conditions, the voting process itself turns into a major means of political manipulation. As such, the legitimacy it confers is as permanent or as fleeting as the power that guides it.

One of the basic premises of this study has been that the people are, in fact, divided into numerous social types. Each social type, having its own values and interests, sees the future in the light of its own world view. In most cases, however, enough values and interests are shared to allow for the establishment of a consensus in terms of which meaningful political transactions could take place. Within Iranian society, for example, noncontrovertible issues pertain essentially to either Islamic fundamentalists, or hard-core Communists. All others may be presumed to be able to accept compromise as an existential feature of political life.

At the level of constitutional engineering, therefore, the value dimension cannot be taken to mean specific prescriptions concerning the mode and the content of socioeconomic relationships. Its point of reference must be the kind of political structure that could facilitate the process of political give-and-take on one hand, and contain the dialectical pressures of systemic contradictions, on the other.

The "democrat's" injunction, therefore, resolves itself into two sets of interrelated propositions. The system must be constructed in such a way as to optimize freedom, by maximizing political participation within the limitations of the socioeconomic setting and the prevailing culture. Second, wisdom suggests that such a propitious situation may be obtained only if political structure and political process are founded on the basic institutions of the society and are supported and strengthened by structural and functional options that attract the contradictory political forces into supporting the integrity of the system. Stated differently, the value dimension of the scenario, cannot be too remote from the characteristics of Iranian society.

Clinically, the above might appear as a futile exercise

belaboring an obvious point. Practically, the connection between normative and existential values has often escaped the attention of the Iranian intellectual. The point is important because theoretical justifications of political options fall essentially within the purview of intellectual expression. When such expressions assume utopian dimensions unrelated to existential conditions, power becomes free to push to its utmost limits, with calamitous consequences for the society.[6]

As may be expected, at the moment there is no consensus on a preferred political system among the Iranians. The existential dimension of the proposed scenario, therefore, must delve into the historically significant characteristics of the Iranian nation in order to identify the salient factors that are relevant to the establishment of an acceptable form of participative polity. Specifically, it must identify the forces and institutions that have historically played a positive role in the preservation of the integrity of the society and rationally assess their relationship to the evolution of a political system in which the optimization of freedom and participation achieve their greatest consonance with the requirements of socioeconomic development for a new Iran. Conversely, it must also determine and harness the centrifugal forces within the society, searching for ways in which apparently disruptive and conflicting tendencies might be brought together to enhance the integrity of the whole system.

In the systemic sense, both kinds of forces are requisites for achieving the desired balance among the seemingly contradictory structural and functional requirements of the system. They ought to be viewed in a dialectical context. The expectation of a static balance or victory of one group over the others will have to yield to the concept of a fluid relationship in which all forces will achieve a part of their desired aims through a changing process of political give-and-take. In this scheme of things, justice is never the interest of the stronger; rather, all interests will have to be served by the mutual recognition of rights and obligations, objectified and safeguarded by the existence of countervailing powers which produce and maintain the dynamic balance referred to above.

Under what circumstances, then, is it possible to construct a political system in which an optimal form of political participation consonant with the requirements of maintaining the integrity of the political system may be secured? The answer must be sought in the relations between two historical factors: the historical ethos of Iranian society manifested in the characteristics of Iranian political culture, and the reality of the prevailing political situation reflected in the relative effectiveness of those socioeconomic forces which will inevitably bear on the country's future political configuration.

Under the confluence of tradition and colonial experience, the nation's natural impulse has been to strive for freedom, that is, to regain an equal status within the world community of nations, and to achieve individual freedom, in moral and material dignity, at home. The fragmented character of the nation's political culture translated this ethos in contradictory ways. Hence, the perpetual conflict between power and justice. It is precisely this conflict that will have to be managed if the historical ethos of the nation is to be realized.

The nation's cultural fragmentation, as we have seen, is manifested in the variety of "social types" constituting the sociopolitical forces which now contend with the prevailing authority, and with one another, for power. Of these, many, including those whose ideological postures make democratic compromises improbable, are armed, thus making military action unavoidable in any future confrontation. This necessity, in turn, favors the savior-hero scenario which, at best, as argued before, throws the country into a new political impasse. These circumstances therefore call for a political approach to the solution of the Iranian question.

The following categories may be identified as the major sociopolitical forces which will play a salient role in the future of the country: the intelligentsia, including the professionals and technocrats; the radical youth, constituting the central core of the present leftist radical movements; the white-collar employees in the private and public sectors; the bazaar, including the guilds and shopkeepers; the clergy; the tribes; the non-Persian Shia or Sunni ethnic minorities; the army; the small landowners; the urban laborers; and the general peasantry. The following figure gives a general picture of the ideological tendencies of these groups and their representatives.

As can be seen, the ideological extremes are represented by the Tudeh, Fada'iyan-i Khalq and other leftist factions, such as the Trotskyites and Maoists, on the secular left; mujahidin, Bani-Sadr and Shari'ati partisans on the religious left; Khomeini

Major Sociopolitical Forces and Their Ideological Tendencies

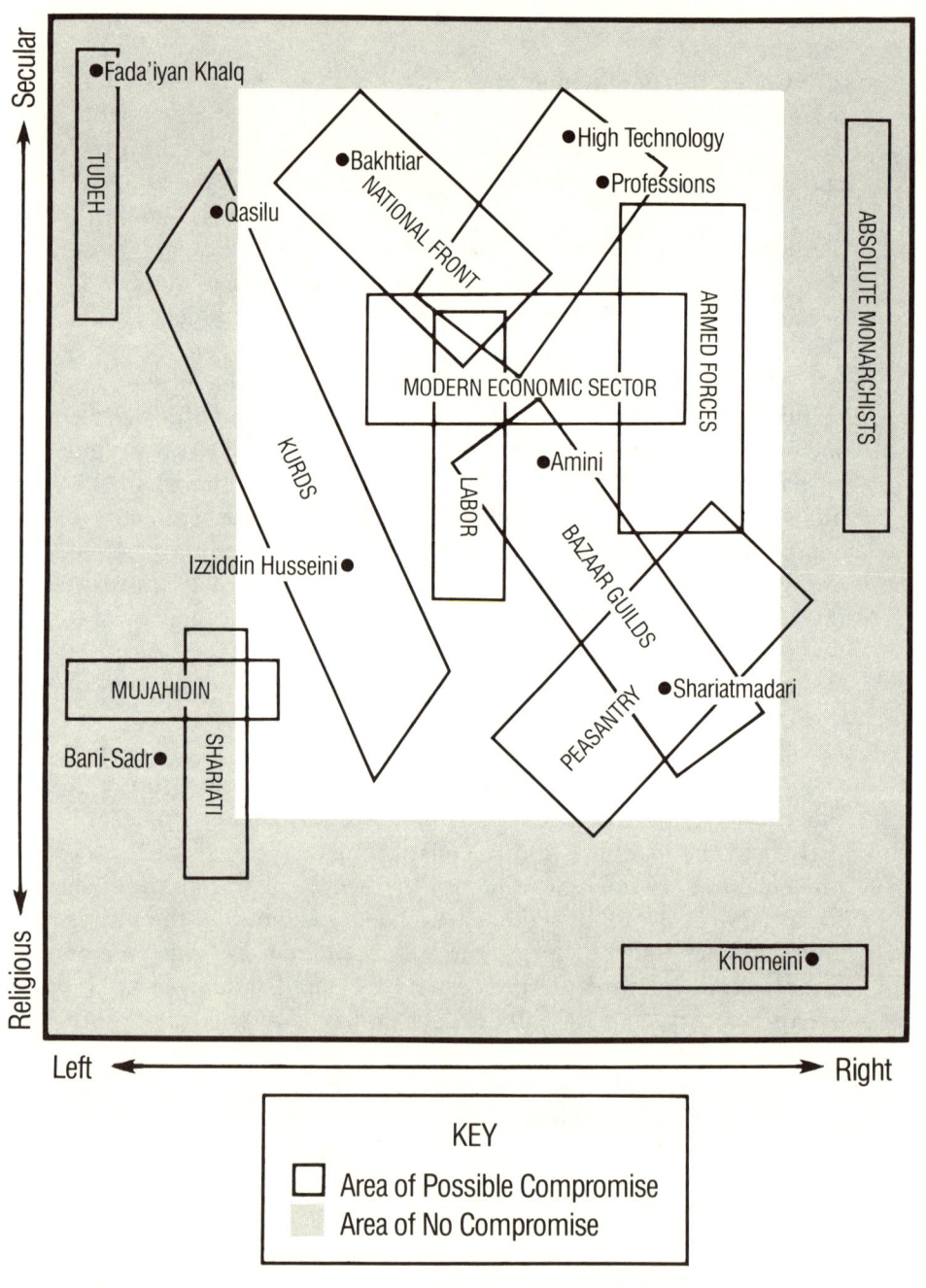

and the Islamic Republican party on the religious right; and, possibly, the absolute monarchists on the secular right. The bulk of the Iranian population fall in between, ranging in ideological terms from the semi-radical secularism of Bakhtiar on the secular left to the religious conservatism of Shari'atmadari on the religious right. That Shari'atmadari's position is shown to lean more toward secularism than Bani-Sadr's does not reflect his relative commitment to religion; only that, in view of his past performance, it is possible to assume that, faced with the cultural characteristics of Iranian society, he may deem a secular government preferable to a theocratic system, provided that the government demonstrates respect for the essential values of the Shia faith.[7] In this sense, his position comprehends the majority of the Iranian peasantry, labor, and traditional elements of the bazaar and guild communities. No doubt, these people thought of, and still consider, 'Ali's *khilafat* as the epitome of justice in government. But the thought is more in the nature of a nebulous yearning for a lost golden age, to be regained only in the semi-mythical conception of the "end of the world" and the reappearance of the twelfth Imam from his long occultation.

From a different perspective, the more moderate 'ulama may recognize, although for obvious reasons not profess, a possible incompatibility between certain Quranic injunctions, such as those pertaining to the relative positions of men and women in society, or to aspects of mode and relations of production and distribution of goods and services, and certain inevitable trends in modern society. Unless religion is divested of its divinity and transformed into ideology, a condition presumably abhorrent to the traditional Shia clergy, compromises on these issues will prove extremely difficult. As the Khomeini experience has already demonstrated, theocracy may, in fact, undermine the whole of the religious edifice by casting doubt on its ethical aspects as well.[8] This genre of questions, now increasingly prevalent among the Iranian intelligentsia, may prove the greatest threat to the foundations of Shiism in Iran.

The relative importance of the above categories varies depending on the stage of political operation. The intelligentsia, for example, will play a very significant role in supporting or opposing the system once power has been achieved, but not in the process of achieving power. Labor and peasantry will remain the basic referents of all operations, but it may be safely assumed that, at least in the initial stages, they will respond favorably to a change in the present system. That response, however, will be determined more by the attitude of other categories than by labor and peasantry themselves. Regardless of what portions of their ranks are organized and controlled by particular ideological factions, for example, the Tudeh, fada'iyan, mujahidin, or the Islamic Republican party, the antisystem response will be affected by the character of the antisystem movement. If the movement represents elements of the archetypal culture, it is likely to elicit a more favorable response. The same argument holds with respect to the traditional middle class.

Of much greater immediate strategic importance are the elements which control public response, or dispose of military and/or parliamentary power. To these belong the legitimate clergy, including their allies in the bazaar, ethnic groups, tribal elements, and perhaps most important of all, the armed forces. The requirement of achieving a viable balance among these groups as well as the others mentioned above, makes Iran's 1906–7 Constitution the most appropriate frame of reference for the political reconstruction of the country.

Analytically, there are two sets of reasons why constitutional monarchy is the form of government most appropriate to Iran. The first set pertains to the characteristics of Iranian popular response. The only political *institution* the Iranian masses can respond to is monarchy. Monarchy is the only archetypal form of government which has been known, felt, and internalized by the masses. Otherwise, among ideology, institution and charisma, the favorable response will be preempted by the charismatic leader, and not by what he represents in terms of ideology or form of government. Routinization of charisma, of course, may take different forms. Under the prevailing cultural circumstances in Iran, the probable pattern will not be very different from the experience of other comparable societies: Charisma tends to fade and be replaced by stark force. We are then back at the impasse discussed in the savior-hero scenario.

Constitutional monarchy, on the other hand, is basically perceived as an institution. The Shah would still represent a father figure, but within a set of expected rules and norms. This is the only explanation for the fact that the young heir to the Peacock Throne remains a viable alternative in the Iranian political psyche, in spite of the fact that he has no political experience, charisma, or force to commend him to the people.[9] His influence derives from a spiritual domain and, under propitious circumstances, could be transformed into the kind of power that would perform the balancing functions required to safeguard the integrity of the political system. It would be only under these circumstances that other political institutions, foreseen in the monarchical constitution, may take root. Whether such a propitious situation obtains, depends more than is generally acknowledged on the awareness and political vigilance of other political actors, rather than on the young prince's personal propensities. Kings, like all others, are subject to the prevailing political culture, and, like others, learn the essentials of that culture through practice and example.

The second set of reasons pertains to the contradictions within the Iranian society. These contradictions manifest themselves in several arenas of conflict. While specifically these arenas may be innumerable, most of them would belong to the realm of problem-solving should a viable political system be established. Thus, conflicts arising from urban and rural policies, labor-management relations, modes of production and distribution of goods and services, or the nation's foreign policy posture, among others, would, one hopes, be managed through the operations of the evolving political institutions.

Of primary significance are the kinds of conflicts which relate to the framework of political decision making. Among these, the following three categories are of overriding importance: tensions between secular and religious concepts of authority, Persian and non-Persian components of the Iranian society, and military and civil preponderance in political power. These three issues remain at the core of the present turbulent conditions in Iran. They may not yield themselves to complete resolution under any political situation, but if the aim is the establishment of a form of participative polity in which socio-economic progress and political freedom are to be secured and the nation's independence and integrity safeguarded, they must be managed within the framework of a political structure suited to that purpose. The analysis of these issues, in turn, suggests that constitutional monarchy, as envisaged by the 1906–7 Constitution, remains the most appropriate frame of reference. Let us now examine each of the above issues in light of the prevailing conditions in Iran.

THE FUTURE: A REASONABLE WAY OUT?

Most of the recent scholarship on the Iranian Revolution has emphasized the conflict between Shiism and the Iranian monarchy. In reality, of course, the contradiction is not between monarchy and religion, as such, but rather between Shia and secular concepts of political legitimacy. It is, therefore, not accidental that within the framework of nontheocratic government, the higher 'ulama in Iran have generally preferred monarchy to other forms of secular government.[10]

The contradiction between Shia and secular concepts of just government may be submerged by preponderance of power for a period of time; but it cannot thereby be resolved. It is an aspect of the dialectical tensions within a changing society that must be managed with the aid of institutions which can maintain the requisite balance between them. Iran's recent history demonstrates that, in the absence of such a "balancer," the integrity of the nation will be in constant jeopardy. Thus, under the Khomeini regime, the "faqih's tutelage" has pushed the country to the brink of disintegration. Fragmented culture has led to fragmented government. The peripheral provinces often operate independently of the central government. At the center, authority is maintained by a group of more or less autonomous kumitihs composed of young men of questionable moral and political character. Opposition is checked by the application of unsavory methods through the employment of the hizbullahi as storm trooper-type thugs whose major mission appears to be to beat up and disperse any political group which opposes the policies of the Islamic Republican party.

On the secular side, the Pahlavi kings were able to override religious contentions, but only as long as they could also hold on to power. Being closer to the mainstream of the nation's historical ethos, they realized great feats of progress. Under their leadership, Iranian society moved forward, until finally it could not bear the burden of external and internal pressure under the deformities of the structure of political power. Still, the failure was the result not of the institution of monarchy, but rather of the abandonment of that institution. The role of balancer, peculiarly geared to the monarchy, was lost in the misinterpretation of the monarch's role as supreme political leader.

Thus, kingship and Shiism, traditionally considered the main pillars of the integrity and independence of Iranian society, have each proved disruptive when operating under conditions of unrestrained power. This kind of perversion, however, does not invalidate the historical roles assigned to these institutions. On the contrary, it underlines the point that, in the absence of other viable political institutions, they remain the main pillars on which a relatively open and participative polity might be constructed.

The Pahlavi kings came into particular conflict with the clergy because, as modernizing kings, they personified secular authority. Nevertheless, it is important to note that between 1941 and 1961 the Shah's relationship with the majority of the higher 'ulama was rather cordial. The point is borne out by the mutual accommodation established between Ayatollah Burujirdi, as the highest authority of the Shia realm (*marja'-mutlaq*)[11] and the Shah, as the head of state, gaining in power, but still far from the absolute authority he became in the late 1960s and 1970s.

The death of Burujirdi in 1961 left the Shia community without a marja'-mutlaq. The leading ayatollahs, including such luminaries as Muhammad Kazim Shari'atmadari, Muhammad Reza Gulpayigani, and Shahab al-Din al-Mar'ashi al-Najafi in Qum; Ahmad Kafa'i and Hadi Milani in Mashhad; Ahmad Khunsari in Tehran; Muhsin Hakim, Abu al-Qasim Khu'i, Muhammad Hussein al-Kashif al-Qita' and Hibat al-Din Shahristani in the *'atabat*, or "shrine towns" of Iraq, each acted as a marja'-taqlid for his group of followers.[12]

The relationship between these *ayati'i-ezam* (exalted ayatollahs) and the court ranged from correct to cordial. In Mashhad, for example, Ayatollah Kafa'i was considered an outright partisan of the court; Milani, on the other hand, was much more reserved. Qum's most influential Ayatollah, Shari'atmadari, had always maintained a very correct relationship with the Shah. Khu'i remained a friend even during the last months of the revolution.[13]

Opposition to the regime's policies was led by a group of less exalted mujtahids, including Khomeini. Their struggle against the system was most vehemently manifested in the 1963 demonstrations against the Shah's White Revolution. Whether the highest-ranking ayatollahs shared this radical movement's conception of Islamic justice remains a moot point; they certainly did not seem to condone its methods. Nevertheless, they felt obliged to protect a fellow cleric and finally succeeded in saving Khomeini from imprisonment. Khomeini was exiled to Turkey until 1965, when he decided to settle in the shrine city of Najaf in Iraq.

THE FUTURE: A REASONABLE WAY OUT?

The years after 1963 saw a radical trend toward the secularization of Iranian society, spearheaded by a power structure which became increasingly symbolized by the person of the Shah. The Shah's successes on the domestic and international scenes overshadowed the essential tensions which existed between secular and Shiite conceptions of justice in the same manner that they tended to camouflage other contradictions of the Iranian society. This situation, in turn, helped convert Shiism into a political tool of the radical movement in Iran. Khomeini's emergence as the supreme religious leader is rather revealing in this context.

Khomeini's political success has somehow obscured the fact that in religious terms he had never been considered a senior colleague of the higher 'ulama either by the religious hierarchy or by the majority of the people.[14] He emerged as the spokesman for the revolution because of his uncompromising opposition to the Shah, whom he had long viewed as the embodiment of modern secular authority in Iran. This uncompromising posture represented his psychopolitical characteristics rather than his Shiism. The latter, essentially informed by *taqiya* or dissimulation and therefore given to compromise, was represented by the positions of the other ayatollahs who recognized, both logically and instinctively, the necessity of achieving a *modus vivendi* between historically determined change on one hand, and Shiite ethics on the other.

As might have been expected, the tension between secular and religious concepts of authority and justice was not resolved with the fall of the Shah. On the contrary, it exploded in the face of the basic postulates of the emerging theocracy. Contrary to the expectations of many who had participated in the revolution, Khomeini proposed to remain true to his beliefs. Supported by revolutionary momentum, he proclaimed the revolution as totally Islamic and defined the future system's governing structure and process on the basis of the concepts he had elucidated in his book, the *Islamic Government*.[15] Faced with his superior power, other ayatollahs gave in to dissimulation. The new prime minister, Mehdi Bazargan, tried vaguely to appeal to the more modern social elements, but was overpowered by the passionate intensity of the new clerical elite. The result was the phenomenal exodus of the modern sector of Iranian society.

In the meantime, Khomeini's intransigence has also created

a deep conflict among the clerics. While the complexities of the present conditions do not allow for a detailed analysis of the points of antagonism, certain general observations may be made. The traditional 'ulama do not hold as vigorously as Khomeini to the doctrine of the illegitimacy of temporal rule. The difference, of course, may be only a matter of degree, but since the present system's claim to legitimacy is essentially based on rigid adherence to the principle of vilayat, derived from religious precepts, it represents an inner threat which cannot be endured by the ruling clergy.

On the other hand, the Khomeini regime has not succeeded in preempting the religious and political influence of the other maraji'-taqlid. The latter's influence remains basically moral, but it is more concentrated and politically quite consequential. Ayatollah Shari'atmadari, for example, still wields unparalleled influence over the country's Azari population in spite of calumnies he has suffered at the hands of the regime. Qumi and Shirazi appear to be in firm control of the shrine city of Mashhad. But, contrary to the radical emphasis placed on the martial aspects of Islam and Shiism by the Khomeini regime, the traditional 'ulama have generally recoiled from violence. *Jihad* is to be waged against the infidels and then only as a last resort. It is, therefore, unlikely that these ayat will initiate an armed struggle against the Khomeini regime. The experience of the Islamic People's Republican Party, based in Azarbaijan Province and associated with Ayatollah Shari'atmadari, demonstrates the point. Faced with resolute opposition from the armed elements of the regime's Revolutionary Guards or pasdaran, Shari'atmadari instructed the party leaders to cease their activities in spite of the party's potential power and the cadres' determination to fight. This decision was characteristic and in tune with his behavior during the Shah's regime. It is a clue to his understanding of his role and responsibilities vis-a-vis his people, that is, to protect them from harm rather than lead them to bloodshed. It is an understanding which is shared, more or less, by the other traditional ayatollahs.

On the other hand, this mode of thinking must be presumed to render these religious leaders favorable to rational propositions. Political rationality, of course, differs from all other kinds of rationality in that it does not derive from the inherent properties of a given proposition, but rather from the manner in which such a proposition affects the congruity of the contending powers and interests. In this sense, if a set of political propositions coincides with the minimal demands of the religious community as well as those of the other interested groups, it is likely to find favor with the moderate ayatollahs. That favor carries with it the weight of the majority of the people. The virtue of the 1906–7 Constitution is that it yields itself to this kind of rationality.

The conflict between Persian and non-Persian components of Iranian society has often been advanced as a threat to the integrity of the nation. This mode of thinking has evolved and gradually become part of the Iranian nationalist creed as a result of the country's colonial experience and its near disintegration in the later Qajar period. Essentially, the centrifugal impulses of various tribes and ethnic minorities were seen to be the result of the gradual erosion of central authority and power. Reza Shah's success in subduing the rebellious khans, chieftains, and other local leaders, through the development and deployment of centrally controlled military force, strengthened that conviction. As the idea of the indispensability of central control, supported by the preponderance of military power, took root in the ruling elite's psyche, it became increasingly difficult to assess correctly the relative weight of other strategic factors. Thus, in spite of the decisive changes that had taken place in Iran's social, economic, technological, political, and military conditions, it remained the preponderant principle of government to the last days of the Pahlavi rule.

Correlatively, the Kurds, Baluchis, Turkomans, Azaris, and others, were depicted as unreasonable, if not anti-Iranian, in their demands for greater economic, cultural, and administrative autonomy.

This kind of perception may be valid only if concepts of "state" and "power" are interpreted in monolithic terms. Then, tensions arising from such conflicts will be naturally judged as disruptive and destructive. Monolithic concepts of polity will find it logical, even an absolute duty of the central government, to overcome such tendencies, if necessary, by force. Just as naturally, under conditions of rapid social mobilization, demands for freedom, participation, and meaningful political choice will rise, changing the relationships between powers that be into aspects of internal subjugation and hegemony.

A different perception of polity may view such tendencies not as disintegrative, but rather as essential for preserving the kind of

THE FUTURE: A REASONABLE WAY OUT?

balance which might be lost in the absence of objective countervailing powers. This mode of perception may initially appear as a form of political expediency. Nevertheless, it modifies notions of legitimate behavior and in this sense helps to transform incontrovertible political postures into mutually accommodating relationships. Tensions will still exist, but their import now will fall within the purview of constructive social conflict.

The ethnic question in Iran puts the problem of modality of power in prominent relief. The monolithic conception of power under the Shah brought into seemingly unresolvable conflict the structure of power and the burgeoning demands of the social base. During the course of the revolution, the ethnic element remained peripheral and appeared rather suspicious of the essentially Shia movement. But in fact it had been an important factor in preventing the process of decentralization and deconcentration of power under the prevailing notions of legitimacy. The regime's concept of Iranian nationalism tended to equate Iranian with Persian. No doubt the ethos of the Iranian nation, in terms of history and life content, is defined largely by its Persian component. But it is one thing to give recognition to reality and quite another to try to stifle all other modes of expression by ineluctable affirmation of the dominant reality. The fear that decentralization might encourage the Azarbaijanis, Kurds, Khuzistanis and others to demand a greater emphasis on their native languages, customs, and mores played an important role in the system's disinclination to effect decentralization. This in turn debilitated the system and helped pave the way for its downfall.

The cause of Iranian national solidarity will not be advanced by the affirmation of Persian hegemony. The nation must come to terms with the fact of cultural diversity and develop the kind of political culture capable of comprehending the idea of unity in diversity. To effect a political synthesis based on the recognition of diversity is not only a prerequisite for establishing a political system consonant with minimal requirements of individual freedom, it has now become a political necessity. Short of long years of military and political struggle which will inevitably eat into the fragile foundations of whatever kinds of political consensus is needed to bind the Iranian people together, the prevailing conditions make it almost impossible to envisage a future political system without substantial freedom for the non-Persian components of the Iranian society. Ethnic freedom is, in fact, a sine qua non of political freedom for all Iranians.

In view of the geographic distribution and manner of concentration of the Iranian ethnic populations, only a decentralized system of government can provide the minimal required structural basis for the satisfaction of demands for effective political participation. The theoretical underpinnings of this proposition have been advanced in the first chapter of this book. Regardless of the characteristics of the decision-making process, under Iranian conditions centralized power simply will not allow for the kind of political participation which can engage ordinary people to satisfy their immediate requirements. The loci of decision-making are too distant to show sensitivity to the demands generated by the special needs of the different geographic and sociocultural sectors of the society. Furthermore, political participation in the "developing" milieu of Iranian society must be viewed in terms of a learning process. Learning, as we have seen, is essentially praxis, contemplation and action brought to bear on the manner of position and solution of problems. Utopian statements of popular capabilities and interests notwithstanding, unless the problems posed for solution are close to the political actors' interests and understanding, the problems tend to bypass the actors and finally be decided, in fact, outside the framework of popular participation. People's reactions to such relatively complex issues as the nation's foreign diplomacy, oil policy, military preparedness, or energy development, will necessarily be haphazard and sporadic, strengthening the position of the false prophets in both secular and religious domains who maintain, for different reasons, that people do not know and must be taught and guided before they can be allowed to assert themselves in the kinds of decisions which affect their lives.

But does not decentralization of power in fact lead to the strengthening of the centrifugal forces and possibly to the dismemberment of the Iranian state? One may begin to address the question by positing its opposite: Will not too much concentration and centralization of power in fact prevent meaningful political participation, lead to greater frustration and cynicism, and finally so alienate the populace that they will rise against the system? Perhaps a more logical way of posing the question would be: Under what kind of political system is it possible to achieve the optimal form of decentralization of power commensurate with the requirements of both political participation and national integrity? The answer must begin with the analysis of the pertinent factors bearing on the response patterns of the elements which have been historically susceptible to separatist movements. The Kurds may be taken as the most relevant prototype.

Two sets of arguments may be advanced as to why, under relatively acceptable political circumstances, the logical assumption ought to be that the centripetal forces pulling Iranian ethnic groups toward integration with the nation will be stronger than separatist tendencies toward independence. The first set relates to the advantages of continuing their association with Iran. In spite of the separatist strains among certain Kurds or Baluchis, instigated by a combination of foreign incitement and ethnic loyalties, historical association with Iran has created significant attachments which should not be taken lightly. Historically, the focal point of that attachment, manifested by Kurdish, Baluchi, or Turkoman tribes, has been the institution of monarchy, a point that will have to be addressed and its political weight carefully measured.

Beyond the psychological attachment, two other basic internal factors must be considered. First, economically, all of the significant ethnic elements have much more to gain by remaining within the Iranian political system than by separating from it. It is a point of considerable importance and, no doubt, will be weighed in any future calculation. Secondly, it must be assumed that no Iranian government, regardless of its ideological proclivities, can allow the separation of a part of the country without a fierce struggle. Insistence on separating from Iran will probably unite all other ideological factions against the separatists. Historical precedents suggest that no such movement has been or will be a match for a reasonably effective central government disposing of a reasonable military might.

Finally, given the pattern of distribution of ethnic groups among the countries of the region, separation from one country does not automatically mean unification with other segments of the ethnic community. The Kurdish population, for example, lives not only in Iran, but also in Iraq and Turkey. Thus, even if the Iranian government remains in its present state of disarray, and therefore incapable of defending the nation's territorial integrity, other countries will still present formidable obstacles to separatist movements. Unless an upheaval of the highest order causes a drastic reorganization of the region's state boundaries, it is difficult to see how separatist movements can achieve their aim of ethnic unification. Rather, their actions will fall in the area of political destabilization, and, in this sense, they become pawns of other interested powers in spite of themselves.

This latter aspect remains a perpetual possibility and should be viewed as an endemic problem of Iranian politics. To the extent, however, that the structure and processes of the political system respond to the basic political needs of the ethnic groups, it is likely that relative local satisfaction, combined with the futility of rebellious acts in the face of internal and external sanctions, will limit the scope and intensity of such movements.

Still, the basic frame of interrelationships among the various ethnic groups may best be understood in dialectical terms. The contradictions between the ethnic and Persian conditions are real and important. Persian hegemony in culture, religion, education, technology, political access, and social standing, must be balanced through the operation of a kind of political system which is structurally capable of providing for arbitration by an office of such national stature that it can stand outside and, in moral and psychological terms, above the everyday political process. Such an office is provided by the institution of monarchy as envisaged in the 1906–7 Constitution.

As history moves on, sociopolitical conditions change. Social mobilization leads to greater political awareness and greater demand for political participation. It also leads to greater diversity and conflict. On the one hand, the growth in communications systems ushers in a higher consciousness of national identity; on the other, threats to traditional values and questions about the past strengthen the subnational communal bonds. As the developing nation assumes greater self-consciousness vis-a-vis the world, ethnic communities also achieve their own greater consciousness. Too often the clash of the two, as an important part of the more general question of cultural fragmentation, has found its political response in authoritarian rule. In certain countries, certain historical institutions may provide an alternative, if they themselves are not overcome by the authoritarian impulse. Iranian kingship is such an institution.

The institution of kingship in Iran has had many functions and, thus, has acquired different connotations during its long history. The idea of "king of kings," ludicrous as it now may appear in its rather pejorative connotation of false pretension to grandeur, also represented the notion of many communities, each enjoying its own form of government, religion, and set of laws, brought together and protected under one political umbrella through the office of the shahanshah. In this second meaning, its basic function still remains.

The third issue addresses the politics of the military-civilian relations in the future of the country. A reasonable scenario will have to approach the military question from three dimensions: First, what would be the most desirable role for the military in Iran's future politics? Second, what would be the probable effects of the actual role the military will be called upon to play—in the process of the establishment of the new regime—on the future of military-civilian relations? And finally, given the characteristics of the Iranian political culture, under what system of government would the desirable role normatively ascribed to the military be most closely approximated?

Presumably, the most appropriate role for the military would be that of the guardianship of the nation's territorial integrity and its constitutional system of government. Within this framework, the military should refrain from interference in the internal politics of the country; it should leave the governing process to civilians who, as the duly elected and appointed servants of the state and the people, are expected to perform their official functions in accordance with the established laws of the land; and it should obey the civilian government regardless of the ideology of the party in power, as long as the constitutional frame of reference is respected.

In fact, in most developing societies, the military either governs directly, or provides the framework and defines the limits within which the civilian government functions. In either case, military preponderance in politics constitutes an essential feature of political life.

The prevailing conditions in Iran preclude the possibility of meaningful change in the present regime without substantial military and paramilitary confrontation. As a general rule, military confrontation facilitates the military's preponderance in politics. Not only does war make heroes of the victorious officers, but conditions in the aftermath of war also tend to favor military control. We have already touched upon these conditions in the discussion of the savior-hero scenario. Neither history nor logic justifies the expectation that the military will abandon power once victory has been achieved, unless moral commitment and environmental pressure combine to force it to act in ways which approximate its normatively ascribed role.

These conditions may obtain only if the solution to the Iranian problem is sought primarily in political rather than military terms. This does not mean that military action is not required, nor even that it may not be of primary importance. It suggests that military operation ought to be viewed as part of a general political package, and should be guided by a decision-making structure which comprehends the military dimension as part of the total political package. Within this package, military and civilian command structures may be defined and separated, and their priorities determined; but every step should be related to the accomplishment of a goal which itself relates to a specific form of political arrangement in which not only the role of the military but also those of other components are more or less clearly defined. This approach, however, becomes practicable only if the proposed political arrangements contain value elements with which the military can identify.

The value preferences of the Iranian military have been clear. Historically, and even more forcefully in recent years, the Crown has been the focus of military loyalty in Iran. While few students of Iranian politics dispute the existence of a special kind of psychomoral relationship between the armed forces and the Crown, the significance of this special relationship for the establishment of civilian supremacy in the Iranian political system has not been properly appreciated. Quite naturally, attention has been focused more on the authority and power this military allegiance had conferred on the Shah. But the inference is not carried to its logical conclusion that, given the characteristics of Iran's political culture and the resulting lack of political consensus, severance of the military's ties to the Crown would not have eliminated the influence derived from military power; it simply would have shifted it to some other focus. Constitutionally, therefore, the relevant lesson to be drawn from the military's apparent total commitment to the Shah is not that it became a pliant tool in the hands of a dictator, but rather that the special relationship between the military and the Crown had created a psychopolitical situation in which the military never contemplated serious interference in the country's political affairs except by specific order from its commander in chief.

The analysis of factors leading to the centralization and concentration of power in the Shah's hands has been the major task of this study. No doubt, the command of the military was a sine qua non of his political control of the country. On the other hand, under present circumstances, the association between the Crown and the military is the only institutional pattern which carries the possibility of developing a political system substantially free from military domination. This is because the Crown remains the only potential institution capable of mediating the military's political pressure on the civilian government.

Interestingly enough, many Iranians, including some among the intelligentsia, see the Turkish military-civilian relations as the proper model for the future of Iran. Struck by the acerbity of the Khomeini assault, they now argue that had the military not been so strictly attached to the person of the Shah, it might have risen in time to avert the approaching disaster. This mode of ex post facto logic is, of course, wanting in consistency. While it is true that a more independent military might have succeeded in deterring the Khomeini assault, it is also true that, had it in fact struck boldly at the revolutionary movement and succeeded, it would now be the main target of attack of many of the present proponents of the military's political activism, who, under a different turn of events, could no longer avail themselves of the benefit of the same hindsight.

The fact is, however, that military government is inherently authoritarian. Its claim to legitimacy is ordinarily upheld by a negative principle, namely, that no other form of government is capable of establishing a minimum of stability and security required for the protection of national integrity and promotion of economic development. Once in power, the military government can relinquish power only at the risk of its own survival. It therefore rarely does so.

Elsewhere in this study we have argued that the Iranian monarchy under the Shah functioned essentially in terms of Hobbesian principles, and also that under the pressure of rapid social and economic change, Hobbesian systems of government will have to yield to more participative forms, either through a tendency to distribute political power (moving toward greater individual freedom) or a tendency toward greater concentration of

THE FUTURE: A REASONABLE WAY OUT?

power (moving toward totalitarianism).

Monarchies appear to be inherently antitotalitarian. In this connection, it may be interesting to note that, historically, all socioeconomically developed societies under monarchial constitutions have evolved into advanced democratic forms. No socioeconomically developed society has remained under purely *authoritarian* rule, while many socioeconomically developed societies find themselves under *totalitarian* systems of government (the differences between these two types of systems are real and important). No suggestion of cause and effect relationship is intended here. Only that, dialectically speaking, it may be argued that, given logical relationships as well as historical tendencies, the chances that under constitutional monarchies socioeconomic development and political freedom will be positively correlated are greater than under any other system. This is essentially because, unless monarchies succeed in opening up their political systems, they will not be able to cope with the emerging requirements of socioeconomic development. Historically, therefore, monarchical systems may be viewed as a hedge, or a form of structural insurance, against totalitarianism.

Notes
Chapter 8

1. See references to Khomeini in such anti-Khomeini weekly newspapers in exile as *Pardis* in Los Angeles and *Iran Azad* in Paris as well as the messages sent by Bakhtiar via radio broadcasts to the Iranian people. The first group praises Iranian development under the Shah, albeit at different levels of emphasis and sophistication. They generally attribute the fall of the regime to foreign connivance and muddleheadness of some Iranian leaders. The Bakhtiar persuasion condemns many of the Shah's policies as the main sources of the uprising, as it also dismisses Khomeini as a revolutionary force. Its position is that of the traditional liberal encumbered by most of the theoretical inconsistencies alluded to in chapter 6, above.
2. This position is perhaps best represented by *Iran va Jahan* presently published by a group of Amini supporters in Paris.
3. See chapter 1, above.
4. See Shahram Chubin, *Soviet Policy Toward Iran and the Gulf*, Adelphi Papers, No. 157 (London: International Institute for Strategic Studies, 1980).
5. See chapter 1, above.
6. See chapter 6, above.
7. For a more balanced view of the Shia conception of temporal authority see Akhavi, *Religion and Politics*, 13; also Fischer, *From Religious Dispute to Revolution*, 5–6.
8. This is a novel phenomenon. Whereas in the past anticlerical expressions were generally directed against the members of the clerical hierarchy and their abuse of Islam and Shiism, such expressions are now increasingly addressed at Islam and Shiism. Many Iranians, in and out of Iran, tend to argue that Khomeini's position in fact represents the true Islam. It is therefore Islam and Shiism that need to be seen and reevaluated in their true light. Paradoxically, they tend to credit Khomeini for his role in laying bare the practical ethics of Shiism.
9. The archetypal attraction of kingship in Iran is manifested in the

steady rise in the popularity of monarchy in the postrevolutionary period. This point is indicated not only by the opinion and behavior of a majority of the middle class in and out of Iran, but also by the statements of certain members of the ideologically antimonarchist left such as the minority Fada'iyan-i Khalq and the Union of Iranian Communists who are in touch with the author as former students. See also William O. Beeman, "Public Support for Restored Monarchy in Iran," *Los Angeles Times*, August 16, 1983.
10. Ibid.
11. Literally meaning "the absolute source (reference)." The position emerges when accepted by all the other main ayatollahs.
12. See Shahrough Akhavi, *Religion and Politics*, 100.
13. In fact, Khu'i received the Shahbanu Farah with much kindness and respect during the latter's pilgrimage to Najaf in late 1978.
14. Shahrough Akhavi, *Religion and Politics*, 100.
15. Ruhollah al-Musavi al Khomeini, *Islamic Government*. (Arlington, VA: US Joint Publication Research Service Translations on Near East and North Africa No. 1897, 1979).

Postscript

Six years have now passed since the establishment of the Islamic Republic in Iran. The regressive aspects of the revolution have been solidified into permanent policy and have become intertwined with the system's claim to legitimacy. In such areas as women's rights, education, and law, as well as in the more technical realms of industrialization and environmental protection, the system has sought justification for its policies in transcendental explanations that are largely irrelevant to the objective needs or demands of the population. In the last two years the war and world market conditions have drastically lowered the country's expected oil income. As a result not only has the mustaz'afin's share of the economic pie contracted, but the subsidies of the families of the war martyrs have also had to be partially curtailed. In spite of the regime's proclamations the gap between the haves and the have-nots has not in fact narrowed, though the prevailing political and social norms hide it partially by discouraging conspicuous consumption.

For a period of time rural contentment was secured by allowing unbridled use of underground water, forests, pastures, and game. Given the scarcity of these resources, subsequent adoption of more stringents regulations by government has now led to a resurgence of discontent. In many cases, land taken from landlords has been returned to them, but the choice of crop still is theoretically determined by the government and enforced by the clerical arm of the regime. In agriculture, as in other matters, the latitude allowed the clerics in meting out justice has had the effect of subordinating the law to the personal whim of the judge. The range of possible verdicts does not allow any one to assess guilt or innocence in a rational manner. The result has been pervasive fear, and a corresponding effort to buy clerical support in any way possible. A *modus vivendi* seems now to have emerged whereby "understanding" between the landlord and the regional clerical potentate affords some lattitude in the choice of crop and a corresponding profit for both.

The Islamic Republic continues to abet terroristic groups in the region and beyond. Inside Iran, political repression in its totalitarian form—social, economic, and cultural—remains the order of the day. Summary executions seem to have abated somewhat. The reason is that the organized left, specifically the mujahidin, have lost much of their effective capability, while the center and center-right have yet to succeed in effectively organizing themselves. The disenchantment with the regime, however, has now become far more diffused and pervasive, including not only the upper and middle classes, but also large portions of the mustaz'afin.

The war with Iraq is now approaching its fifth year. On March 12, 1985, another annual Iranian thrust into Iraqi territory ended in predictable disaster. As expected, against vastly superior Iraqi air, armor, and artillery power, the Iranian attack failed to achieve its stated objective of cutting the Baghdad-Basra lifeline, but it did sate Iraqi marshes once again with the bodies of Iranian and Iraqi youth. Some estimates suggest that between twenty and thirty thousand Iranians and half as many Iraqis fell as a result of the clerics' willful disregard of common logic. Iraq has now escalated the war to a new phase—the war of the cities—where innocent men, women, and children on both sides are targets of unseen bombs and missiles. A stalemate prevails which, death and destruction notwithstanding, is regarded by "objective" analysis of global politics as the best possible outcome!

It is difficult to imagine how the war might end—short of Khomeini's death, or his fall from power. Khomeini appears to remain adamant in his insistence that Saddam Hussein must go; an offer the Iraqi leader, understandably, refuses to accept. In the face of impossible demands, the higher the casualties, and the greater the range of destruction, the more difficult it will be for the belligerents to arrive at mutually acceptable terms. Men of good will have sought, periodically, to detect in Khomeini's statements, or those of his associates, signs of softening, of reason, of recognition of futility. The latest effort to find a point of compromise is now under way pursuant to the UN Secretary General Javier Perez de Cuellar's visit to Tehran and Baghdad in early April. As these words are being written (mid-April, 1985), there is some suggestion that the Secretary General is taking steps to engage the UN Security Council to mediate the conflict. Optimists point to several encouraging signs: Majlis President Hujjat al-Islam Hashemi Rafsanjani's statement in Tehran that the Secretary General's approach to the issue is the only one that may conceivably succeed, Iran's UN Ambassador Said Rajaie Khorassani's suggestion to reporters that the toppling of the Iraqi president, although still an Iranian objective, is "not a political condition" demanded by Iran for a cessation of hostilities, and the lull in the bombing of the cities since Perez de Cuellar's departure from the region on the 9th of April. The underlying assumption, however, is that the apparent death and destruction resulting from a war that cannot be won should encourage reasonable people to try to find a way out. One man's reason, however, may be another's nightmare. Khomeini seems to have endowed the war with a new transcendental meaning: If the war cannot be won, then not the war but victory must be spurned. War must go on for the sake of war, for it is God's work and God's work must be done regardless of the outcome.

In chapter seven of this book I have suggested that the key to understanding Khomeini is not so much Islam or philosophy, but his psychology; that Khomeini is a true believer in the tradition of Hitler. It seems to me that the experience of the past six years supports this point. He does of course routinely draw on verses from the Quran to support his position, but always by imposing his own personal interpretation. It is the measure of Khomeini's psyche that centuries of intercommunal endeavor to soften the "word" have left him untouched. The following excerpt from his speech of December 12, 1984, delivered on the occasion of the anniversary of Prophet Muhammad's birth, is reprinted here from the April 15, 1985 issue of *Harper's Magazine*. It is perhaps an appropriate epithet to the man and his work.

"If one permits an infidel to continue in his role as a

corrupter of the earth, his moral suffering will be all the worse. If one kills the infidel, and thus stops him from perpetrating his misdeeds, his death will be a blessing to him. For if he remains alive, he will become more and more corrupt. This is a surgical operation commanded by God the all-powerful.

"Those who imagine that our time on earth is a divine gift, those who believe that eating and sleeping like animals are gifts from God, say that Islam should not inflict punishments. But those who follow the teachings of the Koran know that Islam must apply the *lex talionis*, and thus that they must kill. Those who have knowledge of the suffering in the life to come realize that cutting off the hand of someone for a crime he has committed is of benefit to him. In the Beyond he will thank those who, on earth, executed the will of God.

"War is a blessing for the world and for all nations. It is God who incites men to fight and to kill. The Koran says: 'Fight until all corruption and all rebellion have ceased.' The wars the Prophet led against the infidels were a blessing for all humanity. Imagine that we soon win the war [against Iraq]. That will not be enough, for corruption and resistance to Islam will still exist. The Koran says: 'War, war until victory.' A religion without war is an incomplete religion. If His Holiness Jesus—blessings upon him—had been given more time to live, he would have acted as Moses did, and wielded the sword. Those who believe that Jesus did not have 'a head for such things,' that he was not interested in war, see in him nothing more than a simple preacher, and not a prophet. A prophet is all-powerful. Through war he purifies the earth. The mullahs with corrupt hearts who say that all this is contrary to the teachings of the Koran are unworthy of Islam. Thanks to God, our young people are now, to the limits of their means, putting God's commandments into action. They know that to kill the unbelievers is one of man's greatest missions."

There may exist a gap between appearance and reality, and men of good will may wish to retain the hope, for the sake of Iran and the world, that beneath the sordid appearance of the Islamic Republic hides some redeeming element as yet unknown to human conscience. A time comes, however, that accepted norms of human decency ought to be allowed to bear on atrocious beliefs leading to atrocious acts that exceed normal ranges of human fall from grace. For Khomeini and the Islamic Republic, that time is long past due.

Select Bibliography

Abrahamian, E. *Iran Between Two Revolutions*. Princeton: Princeton University Press, 1982.

_____"Communism and Communalism in Iran: The Tudeh and the Firgah-i Demukrat." *International Journal of Middle East Studies* 1 no. 4 (October 1970).

_____"Factionalism in Iran: Political groups in the 14th Parliament, 1944–46." *Middle East Studies*, no. 14 (January 1978).

Adamiyat, F. *Amir Kabir va Iran* (Amir Kabir and Iran). Tehran: Kharazmi Press, 1969.

_____*Fikr-i Azadi va Mugaddamih-i Nihzat-l Mashrutiyat-i Iran* (The concept of freedom and the beginning of the constitutional movement in Iran). Tehran: Sukhan Press, 1961.

Afchar, H. *L'Orientation actuel de droit rural en Iran*. Tehran: University of Tehran Press, 1975.

'Ajami, E. *Shishdangi: Pazhuhishi dar Zaminih-i Jami'ihshinasi-yi Rusta'i* (Shishdangi: A study in rural sociology). Tehran: Tus Publications, 2536(1356).

Akhavi, S. *Religion and Politics in Contemporary Iran: Clergy-State Relations in the Pahlavi Period*. Albany: State University of New York Press, 1980.

Al-Ahmad, J. *Gharbzadigi* (Westoxication). Tehran: n.p., 1344.

_____*Dar Khidmat va Khiyanat-i Rushanfikran* (On intellectuals' service and betrayal). Tehran: Ravaq Press, 1347.

'Alavi, B. *Panjah-u sih nafar* (The fifty-three). Tehran: Amir Kabir,

1357.

Algar, H. *Islam and Revolution: Writings and Declarations of Imam Khomeini*. Berkeley: Mizan Press, 1981.

———*Religion and State in Iran, 1785–1906*. Berkeley and Los Angeles: University of California Press, 1969.

American University Foreign Areas Studies. *Area Handbook for Iran*. Washington, DC: 1978.

Amirie, A. *The Persian Gulf and Indian Ocean in International Politics*. Tehran: Institute for International Politics and Economic Studies, 1975.

———and H. A. Twitchell, eds. *Iran in the 80's*. Tehran: Institute for International Political and Economic Studies, 1978.

Amirsadeghi, H., and R. W. Ferrier, eds. *Twentieth Century Iran*. London: Heinemann, 1977.

Amuzegar, J. *Iran: An Economic Profile*. Washington, D.C., The Middle East Institute, 1977.

———"Oil Wealth: A Very Mixed Blessing." *Foreign Affairs*. vol. 60, no. 3, (Spring 1982).

———*Technical Assistance in Theory and Practice: The Case of Iran*. New York: Praeger, 1966.

———and M. Fekrat. *Iran: Economic Development under Dualistic Conditions*. Chicago: University of Chicago Press, 1971.

Arfa', H. *Under Five Shahs*. London: Murray, 1964.

Ashraf, A. *Mavani'-i Tarikhi-yi Rushd-i Sarmayihdari dar Iran* (Historical obstacles to the development of capitalism in Iran). Tehran: Payam Press, 1980.

Avery, P. *Modern Iran*. London: Benn, 1965.

Bahar, M. *Miraskhar-i Isti'mar* (Heir to colonialism). Tehran: Amir Kabir, 1357.

———*Tarikh-i Ahzab-i Siyasi-yi Iran* (History of political parties in Iran). Tehran: Rangin Press, 1944.

Bahrami, 'A. *Khatirat* (Memoirs). Tehran: Mazahiri Press, 1966.

Bakhash, S. *Iran: Monarchy, Bureaucracy and Reform under the Qajars*. London: Ithaca Press, 1978.

Bakhtiar, C. *Ma Fidelité*. Paris: Albin Michel, 1982.

———*Si-u Haft Ruz Pas Az Si-u Haft Sal* (Thirty-seven days after thirty-seven years). Tehran: Radio Iran Publications, 1361.

Baldwin, G. *"The Foreign-Educated Iranian." Middle East Journal* 17, no. 3, (Summer 1963).

———*Planning and Development in Iran*. Baltimore: The Johns Hopkins University Press, 1967.

Bamdad, B. *From Darkness into Light: Women's Emancipation in Iran*. Ed. and trans. F. R. C. Bagley. Hicksville, N.Y.: Exposition Press, 1977.

Bamdad, M. *Tarikh-i Rijal-i Iran* (History of Iranian Statesmen). 6 vols. Tehran: Bank Bazargani Press, 1968–1972.
Banani, A. *The Modernization of Iran, 1921–1941*. Stanford: Stanford University Press, 1961.
_____ed. "State and Society in Iran." *Iranian Studies Special Issue*, 11 (1978).
Bayat, M. "The Iranian Revolution of 1978–79: Fundamentalist or Modern?" *Middle East Journal* 37. no. 1 (Winter 1983).
_____*Mysticism and Dissent: Socioreligious Thought in Qajar Iran.* Syracuse: Syracuse University Press, 1982.
Bayne, E. *Persian Kingship in Transition: Conversations with a Monarch Whose Office Is Traditional and Whose Goal Is Modernization.* New York: American University Field Staff, 1968.
Beck, L., and N. Keddie, eds. *Women in the Muslim World.* Cambridge, MA: Harvard University Press, 1978.
Bemont, F. *L'Iran depuis 1962*. Paris: Fredy Bemont, 1971.
Bernard, C., and Z. Khalilzad. *"The Government of God": Iran's Islamic Republic*. New York: Columbia University Press, 1984.
Bharier, J. *Economic Development in Iran, 1900–1970*. London and New York: Oxford University Press, 1971.
Bill, J. *The Politics of Iran: Groups, Classes, and Modernization.* Columbus, Ohio: Merrill, 1972.
_____"Power and Religion in Revolutionary Iran." *Middle East Journal* 36. no. 1 (Winter 1982).
_____"The Social and Economic Foundation of Power in Contemporary Iran." *Middle East Journal* 17, no. 4. (Autumn 1963).
Binder, L. *Iran: Political Development in a Changing Society.* Berkeley and Los Angeles: University of California Press, 1962.
Blair, J. *The Control of Oil*. New York: Pantheon Books, 1976.
Bonine, M., and N. Keddie, eds. *Continuity and Change in Modern Iran.* Albany: State University of New York Press, 1981.
Bosworth, C., ed. *Iran and Islam: In Memory of the Late Vladimir Minorsky.* Edinburgh: Edinburgh University Press, 1971.
Browne, E. *The Persian Revolution of 1905–1909*. Cambridge: Cambridge University Press, 1910.
Brzezinski, Z. *Power and Principle: Memoirs of the National Security Adviser, 1977–1981.* New York: Farrar, 1983.
Carter, J. *Keeping Faith: Memoirs of a President*. New York: Bantam, 1982.
Chelkowski, P., ed. *Iran: Continuity and Variety.* New York: Center for Middle Eastern Studies, 1971.
Chittick, W. *A Shiite Anthology.* Albany: State University of New York Press, 1981.
Choubine, B. *Tashayyu' Va Siyasat Dar Iran* (Shiism and politics in

Iran). Paris: 1361.

Chubin, S. "The Soviet Union and Iran." *Foreign Affairs* 61. no. 4 (Spring 1983).

――――and S. Zabih. *The Foreign Relations of Iran*. Berkeley and Los Angeles: University of California Press, 1974.

Cottam, R. *Nationalism in Iran*. Pittsburgh: University of Pittsburgh Press, 1979.

――――"Political Party Development in Iran." *Iranian Studies* 1, no. 3 (1968).

Cottrell, A. *Iran: Diplomacy in a Regional and Global Context*. Washington, DC 1975.

Curzon, J. *Persia and the Persian Question*. 2 vols. London: Frank Cass, 1969.

Davudi, M. *'Ayn al-Dawlih Va Rizhim-i Mashrutih* ('Ayn al-Dawlah and the constitutional system). Tehran: Jibi Books, 1357.

――――*Qavam al-Saltanih*. Tehran: Bahar Press, 1947.

Dawlatabadi, Y. *Hayat-i Yahya* (The Life of Yahya). 4 vols. Tehran: Ibn Sina, 1327.

Douglas, W. *Strange Lands and Friendly People*. New York: Harper and Brothers, 1951.

Dreyfuss, R. *Hostage to Khomeini*. New York: New Benjamin Franklin House Publishing Company, 1980.

Eagleton, W. *The Kurdish Republic of 1946*. New York: Oxford University Press, 1963.

Elwell-Sutton, L. *Persian Oil: A Study in Power Politics*. London: Lawrence and Wishart, 1955.

――――"Political Parties in Iran: 1941–1948." *Middle East Journal* 3, no. 1 (January 1949).

Enayat, H. *Modern Islamic Political Thought*. Austin: University of Texas Press, 1982.

Farmanfarmayan, H., ed. *Khatirat-i Amin al-Dawlih* (The memoirs of Amin al-Dawlih). Tehran: Amir Kabir, 1341.

Farrukh, M. *Khatirat-i Siyasi-yi Farrukh* (The political memoirs of Farrukh). Tehran: Sahami Press, 1348.

Faruqhi, A. *Iran Zidd-i Shah* (Iran Against the Shah). Tehran: Amir Kabir, 1358.

Fatemi, N. *Oil Diplomacy*. New York: Whittier Books, 1954.

Fesharaki, F. *Development of the Iranian Oil Industry: International and Domestic Aspects*. New York: Praeger, 1976.

Fischer, M. *Iran: From Religious Dispute to Revolution*. Cambridge, MA: Harvard University Press, 1980.

Forbis, W. *Fall of the Peacock Throne: The Story of Iran*. New York: Harper and Row, 1980.

Frye, R. *Persia*. London: Allen and Unwin, 1968.

Garthwaite, G. *Khans and Shahs: The Bakhtiari in Iran.* Cambridge, UK: Cambridge University Press, 1982.
Ghani, Gh. *Yaddasht-ha* (Memoirs). 12 vols. London: Ithaca Press, 1980–84.
Graham, R. *Iran: The Illusion of Power.* New York: St. Martin's, 1979.
Grayson, B. *United States-Iranian Relations.* Washington, DC: University Press of America, 1981.
Green, J. *Revolution in Iran: The Politics of Countermobilization.* New York: Praeger, 1982.
Grummon, S. *The Iran-Iraq War: Islam Embattled.* New York: Praeger, 1982.
Haddad, Y. "The Qur'anic Justification for an Islamic Revolution: The View of Sayyid Qutb." *Middle East Journal* 37, no. 1 (Winter 1983).
Halliday, F. *Iran: Dictatorship and Development.* New York: Penguin, 1979.
Hariri, N. *Musahibih ba Tarikhsazan-i Iran* (Interviews with makers of Iranian history). Tehran: Amir Kabir, 1358.
Haykal, M. *Iran, the Untold Story: An Insider's Account of America's Iranian Adventure and its Consequences for the Future.* New York: Pantheon Books, 1982.
Hooglund, E. *Reform and Revolution in Rural Iran.* Austin: University of Texas Press, 1982.
International Labour Organization. *Employment and Income Policies for Iran.* Geneva, 1973.
Iranian Plan and Budget Organization. *Iran's Fourth Development Plan, 1968–73.* Tehran.
———. *Iran's Fifth Development Plan, 1973–78,* and *Revised Plan, 1975–78.* Tehran.
———. *Iran's Projected Sixth Development Plan, 1978–1983.* Tehran.
Issari, M., and D. Paul. *A Picture of Persia.* Hicksville, NY: Exposition Press, 1977.
Jabbari, A., and R. Olson, eds. *Iran: Essays on a Revolution in the Making.* Lexington, KY: Mazda Publishers, 1981.
Jacqz, J., ed. *Iran: Past, Present and Future.* New York: Aspen Institute, 1976.
Kasravi, A. *Rah-i Rastigari* (Path of salvation). Tehran: Rushdiyih, 2536(1356).
———. *Shi'igari* (Shiite sectarianism). Paris: 1361.
———. *Tarikh-i hijdah-salih-i Azarbaijan* (Eighteen-year history of Azarbaijan). Tehran: Amir Kabir, 1346.
———. *Tarikh-i Mashrutih-i Iran* (History of the Iranian Constitution). Tehran: Amir Kabir, 1340.
Katouzian, H. *The Political Economy of Modern Iran.* London: Macmillan, 1981.

Kazemi, F. *Poverty and Revolution in Iran: The Migrant Poor, Urban Marginality and Politics*. New York and London: New York University Press, 1981.

Keddie, N. *Roots of Revolution: An Interpretive History of Modern Iran*. New Haven: Yale University Press, 1981.

———ed. *Religion and Politics in Iran*. New Haven and London: Yale University Press, 1983.

———and E. Hooglund, eds. *The Iranian Revolution and the Islamic Republic: Proceedings of a Conference*. Washington, DC: Middle East Institute, 1982.

Kedourie, E., and S. Haim, eds. *Toward a Modern Iran*. London: Frank Cass, 1980.

Khomeini, R. *Vilayat-i Faqih: Hukumat-i Islami* (Tutelage of the jurist: Islamic government). Tehran: Amir Kabir, 1357.

Khusravi, K. *Jami'ih-i Dihgani dar Iran* (Rural society in Iran). Tehran: Payam Publications, 1358.

Kishavarz, F. *Man Muttaham Mikunam* (I accuse). Tehran: Ravaq Press, 1358.

Kissinger, H. *White House Years*. Boston: Little, Brown and Company, 1979.

Laing, M. *The Shah*. London: Sidgewick and Jackson, 1977.

Lambton, A. *Landlord and Peasant in Persia*. London: Oxford University Press, 1953.

———*The Persian Land Reform, 1962–1966*. Oxford: Clarendon Press, 1969.

Ledeen, N., and W. Lewis. *Debacle: The American Failure in Iran*. New York: Knopf, 1981.

Lenczowski, G., ed. *Iran Under the Pahlavis*. Stanford: The Hoover Institution Press, 1978.

———*Middle East Oil in a Revolutionary Age*. Washington, DC: American Enterprise Institute, 1975.

———*Oil and State in the Middle East*. Ithaca, NY: Cornell University Press, 1960.

———*Russia and the West in Iran, 1914–1948*. Ithaca, NY: Cornell University Press, 1949.

Lissani, A. *Tala-yi Siyah ya Bala-yi Iran* (Black gold, or Iran's curse). Tehran: Amir Kabir, 1357.

Looney, R. *The Economic Development of Iran: A Recent Survey with Projections to 1981*. New York: Praeger, 1973.

———*Income Distribution Policies and Economic Growth in Semi-industrialized Countries: A Comparative Study of Iran, Mexico, Brazil and South Korea*. New York: Praeger, 1975.

Mahmud, M. *Tarikh-i Ravabit-i Siyasi-yi Iran va Ingilis* (History of Anglo-Iranian diplomatic relations). Tehran: 1328–1332.

Makki, H. *Kitab-i Siyah* (The black book), vol. 4. Tehran: Sanawbar Press, 1362.

―――― *Tarikh-i Bist Salih-i Iran* (A twenty-year history of Iran). 2 vols. Tehran: Majlis Press, 1323–24.

Maliki, N. *Akhundism: Asrar va 'Avamil-i Suqut-i Iran*. (Secrets and instruments of the fall of Iran). n.p. n.d.

Marlowe, J. *Iran: A Short Political Guide*. London: Pall Mall Press, 1963.

Matini, J. "Bahsi dar barih-i Sabiqih-i Tarikhi-yi Alqab va 'Anavin-i 'Ulama dar Mazhab-i Shi'ah" (A study of the history of 'Ulama titles in Iranian Shiism). *Iran Nameh* 1, no. 4 (Summer 1983).

McDaniel, R. *The Shuster Mission and the Persian Constitutional Revolution*. Minneapolis: Bibliotheca Islamica, 1974.

Miller, W. "Political Organization in Iran: From Dowreh to Political Party." *Middle East Journal* 23 nos. 2 and 3 (Spring and Summer 1969).

Millspaugh, A. *Americans in Persia* New York: Da Capo Press, 1976.

―――― *The American Task in Persia*. New York and London: The Century Company, 1925.

Miskub, S. *Sug-i Siyavash* (Mourning for Siyavash). Tehran: Amir Kabir, 1355.

Momeni, D., ed. *The Population of Iran: A Selection of Readings*. Honolulu: East-West Center, 1977.

Naipaul, V. *Among the Believers: An Islamic Journey*. New York: Knopf, 1981.

Nakhleh, E. *The Persian Gulf and American Policy*. New York: Praeger, 1982.

Nashat, G. *The Origins of Modern Reform in Iran*. Urbana: University of Illinois Press, 1982.

Nasr, S. *Islamic Life and Thought*. Albany: State University of New York Press, 1981.

―――― *Sufi Essays*. Albany: State University of New York Press, 1973.

Nasri, F. "Iranian Studies and the Iranian Revolution." *World Politics* 35, no. 4 (July 1983).

Nirumand, B. *Iran: The New Imperialism in Action*. New York: Monthly Review, 1969.

O'Donnell, T. *Garden of the Brave in War*. New Haven, CT: Ticknor and Fields, 1980.

Pahlavi, M. *Answer to History*. New York: Stein and Day, 1980.

―――― *Bih-su-yi Tamaddun-i Buzurg* (Toward the Great Civilization). Tehran: Imperial Pahlavi Library, 1978.

―――― *Mission for My Country*. London: Hutchinson, 1961.

―――― *The White Revolution*, trans. Imperial Pahlavi Library Tehran: Kayhan Press, 1967.

Pesaran, M. *World Economic Prospects and the Iranian Economy.* Tehran: Institute for International Political and Economic Studies, 1976.

Qanun-i Asasi va Mutammim-i An. Tehran: Majlis Press, 1355.

Qarabaghi, A. *Hagayiq dar barih-'i Ingilab-i Iran* (Facts about the Iranian Revolution). Paris: Suhayl Publications, 1984.

Radji, P. *In the Service of the Peacock Throne: The Diaries of the Shah's Last Ambassador to London.* London: H. Hamilton, 1983.

Rahimi, M. *Qanun-i Asasi-yi Iran va Usul-i Dimukrasi* (Iranian Constitution and Principles of Democracy). First published in 1347, n.p., n.d.

Rahman, F. *Islam.* 2nd ed. Chicago: University of Chicago Press, 1979.

Ra'in, I. *Faramushkhanih va Framasuniri dar Iran* (The house of oblivion and Freemasonry in Iran). 3 vols. Tehran: Amir Kabir, 1347.

Ramazani, R. *The Foreign Policy of Iran, 1500–1941.* Charlottesville: University of Virginia Press, 1966.

———. *Iran's Foreign Policy 1941–1973.* Charlottesville: University of Virginia Press, 1975.

———. "Who Lost America? The Case of Iran." *Middle East Journal* 36, no. 1 (Winter 1982).

Ravandi, M. *Tafsir-i Qanun-i Asasi-yi Iran* (Interpretation of Iran's constitution). Tehran: Amir Kabir, 1357.

Rawhani, F. *San'at-i Naft-i Iran: Bist Sal pas az Milli Shudan* (Iran's oil industry: Twenty years after nationalization). Tehran: Jibi Books, 2536(1356).

Razi, H. "Genesis of Party in Iran: A Case Study of Interaction between the Political System and Political Parties." *Iranian Studies* 3, no. 2 (Spring 1970).

Roosevelt, K. *Countercoup: The Struggle for Control of Iran.* New York: McGraw Hill, 1979.

Rubin, B. *Paved with Good Intentions: The American Experience and Iran.* New York and Oxford: Oxford University Press, 1980.

Rubinstein, A. *Soviet Policy Toward Turkey, Iran, and Afghanistan: The Dynamics of Influence.* New York: Praeger, 1982.

Sablier, E. *Iran: La Poudrière.* Paris: Editions Robert Laffont, 1980.

Sadiq, I. *Modern Persia and her Educational System.* New York: Columbia University Press, 1931.

Saikal, A. *The Rise and Fall of the Shah.* Princeton: Princeton University Press, 1980.

Salinger, P. *America Held Hostage: The Secret Negotiations.* Garden City, NY: Doubleday, 1981.

Sampson, A. *The Seven Sisters: The Great Oil Companies and the World they Shaped.* New York: Bantam Books, 1975.

Sanasarian, E. *The Women's Rights Movement in Iran: Mutiny, Appeasement, and Repression from 1900 to Khomeini.* New York: Praeger, 1982.
Sciolio, E. "Iran's Durable Revolution." *Foreign Affairs*, 61, no. 4 (Spring 1983).
Shafa, S. *Paykar ba Ahriman* (Battle with the Devil). Paris: Iranshahr Publications, 1362.
———*Tawzih al-Masa'il.* Paris: Imprimerie Herissey à Evreux (Eure), 1362.
Shafaq, R. *Khatirat-i Majlis va Dimukrasi Chist?* (Majlis memoirs and what is democracy?). Tehran: Shafaq Press, 1334.
Shaji'i, Z. *Nimayandigan-i Majlis-i Shura-yi Milli dar Bist-u-Yik Dawrih-i Qanunguzari* (Deputies to the National Consultative Assembly during twenty-one legislative sessions). Tehran: Tehran University Press, 1344.
Shari'ati, A. *Majmu'ih-i Asar* (Collected works) 8 vols. Tehran: Husseinieh Irshad Press, 1358–1359.
Shayigan, D. *Asia dar barabar-i Gharb* (Asia faced with the West). Tehran: Amir Kabir, 1356.
———*Qu'est-ce qu'une révolution religieuse?.* Paris: Les Presses d'Aujourd'hui, 1962.
Shuster, W. *The Strangling of Persia.* New York and London: The Century Company, 1912.
Stemple, J. *Inside the Iranian Revolution.* Bloomington: Indiana University Press, 1981.
Sullivan, W. *Mission to Iran.* New York: W. W. Morton and Company, 1981.
Tabari, A. and H. Yeganeh. *In the Shadow of Islam: The Women's Movement in Iran.* London: Zed Press, 1982.
al-Tabataba'i, Allameh M. *Shiite Islam*, trans. S. H. Nasr. Albany: State University of New York, 1975.
Upton, J. *The History of Modern Iran: An Interpretation.* Cambridge, MA: Harvard University Press, 1968.
Vance, C. *Hard Choices: Critical Years in America's Foreign Policy.* New York: Simon and Schuster, 1983.
Vreeland, H. *Iran.* New Haven: Human Relations Area Files, 1957.
Wall, P., et al., eds. *The Indian Ocean and the Threat to the West: Four Studies in Global Strategy.* London: Bayard Books, 1975.
Wilbur, D. *Iran, Past and Present.* 7th ed. Princeton: Princeton University Press, 1975.
———*Riza Shah Pahlavi: The Resurrection and Reconstruction of Iran.* Hicksville, NY: Exposition Press, 1975.
Women's Organization of Iran. *Karnamih-i Saziman-i Zanan-i Iran* (The balance sheet of the Women's Organization of Iran). Tehran:

Center for Research on Women Issues, 1978.
Yar-Shater, E., ed. *Iran Faces the Seventies*. New York: Praeger, 1971.
Zabih, S. *The Communist Movement in Iran*. Berkeley: University of California Press, 1966.
_____*The Mossadegh Era: Roots of the Iranian Revolution*. Chicago: Lake View Press, 1982.
Zonis, M. "Iran: A Theory of Revolution from Accounts of the Revolution." *World Politics* 35, no. 4 (July 1983).
_____"The Political Elite of Iran: A Second Stratum?" In *Political Elites and Political Development in the Middle East*, ed. Frank Tachau. New York: John Wiley, 1975.
_____*The Political Elite of Iran*. Princeton: Princeton University Press, 1971.

Index

Abbasid Caliphate, 228
Abu Muslim of Khurasan, 228
Adorno, Theodore W, 52
'Alam, Asadollah, 27, 53, 94, 187
Alburz College, 49
Algiers Agreement of 1975, 152, 153
'Ali, Shiite Imam, 22, 90, 104, 237
American influence—on Iranian political culture and intellegentsia, 48–51
—on Iranian politics, see also US relations, 28, 157, 162–163, 165
Amini, 'Ali, 27, 28, 101–102, 166, 182
Amnesty International, 185, 187
Amuzigar, Jamshid, 53, 66, 74, 107, 187
—Premiership of, 85, 86, 87–88, 89, 93, 95, 191
Anglo-Iranian Oil Company, 23, 25
Anglo-Russian Agreement of 1907, 216
Ansari, Hushang, 53, 74, 187
Azhari, General Gholam Reza, 85, 103, 120, 185
Azmun, Manuchihr, 71, 100

Baader-Meinhoff Group, 87
Badri'i, General 'Abdollah, 114, 124, 132
Baghdad Pact, 148
Bahais, 206
Bahiri, Muhammad, 100
Bakhtiar, Shapur, 85, 102, 107, 108, 113, 115, 116, 122, 123, 124, 125, 127, 129, 130, 132, 133, 135, 136, 138, 139, 140, 166, 182, 192, 226, 237
Ball, George, 134
Baluchis, 153, 211, 213, 214, 230, 244, 247
Bani-Sadr, Abul Hasan, 166, 199, 204, 205, 226, 235, 237
Barzani, Mullah Mustafa, 152
Basij, 209

269

INDEX

Bazargan, Mehdi, 5, 92, 108, 116, 117, 132, 135, 138, 140, 166, 190, 191, 199, 204, 226, 242
Beheshti, Ayatollah Muhammad Hussein, 135, 201, 202, 207
Biglari, General, 114, 123
Bihisht Zahra Cemetery, 108
Black Friday incident, 97–98
Blumenthal, Michael, 134
Boumediene, Houari, 152
Britain, see Great Britain
British Broadcasting Corporation (BBC), 135, 167
Brown, Harold, 130, 131, 136
Brown, Lord George, 123
Brzezinski, Zbigniew, 115, 130, 134, 136
Bunyad-i Mustaz'afin, 209
Burujirdi, Ayatollah Sayyid Muhammad Hussein, 21, 241

Callaghan, James, 123
Carter, President Jimmy, 10, 92, 114, 115, 123, 129, 130, 134, 135, 146, 148, 157–158, 161, 164
Ceaucescu, Nikolai, 147
Central Intelligence Agency (CIA), 94, 159, 164
Central Treaty Organization (CENTO), 148, 153
Centralizing tendencies, 11, 18, 28, 39, 40, 60, 76, 83, 223–224, 244, 251
—political consequences of, 76–77, 224
Che Guevara, Ernesto, 174
Christopher, Warren, 131
Churchill, Sir Winston, 32
Cinema Rex incident, 95
clerical forces, relations with the monarchy, 21, 22, 23, 24, 96, 121, 241–244
Constitution of 1906–07, 8, 10, 17, 25, 27, 61, 68, 69, 70, 125, 126, 129, 180, 190, 191, 192, 227, 238, 239, 244, 248
constitutional monarchy, see the political opposition, the Constitutionalists
Constitutional Revolution of 1905–06, 17, 227
Cyrus the Great, 1, 26

Daoud, Muhammad, 153
De Gaulle, Charles, 147
The "Democratic Era," 20–26
Desai, Muraji, 154
Détente, 162
developmentalism, 3, 7, 11, 34, 35, 64, 181, 198
—and foreign policy, 146–147, 198
Dhofar insurgency, 151, 152
Dubcek, Alexandre, 147
Duncan, Charles, 131

Fada'iyan-i Islam, 21, 200
Fada'iyan-i Khalq, 108, 174, 202, 235, 238
Faqih, concept of, 177
Farah-Abad incident, 108
Fardust, General Hussein, 107, 114
Farsiu, General Zia al-Din, 186
Ford, President Gerald, 148, 157
Foundation of the Oppressed, see *bunyad-i mustaz'afin*
Freemasonry in Iran, 95, 96
French Revolution, 175, 225
Frost, David, 187
Furuhar, Daryush, 166

Ganji, Manuchihr, 100
Gast, General Philip C., 133, 135
Giscard d'Estaing, Valery, 123
Great Britain, influences in Iran, 23–24

INDEX

The "Great Civilization," 33, 36
Guadeloupe Meeting, 123, 134
Guardian Council, 206, 207
Gulpayigani, Ayatollah
  Muhammad Reza, 241

Habibollahi, Admiral Kamal al-
  Din, 124, 132
Hafiz, Iranian Poet, 2
Haig, General Alexander, 129
Hakim, Ayatollah Muhsin, 241
Hashimi-Rafsanjani,
  Hujjatul-Islam 'Ali Akbar, 207,
  257
Hatam, General Hushang, 139
Hitler, Adolf, 88, 181, 198, 257
Hizbollahis, 205, 209, 240
Hoveida, Amir 'Abbas, 27, 47,
  66, 67, 86, 103, 109, 114, 140,
  187
—role in Iranian politics, 53–57,
  71
Hua Kuo-Teng, 31
Hujjatiyah, 206–207
Hussein, Saddam, 81, 153, 256,
  257
Hussein, Shia Imam, 91, 104
Huyser, General Robert, 114,
  115, 116, 117, 122, 123, 127,
  129, 130, 131, 132, 133, 135,
  136, 137, 140

Imperial Commission, 83, 85, 98,
  185
Indian Ocean Common Market
  Proposal, 150, 154
Iqbal, Manuchihr, 27, 53, 187
Iran—changing role in
  international affairs, 31–32, 214
—foreign policy, global, 31,
  147–148, 149, 156, 214
—foreign policy, regional, 31,
  148, 150, 151–154, 214–215
—geopolitics of, 18, 148, 155,
  164, 165, 198, 230
—oil policy in the 70s, 154–155,
  157
—policy towards ethnic groups,
  152, 153, 211, 240, 244–246,
  247–248
—prospects for the future,
  201–217, 224, 228–238, 243–244
—relations with the Arab world,
  150–153
—relations with Great Powers,
  19, 23, 145
—relations with India, 150, 154
—relations with Iraq, 151–153
—relations with Pakistan,
  153–154
—role in the United Nations, 32
—views of America, 158–168
Iran Freedom Movement, 117,
  204
Iran-Iraq War, 152, 207, 211,
  212, 214, 256–257, 258
Iran Novin Party, 47, 51, 54, 55,
  67, 71
Iranian bureaucracy, political
  role of, 47, 50, 53, 57, 58, 61,
  62, 63, 68
Iranian intelligentsia, 176–182,
  185–193, 213, 235, 237
Iranian monarchy—alliance with
  the bureaucracy, 58–60, 85,
  184
—institutional characteristics, 11,
  12, 26, 27, 28, 40, 58–59,
  64–66, 68, 75–76, 182–185,
  187–188, 193, 238–241, 247,
  248, 251–252
—prospects for the future, see
  the political opposition, the
  constitutionalists
—relations with political parties
  58–59, 66–71, 73, 76
—relations with religion, 239–241
—response to the Revolution,

92–109
Iranian Oil Consortium, 145
Iranian political culture, 5, 8, 9, 26, 27, 47, 68, 88, 146, 173, 229, 235, 237, 238
—influences of foreign political cultures, 48–53
Iranian political elite, authoritarian tendencies, 51–53
Iranian political structure, 4–6, 9, 10, 11, 17, 18, 20, 24, 48, 50, 63, 65, 74–75, 182–185, 187–188, 238, 241–243
Iranian Revolution, 2, 5, 92–109, 173, 223–224, 226, 227, 239
—ideology of, see Khomeini, ideology
—role of political structures and processes, 10, 11, 12, 39, 224
—role of religion, 5, 197–199, 201, 206–207, 227, 242
—role of revolutionary organizations, strategy, personalities, 10, 89, 91–94, 97, 99, 105, 108, 121, 127, 158, 173–175, 181, 190, 191
—role of the Shah's leadership style and ideology, 33–34, 40, 92–104, 224, 227
—role of socio-economic developments, 3, 7, 8, 9, 10, 37–38, 84–85, 200–201, 224, 227
—role of the West, 4–5, 11
—succession issue, 201–217
Iranian society, demographic characteristics, 100, 200, 202–203, 204
Iskandari, Iraj, 203
Islam, views on politics, 22, 197, 258
Islamic Assembly, 206, 207
Islamic Courts, see Revolutionary Courts

Islamic fundamentalism, 13, 68, 117, 175, 189, 191, 198, 200, 201, 205, 209, 210, 233
The Islamic Government, 181, 242
Islamic People's Republican Party, 243
Islamic Republic of Iran, 12, 13, 122, 198–199, 201–202, 203, 204, 205, 206, 209–210, 212, 213, 214, 215, 224–225, 233, 255–256, 258
—foreign policy, 197, 214–215, 256
—inherent limitations of, 209–217, 224–225
—succession issue, 201–217
Islamic Republican Party, 201, 202, 209, 237, 238, 240
Ivan the Terrible, 176

Jam, General Firaydun, 102
Jihad, 22, 197, 243
Jihad-i Sazandigi, 206, 209
Jones, General David, 129, 131
Jordan, Samuel, 49

Kafa'i, Ayatollah Ahmad, 241
Kashani, Ayatollah Sayyid Abul-Qasim, 24
Al-Kashif Al-Qita', Ayatollah Muhammad Hussein, 241
Kennedy, Edward, 159
Kennedy, President John F., 28, 156
Kerenski, Aleksandr, 176
Khajih-Nuri, General 'Ali-Muhammad, 137
Khalkhali, Sadiq, 199
Khaminih-'i, Ayatollah 'Ali, 207
Khomeini, Ayatollah Sayyid Ruhollah Musavi, 5, 13, 91, 92, 93, 94, 95, 96, 97, 102, 103, 108, 113, 116, 117, 127, 129, 130, 132, 134, 135, 136, 137,

INDEX

138, 139, 153, 166, 167, 168, 175, 177, 179, 181, 190, 191, 197, 198–199, 201, 202, 203, 204, 205, 206, 207, 208, 209, 213, 214, 215, 224, 225, 226, 227, 228, 230, 235, 237, 240, 242, 243, 251, 256, 257, 258
—ideology of, 181, 197–199, 213–215
Khrushchev, Nikita, 28, 162
Khu'i, Ayatollah Abu Al-Qasim, 241
Khunsari, Ayatollah Ahmad, 241
Kiyanuri, Nuriddin, 203, 204
Kumitihs, 202, 205, 206, 207, 208, 209, 210–211
Kurds, 152, 211, 213, 214, 230, 244, 245, 247

Lenin, V. I., 175
"The Libertarian Model," 173
Local Councils, 61
Louis XIV, 175

Madani, Admiral Ahmad, 226
Mahdavi, Firaydun, 84
Mahdi, Twelfth Imam, 22, 237
Majidi, 'Abdul Majid, 85
Majlis, National Consultative Assembly, 17, 18, 19, 21, 23, 25, 26, 28, 29, 87, 96, 98, 103, 128
Maktabiyun, 205–206
Maliki, Khalil, 24
Mansur, Hasan 'Ali, 54, 55, 186
Mao Tse-Tung, 147, 174, 175, 225, 235
Al-Mar'ashi al-Najafi, Ayatollah Shahab al-Din, 241
The Mardum Party, 56, 67
Matin-Daftari, Hidayat, 166
Milani, Ayatollah Hadi, 241
Military—influence in politics, 24, 26, 238, 244, 249

—and the Iran-Iraq War, 212, 256–257
—organizational structure, 117–120
—response to instabilities of 1978–79, 93, 94, 103, 105–106, 107, 108, 113–128, 132, 134, 135, 137–138, 139, 140–141
—role in the future of Iran, 249–251
Minachi, Nasir, 136
Mondale, Walter, 131
Mossadiq, Muhammad, 20, 24, 25, 28, 29, 94, 95, 101, 106, 107, 118, 125, 128, 145, 147, 166, 167, 182, 201
Mu'azzami, 'Abdollah, 95
Muhammad, Prophet of Islam, 22, 104, 257, 258
Muhaqiqi, General Ahmad, 120
Mujahidin-i Khalq, 108, 174, 186, 202, 205, 206, 235, 238
Mujtahid, 22, 243
Muntaziri, Ayatollah Hussein 'Ali, 207
Muqaddam, General Nasir, 140
Musavi Ardabili, Ayatollah Abul-Karim, 207

Nadir Shah Afshar, 27, 228
Nahavandi, Hushang, 100
Napoleon Bonaparte, 175
Nasiri, General Ni'matullah, 53, 103, 141, 187
Nassir, Gamal Abdul, 147, 150
National Front, 12, 28, 51, 92, 102, 106, 107, 136, 166, 181, 190–192
National Iranian Oil Company, 101
Nationalism, 7, 11, 25, 146, 148, 215, 244, 245
NATO, 148
Nazih, Hasan, 166, 226

INDEX

Nehru, Jawahir La'l, 147
Newsom, David, 131
Nicholas II, 176
Nixon, President Richard M., 11, 149, 156, 157
Nixon Doctrine, 148
Nkrumah, Kwame, 147

OPEC, 86, 155
Oveisi, General Gholam 'Ali, 103

Pahlavi, Farah, the Shahbanu of Iran, 67, 70, 72, 107
Pahlavi, Muhammad Reza Shah, 1, 2, 3, 4, 5, 11, 12, 17, 19, 20, 24, 26, 27, 51, 56, 63, 70, 92, 93, 95, 100, 103, 105–106, 107, 113, 114, 115, 117, 118, 119, 120, 121, 122–124, 125, 126, 128, 129, 130, 131, 132, 133, 134, 135, 136, 137, 139, 150, 154, 155, 156, 157, 158, 160–162, 164, 165, 167, 168, 177, 182, 187, 200, 212, 223, 224, 225, 226, 231, 241, 242, 245, 250–251
—leadership style, 26, 28, 40, 47, 88, 187–188, 251
—popular and international image, 32, 33, 40, 89, 155, 158–168, 184, 189
—relations with the military, 113, 117–119, 122–127, 136, 141, 250–251
—response to Revolution, 33–34, 92–109
—views on arms build-up, 155–156, 157
—views on foreign policy, 147–154
—views on oil, 154–155, 157
—views on politics, 32, 33, 148
Pahlavi, Reza Shah, 18, 19, 20, 25, 26, 118, 228, 240, 244

—leadership style and policies, 18, 19, 20, 27, 117, 147
Pahlavi Dynasty, 17, 93, 176, 199, 210, 225, 227, 244
Pahlavi Foundation, 95, 103, 209
Pahlavi regime, see Pahlavi Dynasty
Parliamentary elections of 1975, 73–74
Pasdars, 202, 205, 207, 208, 209, 210–212, 243
Perez de Cuellar, Javier, 257
Persian Gulf, 13, 137, 148, 150, 151, 152, 215, 230
The Plan and Budget Organization, 61, 188
PLO, 158
political opposition in Iran, 23, 51, 52, 86, 87, 121, 127, 133, 135–136, 158, 161, 162, 184
—Constitutionalists, 226, 238–239, 247
—cooptation into the system, 51–52
—ideas of, 173–175, 190
—leftist groups, 87, 158, 174, 190, 202, 203–204, 213, 228
—liberal forces, 12, 92, 140, 158, 174, 176, 179–182, 185–193, 204–206, 226, 228
—origins of, 158
—terrorist groups, 87, 108, 133, 137, 139, 158, 162, 185, 186, 188
—transformation into a religious movement, 86, 87, 89, 90–92
political participation, 10, 33, 53, 59, 63–64, 68, 69, 71, 75, 76, 178–181, 184, 246–247
Pol Pot, 202
Progressive Circle, 54

Qabus, Sultan of Oman, 151
Qajar Dynasty, 27, 75, 244

Qarabaghi, General 'Abbas, 114, 115, 116, 123, 124, 125, 126, 127, 132, 133, 135, 136, 137, 138, 139, 140
Qasim, Abdul-Karim, 151
Qavam, Ahmad (Qavam Al-Saltanih), 23, 24, 94
Qumi, Ayatollah Hasan, 243
Qutbzadih, Sadiq, 166, 205

Rabi'i, General Amir-Hussein, 124, 132
Rahimi, General Mehdi, 140, 141
Rajaie Khorassani, Said, 257
Rastakhiz Party, 33, 51, 52, 56, 61, 66, 67, 71, 73, 84, 96, 98, 184
—limitations, 73, 74–75, 87–88
—main tenets, 70, 71
—organizational structure, 72–74
—origins of, 66–67
—theoretical basis of, 68–69
Razmara, General Haji 'Ali, 24, 25
Reagan, President Ronald, 11
Regency Council, 108, 124
Regional Cooperation for Development (RCD), 150, 153
Revolutionary Courts, 205, 207, 208
Revolution's Guardians, see the *Pasdars*
Roosevelt, President Franklin D., 32, 156
Russian Revolution, 175–176

Sadat, Anwar, 31, 150, 151
Sadiqi, Gholam Hussein, 106
Safavid Dynasty, 90, 228
SALT, 162
Samadiyanpur, General Samad, 120
Sanjabi, Karim, 102, 106, 107, 166, 181, 182, 191, 192

Saunders, Harold, 131
SAVAK, 87, 95, 96, 99, 103, 108, 114, 128, 140, 168, 185–187, 188
SAVAMA, 114
Schlesinger, James, 131
Schmidt, Helmut, 123
SEATO, 148
Shaffaqat, General Ja'far, 125
Shafiq, Prince Shahriyar, 114
The Shah, see Pahlavi, Muhammad Reza Shah
Shahristani, Ayatollah Hibat al-Din, 241
Shahsavar by-election of 1974, 66–67
Shari'ati, Ali, 90–91, 235
Shari'atmadari, Ayatollah Muhammad Kazim, 201, 237, 241, 243
Sharif-Imami, Ja'far, 27
—Premiership, 85, 95–103, 105, 185
Shatt al-Arab Issue, 151, 152
Sheikhul-Islamzadih, Shuja'iddin, 109
Shia Islam, 5, 11, 21, 22, 89, 90, 104, 152, 166, 177, 201, 203, 213, 214, 235, 237, 240, 241, 242, 243, 245
Shia political ethos, 21, 22, 237
Shiism, concept of *Imam*, 21, 22, 90
Shirazi, Ayatollah Abdollah, 243
Shuster, Morgan, 48
Sisco, Joseph, 148
"Siyahkal incident," 87, 186
socio-economic development in Iran, 6, 9, 19, 29, 30–31, 34, 37, 62, 178, 200, 203, 223, 231, 234, 255
—assessment of, 38, 39, 178, 200, 223
—ideology of, 34

—influence on agriculture, 35–36
—influence of oil, 35, 36
—influence of Westernism, 34–35, 178–179
—planning and management issues, 37
—political consequences of, 39, 62, 75
—role of the private sector, 36
Soviet Union—influences in Iran, 23–24, 203
—relations with Iran, 32, 149, 203, 204, 230
Stalin, Joseph, 23, 32, 88, 147, 175, 176, 225
Sukarno, 147
Sullivan, Ambassador William, 115, 116, 123, 129, 130, 134, 135, 136, 137, 138
Sunni Islam, 21, 152, 213, 235

Tate and Lyle Sugar Company, 190
Tehran University, School of Public Administration, 50
Tito, Josip Broz, 147
tribal forces, 18–21, 26, 211, 213, 238, 244
Trotsky, Leon, 174, 235
Truman Doctrine, 145
Tudeh Party, 23–24, 26, 48, 51, 118, 201, 202, 203–204, 206, 235, 238
Tufaniyan, General Hasan, 124, 125, 132, 136–137
Turkoman, 211, 213, 214, 244, 247

Umayyad Caliphate, 104, 228
United Nations Security Council, 257
United States, see also America,
—relations with Iran, 3, 11, 24, 28, 48, 118, 132–133, 156, 157, 158–168
—Point Four Programs, 24, 49
—response to the Revolution, 127–138

Vance, Cyrus, 115, 130, 131
Von Marbod, Eric, 136

White Revolution, 1, 18, 28–31, 39, 47, 53, 58, 64, 65, 68, 70, 93, 119
—effect on the society and the economy, 30–31, 68
—points of, 29–31
Women's Organization of Iran, 30
women's rights, 30, 206, 255
World War II, 19, 146

Yazid Ibn Mu'awiyyah, 104
Yazdi, Ibrahim, 166

Zahidi, Ardishir, 187
Zahidi, General Fazlollah, 27